YOUNG
AMERICA
IN
WALL-STREET.

BY

GEORGE FRANCIS TRAIN

GREENWOOD PRESS, PUBLISHERS
NEW YORK

Originally published in 1857 by Derby and Jackson, Publishers

First Greenwood reprinting, 1968

Library of Congress catalogue card number: 68-28649

Printed in the United States of America

INTRODUCTION

THE time-worn adage that "young men should be seen and not heard," has closed many a young man's mouth. The sage who made it, forgot to mention the maxim in the succeeding chapter—that "gravity was often a mysterious carriage of the body to conceal the defects of the mind." "Young men *think* old men are fools—old men *know* that young men are," was rub number two for "Young America." If young men are fools, could their fathers have been sages? "A little knowledge is a dangerous thing" is another apothegm of sham philosophy. Is not, I ask, in all reason, a little knowledge of the present state of our financial affairs better than none at all?

During the last generation the young man has had a hard fight in the battle of life, and met with little or no encouragement from the old. If he kept the old track he was all right, if he struck out a new path for himself he was all wrong. If he asked to be taken into the firm, he was met with a volume of unprofitable good advice. But was he taken into the firm? Oh, no! Anything but that. He was told to be conservative—to be prudent—to be cautious—to keep cool, and not to get excited—to listen rather than to talk—to speak only when he was spoken to—to observe what was passing, and warned against the audacity of commenting on what he saw; and if, daring to walk more rapidly than the rule, he disobeyed in any of these particulars, he was, in the estimation of the savans of commerce, rushing recklessly and rapidly to ruin! How often has such admonition, good of itself, but having nothing substantial to back it, chilled the heart and cramped the ambition of the young man, who, without rich friends or rich connections, has striven in vain to make a start in life!

The young man has thus been taught, in the roughest school, that he "must learn to labor and to wait" if he expect to be successful. While laboring hard and waiting long, if he have the temerity to print a letter—he is censured! If he express an opinion—he is sneered at. If he make a speech, he is ridiculed. If he write a book, the chances are that he will be ruined for life, as far as the sage opinions of his elders can suffice to ruin him. His notes don't pass,—that freezing, contemptuous, and suggestive shrug of the shoulder of the great man on 'change cramps all his energies. Poor fellow, he must not complain; he forgets that he is young. Let him expect advancement when his hair is grey and his brow is furrowed,—let him live in hope even if he die in despair. He may be a junior partner some day, perhaps even before he is sixty!

I am a Bostonian, and know how hard it is to penetrate through the powerful freemasonry of a Boston firm. Returning from abroad after an absence of several years, I find the same clerks on the same wharves, in the same counting houses, with the same thread-bare coats on— the same salaries — living from year to year on pro- mises — promises that cheer them till life is worn away in the service of others, who, when at last an opportunity arrives to advance them, have not the will to do it!

The New-York merchants may take more interest in the young man's welfare than the " solid men of Boston;" but even in this progressive city I fear that youth is a drug in the market. Pray do not suppose for a moment that I do not respect the counsels of the old; I have ever sought their society—ever associated with those older than myself—ever listened when they advised—ever striven to profit by their experience; but the moment the young man dares to express an opinion of his own he is at once considered a fit candidate for a lunatic asylum. My object in publishing these letters is to show at least a shade of " method in my madness."

Hard mental labor, in the three great Anglo-Saxon lands, America, England, and Australia, under the weighty responsibility of an extensive House, unless I was more stupid than the common herd, should have given me some practical experience in the way of managing business. From Australia I stepped into Asia, saw Africa, passed through Europe into England, and returned last year to America,—my eyes wide open, as I hurried round the world. While here I made arrangements to establish a commission and banking-house in London. Returning to England, I imagined the times were changing. An inward voice said, Don't be in a hurry, wait. I suddenly became an old fogy, and went to the Continent, where I have spent a twelvemonth in improving my knowledge of the European languages. Freeman Hunt, of the Merchants' Magazine, wrote me, with the request that I would throw him off an occasional article on European Finance. When tired with poring over French, Italian, and German verbs, I changed the course of my thoughts by diving down into the archives of the *Crédit Mobilier*, the Bank of France, and the Bank of England. The moment I examined the statistics I thought I saw breakers ahead; and having seen the leading merchants and bankers, from Melbourne to Manhattan, from Batavia to Amsterdam, from Canton to Constantinople,—having talked with peasant as well as prince, from Shanghai to Stock- holm, from Hobart Town to London, from New South Wales to St. Petersburg, I came to the conclusion that the panic of 1857 must be more terrific than anything be- fore! Why? Because the application of high pressure to machinery had been paralleled by a high pressure to finance. The moral world has shared the impetus of the physical; and there is a bursting of the boiler in the one case, as well as in the other.

I found over-stocked markets everywhere, ruinous com- petition and extravagant living in all lands ; no wonder it made me croak!—the raven was always "at my chamber- door,—croaking, croaking, evermore!" When a man of sense and observation was thrown into my company, I nailed him for a financial argument. I talked on all sides of a Panic, to get from different minds sound views. Politics I discussed with the Herald, finance with Hunt, and if I have foreshadowed what has come to pass, don't think I am so egotistical as to take to myself any credit for particular foresight on the subject. I only produced a digest from the minds of others. I talked with older men,—men who had notes to meet,—men, who could not see a panic coming, because it was not their interest Neither was it mine. Yet I could not shut my eyes to the fact that was staring me in the face. When making assertions I gave the figures; when talking of a crisis, in the absence of facts I argued from reason ; I marked the cause, and saw the effect : such views led me to examine the workings of commerce, and the more I sought, the less confidence I had in the future. Most of the London journals argued exactly against me ; one of the leading minds of the London Times told me he expected a crisis, yet the " City Article" went on the even tenor of its way. Bennett was the only man who saw the approaching storm, and boldly made the signal to take in sail ; but who regarded him ?   Even now there are many who give him the credit of the whole disaster—*just as though an individual mind could break a solvent nation !*

The truth is we are a fast people, bound to beat the world, even in the abysses of our insolvency. The most surprising thing to me is, that an intelligent community, a mercantile people, could march on with a steady tramp to the brink of a precipice, blindfold their eyes, recklessly advance, deliberately step over, and fall into an almost universal bankruptcy, without being aware of it themselves !

Mr. Stevens, Mr. Appleton, Mr. Leavitt, say they have never seen such times. Indeed ! what a remarkable discovery ! How, for a moment, can an intelligent man compare this panic with that of 1837 ? Our commerce was then in a nutshell, now it covers a world.

These were my arguments in continental Europe, in England, and in America, viz.: that the credit bubble to-day has been inflated in proportion to the progress the nation has made *since that day.* Tom Thumb and the Belgian giant are very poor comparisons. At that time Biddle and the National Bank were the scapegoats. Yet large as were their transactions, the Illinois Central and another Western railway or two would swallow up the entire Biddleisms of that day. Eastern lands in 1837 comprised a few thousand square acres in Maine. Western lands to-day are in the hands of several great States, each competing with the other to see who can speculate the most wildly !

Our financial leaders seem to have forgotten that our twenty-five thousand miles of railway have been constructed *since that day !*

That our immense steam fleet has been sent to sea *since that day !*

That our gigantic shipping interest, comprising some five millions of tons, has been launched *since that day !*

That our extensive manufactories have been erected *since that day !*

That our enormous dry-goods trade with England and Europe has been proportionably expanded *since that day !*

That the marble palaces on Broadway, and the brown-stone houses on Fifth Avenue, have sprung into existence *since that day!*

That silks and satins, laces and crinoline, hoops and diamonds, fast horses, clubs, and brandy smashes have been introduced *since that day!*

That steam, the telegraph, and patents for everything in Christendom have come into life *since that day!*

That three millions of foreigners have arrived amongst us—some three millions, who displaced some two millions of Americans, who were forced to gain their living by their wits—*since that day!*

That we have imported some three million tons of rails to employ the workmen in building the roads —the iron in the hold, the passengers between decks,— the transportation of which (together with Irish famine and Mexican war in 1847, California in 1849, navigation laws in 1851, Australia and Guano in 1852,) has given a startling impetus to the shipbuilders of New-England and the mechanics in their various trades employed in this way, at the same time that the railways, canals, factories, and palaces were being completed, creating a great demand for labor; hence that heavy staple of a nation's wealth has become as much inflated as the works which laborers' hands have completed, *since that day!*

Gilded churches for gilt-edged sermons, aristocratic colleges and institutes for aristocratic children of aristocratic parents, who live in aristocratic avenues, and aristocratic cities, have been brought upon the scene, *since that day !*

And to sum up in a word, all this astonishing progress, in everything, and everybody, could not have been made, unless finance had been reduced to as much of a clipper science and a clipper system as the clipper ship, the clipper railway, the clipper factory, the clipper church, the clipper government, the clipper merchant, and the clipper banker, *since that day !* the memorable mile-stone year of eighteen hundred and thirty-seven !

The brandy of bubbling speculation has stupefied our reason, and *delirium tremens* has overtaken the nation !

Like a balloon allowed to expand too far, its explosion brings from the clouds to the ground the daring æronaut !

Like a ship under full sail, the compass of sound sense gone, and no officer in command, no wonder the ship went upon the rocks !

New-York was the locomotive of these United States ; Wall street was the steam ; twenty miles an hour—thirty —forty—and we were ambitious to make it fifty, when Bennett said, " Look out for the engine while the bell rings!" Stop her!—ease her!—half speed!—and off the track she went; smashing cars, killing passengers, and creating almost universal calamity!

Everybody has gone joint-stock mad! The man who *owed* a hundred thousand dollars imagined himself worth half a million; and the unreflecting outsider pointed to him and said, There goes *Bubble*, the millionaire! Like the Gobelin tapestry of Paris, the mosaic work of Rome, every interest was dovetailed into every other interest; so much so that no man could tell when he was conducting a legitimate trade; and yet, notwithstanding all these changes *since that day*, our financial sages are surprised that this crisis is grander in its immensity than that petty little affair of twenty years ago!

Where, I ask, is the analogy with the past? There is none. But I will qualify that assertion: in each case the time consumed in bursting the bubble is about the same.

Josephs failed on the 17th of March, 1837, the banks followed suit on the 10th of May—just fifty-three days between the Alpha and the Omega! The Ohio Life and Trust Company came down on the 24th of August, 1857, the banks broke on the 14th of October—just fifty-one days between the first and the last! So much for the past! So much for the opinions which I have been advancing during the past twelve months, the expression of which on all occasions led my friends to doubt my judgment.

So much, then, for the past. What of the present? I answer : paralysis !—stupefaction !—dread ! The banks suspend—(a legal swindle ?)—the merchants tremble— Banquo's ghost will not down. A public meeting is called in Wall street, to get an independent expression of opinion on financial affairs. One clever mind, cleverer than the rest, writes some resolutions ; A, B, C and D approve. Two thousand merchants—New-York merchants—merchants whose minds are wrought up by the excitement of the times to intense reflection, assemble in the Exchange.

Mr. A. calls the meeting to order ; Mr. B. takes the chair : " All those in favor of these resolutions, say Aye ! — Contrary-minded, No !" 'Tis a unanimous vote !

Mr. C. makes a speech—" Owing to the peculiar formation of this building, it is well known that *my voice cannot penetrate thirty feet from where I now stand*— therefore I will only say that the banks are right—and in our afflictions we must be kind to one another !" (Cheers from the right.)

Mr. D. immediately moves an adjournment. " All those in favor say Aye !—Contrary-minded, No !"—'Tis a vote !

" Gentlemen, this meeting is now adjourned," and more than nine-tenths of the audience leave the Exchange *without having heard a single word of the resolutions!* And yet these same resolutions go to the press, from the press to the country, from the country to the Old World, as the intelligent independent opinions of the New-York merchants on our present financial affairs!

I have carefully read the resolutions, the essence of which, to my mind, seems to be, that "*whereas we are a free and independent people, we freely and independently declare ourselves bankrupts.*"

The position of matters to-day is, the illegal suspension of the banks, and the approval of the measure by the merchants.

The judges applaud, and by their decision have made themselves famous. This is their judgment : " *One murder makes a villain — millions a hero!*" Three cheers for the progress of morality, and a strong, ablebodied, athletic groan for the judges !

This "*extra-judicial opinion*" justifies the man who owes a penny, and cannot pay, to balance off his account ; for, certainly, what is a *virtue* in the corporation cannot be a *crime* in the individual. The debtor may now say to the creditor, under the new banking decision : " My dear fellow, I am short ; in fact I may tell you in confidence that I am burst,—expect to pay every red ; and, in consideration of our long friendship, I will ask you to call upon me, if you have the time, this day two years, and, should I be in funds, I will be most happy to *pass the amount to your credit!*"

Carlyle criticises : he never creates. If Carlyle takes such liberties, why should I be censured for following his example ? However, if the reader will wade through the following letters—some financial, some commercial, some political, and some descriptive—noting when and where they were written, I will promise to give the best remedy I can discover for the disease which I have described.

To my mind, the fog still enshrouds the icebergs.

The earthquake has only loosened the plaster on the ceiling—the walls still stand.

The burning lava has not commenced to run down the mountain towards the village on the plain.

The rattling of the thunder is not the thunderbolt.

Therefore, in a concluding chapter, I propose to show that we have not seen the end of the beginning, much more the beginning of the end.

St. Nicholas Hotel,
New-York, Nov. 1st, 1857.

YOUNG AMERICA

IN

WALL STREET

ARTICLE I.

Politics—Finance—Bullion in National Banks—Austria--Treaty of Paris
—Bolgrad the Little not Bolgrad the Great—Reasons for expecting a Crisis in financial affairs—Panic comes round every ten
years—Bank of England less Bullion than before discovery of
Australian and California Mines—Rate of Interest—Two and a
half to seven per cent.—Bank of France as strong as Bank of Eng-
land—Why a crisis may be expected in France—*Pereire* and the
Crédit Mobilier—Russian Railways—Iron produced in England—
Silver question—Opium heretofore prevented the drain—Exports and
Imports to India and China—Tea—Silk—Balance of Trade against
the West—Sixty-five millions Silver exported in sixteen months—
Hamburg Bank declares a Gold Standard— *Crédit Maritime*—
French Merchants buying New-York Clippers—The gloomy aspect
of the financial sky.

GRAND HOTEL DU LOUVRE,
Rue de Rivoli, Paris, Nov. 13, 1856.

MY DEAR SIR :—There's no better way of dissipating
the *ennui* of Parisian life, than an occasional use of the

pen; for journalizing stimulates reflection, and there's real pleasure in the knowledge that one is doing anything to expand the mind, or add to the book of knowledge. The morning has gone in discussing the causes of the political mist that fairly chills the atmosphere in all the capitals of Europe; for the New-York Herald and I propose to spend the evening in following out the train of thought which such reflections have given rise to, and try and meet my promissory note due for the December number of the Magazine.

So from *politics* let us turn to *finance*—simply remarking that just now they are most intimately associated—like England and America—a Siamese Twins connection; cut the band and thrones will tumble! The stock exchange is more powerful than the monarch—and the treasury has always had a wonderful influence on the cabinet. At present the peace and happiness of Europe depend somewhat upon the amount of bullion in the National Banks! Austria has *forty millions of dollars* in her vaults, yet she does not resume specie payment. France has but *thirty millions*, yet she still lives in spite of croakers, by buying gold at a loss (?), which by the way I don't believe—for if I understand the exchanges between the countries, France makes money by every operation;

while England, who rules them all, shows but *forty-seven millions of dollars* in the bullion department of her distinguished protegé—*a lesser sum than she has seen for the last nine years.* And so long as the Bank of England persists in keeping the price at which she purchases gold at £3 17s. 10½d, or at the par of exchange $18 69, there is little chance of her getting hold of the continued arrivals by transatlantic steamers or Australian clippers; for Continental buyers are more liberal, and give better prices. Exchange brokers must be accumulating fortunes, when such heaps of treasure are passed from hand to hand!

Having taken the position that disordered politics embarrass finance, you may ask, why? Simply by creating distrust, where everything is so uncertain. A want of confidence is sure to give birth to rumors—and rumors paralyze the money market. And since Fox & Henderson came down other names are mentioned.

Had the treaty of Paris been written as carefully as its importance demanded, no confusion would have arisen. But now serious disputes are talked of. The great Powers differ. What then? Why, Russia says: "Another conference, of course. Let us see 'who has broken the' treaty.' Austria, by arming the disputed 'Provinces?' or England, by sending her fleet into the Euxine? For what have I done? Bolgrad the Little, on the banks of the Danube, don't mean Bolgrad the Great, a few miles distant from the river." England disdains to answer; and Austria does what England wishes, and both reply by pointing to the sword! France appears indifferent, but is not; for her every action shows she sides with Russia! Napoleon must do one of two things : break the alliance with England (where lies his great strength), and get up a war some distance from his frontier, farther off than Italy ; or prepare for shooting down a few thousands of enthusiastic workmen who will be crying for bread. For 'tis plain that the seed of Revolution is sown broadcast! Can you doubt which he will choose ? Has loss of life anything to do with an Emperor's pleasure ? Besides, Napoleon must find amusement for his army! *To say the least, the future is somewhat misty, and that, in part, is why the financial world is trembling. Added to this is the fact that 1857 is the year—the one in ten—when a crisis purifies trade and commerce, and the machinery gets oiled, only to be clogged some ten years later ! Am I dreaming, or stating facts ?* Read McCulloch, and the history of the Bank of England. I wish I had a copy—but must trust to memory. Some sixty years ago, when Bonaparte threatened England with invasion, the habit commenced :—in 1797, when William Pitt issued the order in council for the

Bank to suspend specie payments for four months, to arrest the general bankruptcy of the kingdom. Only for four months. But some twenty-two years went round before it opened its vaults again!—not till 1819, under Sir Robert Peel's bill, who said that there was one thing more stubborn than figures—facts! So let us deal with them, and recall some old associations.

The panic of 1825–'27 was in your day, and I was too young to remember even '37, when the credit of London itself was shaken to its centre, bringing down the W.'s and making the B.'s tremble. But ten years after I was in the counting-house, and remember well how leading bankers, both in London and Liverpool, found a friend in the Bank of England in '47. The finances of the kingdom were in a bad way at the close of the last century; and history says that every ten years the lamp goes out. Do you not see that the elements are again concentrating? Or is it monomania with me? If I take a sombre look at affairs to-day, don't write me down a Dogberry. I assure you I have no scrip to sell—no notes to meet—never belonged to the Brokers' Board, —consider the Stock Exchange forbidden ground, and would not be an alarmist: so don't accuse me of raising the mad-dog cry! All former panics came before California and Australia opened their vaults.

And what a strange anomaly ? When *twenty millions*
of dollars were all we could get from the Ural Mountains, the Bank of England showed *one hundred million* dollars of bullion : now, when these two countries
turn out an *an annual production of one hundred and
twenty-five million dollars*, there's less than *fifty millions* in last week's balance, and the drain grows
more alarming daily.   The Bank Directors are in a
quandary.   What is to be done ? say they.

For over a century the rate of interest never varied but
one per cent. ; never, before 1835, below four per cent., and
never above five.   But during the last twenty years it has
ranged all the way from *two-and-a-half* to *eight* per
cent. ; (this last point only for a few months in 1848.)
Now the Court have made it seven per cent.   But still
the gold and silver leave the kingdom ! *Bankers, ship-
owners, merchants and manufacturers show discontent—
each distrusts the other—and all fear the next action of
the Bank.   The Directors have had several meetings since
last balance day, and great uncertainty prevails.   In
such a state of matters, would you be surprised to see
them raise the rate to ten per cent.?   The commerce of
England waits impatiently to know what next is to
be done.   Foreign securities, and even local stocks,
are choking for a decision, and England puts it all
on France.*

I certainly don't see but that the French Bank shows as good a balance as the English. What are the causes of the crisis in France ? These are some of them. Five hundred millions of dollars for the late war paid or to be provided for ! (England is the only nation that understands the art of raising the wind, and growing richer and richer the more she owes to her own people and trusts other nations.) A deficient harvest, the almost total loss of the silk crop, while the grapes are bad, and the inundations were disastrous—all these ; together with the natural impetus given to credit by the Nic. Biddle, of France, *M. Isaac Pereire*, the most wonderful magician of the century, the manager of the *Crédit Mobilier*—a financier who bids fair to take away the hard-earned laurels of a Rothschild, a Baring, a Steiglitz, and a Hope. For has he not beaten all these rulers of the world in the late Russian railway grants ? Yes, he has the contract, and is willing to give them a share ; " only think of it"— twenty-five hundred miles, a single track, to be built in ten years, at a cost of only *two hundred millions of dollars !* But what of that ? the government guarantees *five* per cent., and the concession is for almost a hundred years ! Two hundred and fifty thousand tons of railway iron are wanted ; but that is nothing. Hitherto America required as much for an annual supply, simply to relay her worn-out plant for her twenty-five thousand miles of rail. Russia produces but 250,000 tons a year, and few of her serfs possess iron implements for agriculture. If she wants England to give her rail she must change her tariff, for now it is prohibitory. England turns out 4,000,000 of pig and 2,000,000 of bar iron annually, of which 300,000 tons is of the former, and one-half the latter finds a foreign market. But I am wandering from Monsieur Pereire and the *Crédit Mobilier.* Really it is a gigantic institution! With only a capital of twelve million dollars, it can increase by charter ten to one, something like the New-York banks, and as much more on the strength of its deposits, giving a capital equal to the public debt of the Hon. East India Company—say *two hundred and eighty millions of dollars!* England fears its power, and every day her journals caution capitalists against dabbling in foreign speculations. But who can say but what *Pereire* is hand and glove with all the bankers of England and the Continent, great and small? For the ramifications and operations of the financial system are as widely diffused and as closely connected throughout the commercial world, as the nerves and veins are over the animal body. No matter whether it is a Russian railway or the sugar crop, the building of this hotel, or the establishing of a steam fleet, beautifying the city of Paris, or buying up the Spanish papers: *Pereire* is equal to it all.

This terrible engine for inflating credits, added to the causes which I mentioned, has occasioned the crisis which is being worked out in France. But perhaps the

most serious cause is the political distrust that makes
the people *hoard* their earnings. The building up of
the city is, in my opinion, a financial and commercial,
as well as architectural failure. The population has
not increased with the boundaries of the city. Winter is
approaching ; the workmen are cold, and bread at *ten
sous !* Everything helps to hasten the crisis. Silver
comes into the country to-day, is coined, and the five-
franc pieces are melted down, and shipped to India
on the morrow. Napoleon tries to stop it, but he
don't know how. Who does ? Can you spare a par-
agraph on the silver question ? Let us then leave
France to squeeze through the panic, if she can, and
return to England.

In my letters from China and India, at the com-
mencement of the year, which you did me the honor
to edit and publish, I alluded to the fact, that the
importation of opium into China saved the Western
world from sending out every year some forty millions
of dollars, to help make up the indebtedness to China.
What are the facts ? Let me make a few figures.
Take India first : England has managed that country
better than China, for her exports average *forty million
dollars.* In '48, British exports to India were *twenty-five
million dollars.* But last year they reached some *fifty-
two millions*, notwithstanding which the imports are

against her. In 1855, India gave to England some *sixty-three millions* of produce,—showing a balance of *eleven millions* to be paid in silver! Now in China the balance is far greater. China wants nothing from the West. I may be wrong; but my observations, when there some months since, go to show an enormous indebtedness to the native from the foreign merchant. And when domestics came in, it was something like this: "I owe you money for tea and silk, and have done so for years; now you must take these goods or nothing." The Chinaman no longer hesitates; and this is our famous export trade! Then, while the exports to India are on the increase, China gives no real signs of life. Fourteen years ago England sent out as much as now. Just after the war English exports to Canton were only some five million dollars! They are no more now, taking the last two years for a guide, while imports extend from year to year.

Take *Tea*. Sixteen years since, only 31,000,000 lbs. were imported; ten years after, it reached 70,000,000 lbs., and last year the tables show an import of 91,000,000 lbs., and the United States annually 40,000,000 lbs.—all of which, under the documentary bill sytem, is paid for through England! Silk also comes over more freely than formerly. Eight years ago, in 1848, England got but 17,000 bales. Now, last year she took 50,000, and this year something more.

Add these two articles up, and there is a sum of $43,000,000 for imports! And what is there to off-set it? Why only the paltry sum of some six or seven millions of dollars exports! The balance of course must go out in silver, for gold is not current in India, and the Chinese don't like it. Here then is some $47,000,000 per year against England. Ex-penses may reduce it some, but not much. No wonder then that every overland mail takes out some *three million dollars;* making a fearful sum at the end of the year! Thus far twenty-one steamers have left Southampton, one every fortnight, since January 1856, and the export list shows "Treasure, *sixty-five millions of dollars!*"—a good thing for the P. & O. One per cent. would give them a freight of over half a million. No more of this.

Have I encroached too far upon your space? I will only stop to remark: That the Hamburg Bank, after battling with a silver ore for the last *two hun-dred years*, has decided on a gold standard. That *one hundred million dollars* are wanted to finish the net-work of railways in Austria and Germany. That the *Crédit Maritime* of France have just received an order from Russia to build sixty steamers, to compose

the Black Sea fleet! That France also is buying some
of our transport clippers for the India trade, — the
" Ocean Herald " and " Queen of Clippers " of N. Y.,
both over two thousand tons—the former bringing
about $65,000 the latter $70,000, cash. That England and France will require all our surplus breadstuffs—for they get none from Russia since the war.
In 1853, England alone received some *four-and-a-
half millions of quarters* from the Euxine ; now, Russia requires it all. *And to conclude, I think, upon
the whole, the financial sky all over the world (why
should I except America ?) is somewhat clouded, and
will be, so long as the merchant who makes* $10,000
spends $20,000, *and tells his friend in confidence his
wonderful gains, but forgets to mention his losses !*
The hour is late, and I have my French lesson before
me, so I bid good night to finance.

ARTICLE II.

Australian Treasure Ships—$8,000,000 in one day—"Sick Man" no better
—Disease chronic—Gold displaces Silver on the Continent—China
wants nothing from us—Exportation a forced process—Silver Produc-
tion—Continental States refuse Gold Standard—Gold Production—
Interest at Bank of England—Money wanted by needy borrowers—
Crimean War—Rothschild still buying Bullion for the Bank of
France—England has not escaped the Panic—Bank issues One
Pound Notes when in a tight place—Former Panics—Peel's Cur-
rency Bill of 1844—British Exports then compared with now—Ex-
ports this year—Statistics of Board of Trade—French Commerce—
Belgium—Shaving rates of Interest—Difference between Panic of 1847
and the one expected this year—The more Commerce increases, the
more we have to pay for money—History of Bank of England—Joint-
Stock Banks and Private Bankers—Royal British and Tipperary
Banks—Strahan, Paul, Bates & Co.—Commercial stimulants—England, Holland, and Spain—Steam Engine—Discovery of Gold—
Facilities of the Joint-Stock Banks—Englishman's word as good
as his Bond—National Debt—America and Australia—Telegraphic
Cable —Mr. Field's Prophecy.

PARIS, FRANCE, *January* 1, 1857.

MY DEAR SIR :—Opportune arrivals of Australian
treasure ships, more confidence in the stability of the
French alliance, and comparative quiet among the des-

potic powers, are, no doubt, the principal causes of the present firmer tone of the money market. *London insists upon it that the panic is past, and Paris has a great respect for the opinion of her distinguished friend. Certainly, on the face affairs look better—but it is only on the face. The sick man may be better, but he is far from well. The disease is chronic, and the remedy—the arrival of $8,000,000 of gold at Liverpool between the rising and setting of a sun, an amount unprecedented in a single day—only touches the outer man, leaving the malady to gnaw away at the vitals of commerce for awhile, and then burst out again with more violence than before!*

When I wrote you, I endeavored to show that however bad matters were at home, they were far worse abroad, and that a gold drain to, was nothing more than a silver drain from, the Continent. So long as we continue to import Oriental luxuries, we must continue to put our hands in our pockets, and established European coins must continue to be thrown into the melting-pot to supply the ravenous demand for silver which such importations are sure to create, and that silver must be replaced with Californian and Australian gold. Am I not right? The disease is therefore chronic, and the temporary relief afforded may only deceive the public, and take the issue away from the

East, where it belongs, and solve the problem nearer home. China wants nothing from the West. That wonderful land is only a gigantic Japan; the Emperor and his cabinet to-day, I have no doubt, would give the world many hundred millions if every European would quit the soil. But England forced the trade fourteen years ago, and the Chinese retaliate by selling her goods at high prices, and taking nothing but hard cash for payment.

Every mail, regularly twice a month, the treasure goes away. To-day the amount by the overland is $4,000,000, the next the same, and most likely so on during 1857—about $60,000,000 or $70,000,000 in a twelvemonth! But even at this rate, it will take many years to exhaust it; for we continue to extract out of the old mines some $40,000,000 per annum—and the quantity has been increasing for centuries; and when the coin grows scarce, high prices will tempt the owner of silver plate to take the gold instead. It is said that France alone has some $600,000,000 in silver, the collection of ages; and all the Continent—Germany, Austria, Prussia, and Russia, as well as minor States—have refused aught but a silver standard—Hamburg alone having broken the chain, and at last followed the example of England and America. They must all come to it, sooner or later; for the pouring

in of some $600,000,000 in gold since old Sutler saw
the dust on his mill-wheel, in 1848, is sure to revo-
lutionize rusty and time-worn habits. Since Louis
Philippe made way for Louis Napoleon—

> California has turned out, up to 1856.............$321,000,000
> Australia... 208,000,000
> Add for both El Dorados for 1856............... 100,000,000

—Making, in less than eight years, more gold than
France collected in silver in as many hundred!

*The rate at the Bank of England for " gilt-edged"
paper may be half per cent. less to-day ; but the Directors never made so false a move as when they dropped
it to six and a half, until there is more certainty for
the future ; for exchange on all sides is against England, and Continental money-seekers are on the increase.*

*Operations now are giants to what they were only
a quarter of a century since ; for, while England
and America have macadamized their soil with railways, Europe and Asia have only inserted the wedge.*
In round numbers—why not put down the figures?
there's no harm if it amounts to a few millions more
or less. Governments, corporations, and financial leaders are putting out their baits ; and, from what I
note, I feel authorized in issuing the following adver-
tisement :—

MONEY WANTED—For Railway and other Enterprises, during the coming year.

Commence with England—Branch Railways and New Joint-Stock Companies, under the Limited Liability Act—About 410 Prospectuses issued.... $50,000,000

France calls for 40,000,000 officially, for Railways, Branches from the Trunk Lines, (which will serve to take away her 10 and 15 per cent. dividends, as they have always done in railway enterprise,) and will want as much more for other projects—say for France................................... 80,000,000

Russia, at least, for Railways and Steamships, must commence with............................. 60,000,000

Austria, for her Railways, &c.................... 50,000,000

And take America, India, Australia, and other countries—you should give them.................... 80,000,000

$320,000,000

Here you have some $320,000,000 to furnish during the twelve months ending 1st January, 1858! But you answer: "That is nothing; the world dropped about as much each year of the war upon the Crimea." Admit it; but war spreads disaster; and its commerce is as unprofitable as it is immoral. One nation's happiness is marked by the misery of the other. The one amount is sunk, the other to be raised. Taking, then, these sums for great national enter-

prises, and then adding what is wanted to carry on
the *legitimate trade of the world, in its present inflated state*, money in 1857 will command at least
twice as much as it did five years before. I much
doubt if the rate in Threadneedle-street drop below
four per cent. for many years, and during the coming
year certainly not less than five. The French Bank
has paid away during the last sixteen months enormous sums for gold; and now, it is said, that Rothschild has contracted to supply her with $40,000,000
during the next year. At this rate the Bank of England will find it difficult to lower her rate of interest, without losing her bullion, for she never likes to
have less than $70,000,000 in the vault, and now it
is only $50,000,000.

*England may have escaped a panic, but I don't be-
lieve it notwithstanding.* Whenever there is a *bona
fide* crisis in England, it is thrown upon the Bank as
the chief cause. The old lady gets crowded, Government helps her, and then all goes smoothly on until
something new comes up, and she is as weak as the
most rotten of her securities. In 1822, she avoided a
panic by issuing $20,000,000 in small notes, but the
Directors forgot that sudden contraction produced just
what they tried to avoid; for it was only three years
later when they called in the same notes that caused

that terrible panic of 1825. Instead of suspending cash payments as before, they again issued small notes, some $23,000,000, which averted a national bankruptcy. In December, 1825, its circulation was $98,000,000, and during the next three months it reached $122,000,000; but before the end of the year, it fell off to the old figure; and it was then that the one, and all under five, pound notes were abolished, and have never been since used in England.

Again, during that memorable period, 1836 to 1840, the sudden contraction of bank-notes, it is said, created the disaster. In 1839, the notes only amounted to $76,000,000; but after the panic occurred, as usual, they tried once more the old remedy, and issued some $20,000,000 new notes, so that in 1843, about the time that Mr. Miller was to take his celestial flight, their notes showed the sum of $96,000,000. Go back, if you like, to earlier dates, you find it much the same. The course of the bank has been to arrest panic by the issue of more notes. Was not the crisis arrested in 1793, (when George and Napoleon got mad with each other and went to war,) by issuing the exchequer bills? Four years later she had no gold, and out came one pound notes again, with suspension of specie payments. In 1810, the same course was pursued; then the notes reached the enormous sum of $240,000,000!

Well, when contraction came, it occasioned a smash; and the resuming of cash payments, in 1819, brought the English people almost to rebellion,—money was so scarce and the times so hard.

But to return to 1843. The times required some new legislation, and Peel was at hand with his Currency Bill of 1844, under which the councils of the Bank of England are now governed. That Act prohibits expansion. Hence the difference. With $50,000,000 bullion, she can only discount $150,000,000; while New-York, with only $10,000,000 specie, has a discount line of nearly $100,000,000! Thus in the former case it is only three to one, in the latter ten to one. Such being the fact, many of the London financiers are crying for a change; and sound enough is the argument, that bank facilities sufficient for England's commerce in 1844 are by no means adapted to England's commerce in 1857. Why, look at the fact. Previous to that time, say 1841, British exports did not exceed $250,000,000, and they only reached $10,000,000 more in 1845, but sprang ahead, under free trade, to $350,000,000 in 1850; 400,000,000 in 1852; and in 1853, during the Australian panic year, the last of the peace, they reached $494,000,000! But during the war they fell off again,—in 1854 by some $8,000,000; and in 1855 the entire export was but $478,000,000—showing how war operates upon commerce. For this year, the year of peace and plenty, Old England will out-herod Herod. The Report of the Board of Trade is most instructive, as showing the increasing commerce of the Merchant Island or, in Napoleon's words, the "nation of shopkeepers."

During the first ten months of the present year, British exports amount to as much as the entire exports of last year. Already the tables show four hundred and seventy-seven millions to the 1st of November, 1856 ; an increase of nearly 22 per cent. over 1855. Again, look at the imports ; seven hundred and sixty-two millions in 1854, forty-four millions less the following year ! The decrease was from foreign lands (not colonies), half of which was for cereals.

The commerce of France has also received a powerful impetus. I note her imports and exports are returned in one sum. In 1854 the tables show a trade of seven hundred and fifty millions,—five millions less in 1853, and only six hundred millions in 1852 ; while last year (1855) the exports and imports of France amounted to eight hundred and sixty-five millions of dollars,—for a population of thirty-six millions of people ! Even little Belgium, during 1855, exported one hundred and forty millions, and imported five millions less.

The extraordinary increase in the commerce of the

world must create a *pro rata* demand for money to carry on that commerce ; and, from the figures which I have given, it will be seen that we require more extensive banking facilities now than when the Act was passed, and may naturally enough look for a higher rate of interest. When the Bank Court placard 7 per cent., many shavers in England squeeze out 12. The Committee of the House of Lords reported in 1847 that the panic of that year was caused by the restrictive measures of 1844. *But then the losses were from one Englishman to his brother merchant; now it would be a loss to the nation, for the balance of trade is so against her.* England has credit enough, but not currency. If she would issue one-pound notes again, she would at once release millions of sovereigns ; for who will cart round gold when he can have sound paper ? During the coming parliamentary session, I think the question of currency will be taken up. It certainly requires some healthy regulations. Now the Bank of England depresses or inflates the money market—pushes all stocks up or down, just when she happens to have the fancy. Supposing the Manager of the Bank of France gave the wink to the Governor of the Bank of England ; or— let it go deeper—the Directors were in the secret, and they put up the rates, and down the screw—what

a nice game they could play with rents and consols,
private stocks, and American securities!

Yes, bullionists and finance writers lay all changes
in the money market at the door of the Bank of
England. But what does she care?—her policy is to
make money; and if she brings on a crisis, how
simple it is for her to get an order in council to
suspend specie payment! She has done it before, she
can do it now! How strange it is that her private
securities, now that money is high, roll up so! Why,
in '51 and '52, when money was 2 and 2½ per cent.,
private securities were only from fifty to sixty-five
millions; but during the last year and a half, when
the rate has been backing and filling between five
and seven per cent., the private securities come up
to ninety-five, to one hundred and five, millions! But
the exports then were only three hundred and fifty
millions; now this year they are at the rate of five
hundred and fifty-five millions!—showing that the
more commerce increases, the more we have to pay
for money. Is it not so? Hence, I do not think we
shall get the old rate again for a long time.

The history of the Bank of England would read
like a romance,—so many are its thrilling scenes, so
numerous are its individualities, so gigantic are its
operations. In times of peril, it holds up great names,

and deals out millions as smaller corporations would thousands; but her greatness is of the past—yet her influence still shakes the kingdom. Through a dozen kingly reigns, private bankers and the Bank of England have managed to rule the financial world, and pocket all the banker's profits; but during the last quarter of a century a new element has been introduced, which has given a wonderful impetus to trade, and somewhat startled private bankers with the fact of their possessing a powerful competitor, that bids fair to swallow up all the time-worn names. I allude to the joint-stock banks in England, with branches in all the colonies. Allowing interest on deposits, giving great facility in discounts, and declaring satisfactory dividends, the joint-stock bank and the private banker, so long as they are rivals, cannot be friends. When the one sneeringly alludes to the gigantic swindles of the Royal British and Tipperary banks, the other remembers one Strahan, Paul, Bates & Co.; so each has a piece of the argument for illustration.

Most interesting is it to trace the stimulants to commerce. England first, and Holland, and once Venice, and old Spain. The discovery of the North American continent was a powerful stimulant. Another, of smaller proportion, the conquest of India. Then came that mighty agent, the steam-engine; afterwards the opening of China; and then gold in the Pacific, gold in the Indian Ocean. The last four agents spurred on and pushed, to their working capacity, the acknowledged potency of the joint-stock bank. England may, therefore, give that institution some credit for the astonishing and unhealthy impetus given to her commerce, as shown by the Tables of the Board of Trade. Most of the heavy enterprises of the day, have been completed by the joint-stock bank. To a man of standing, they are not mean in their facilities. Overdraw your bank account in State or Wall streets for one half-eagle, and a red mark is placed against your name. Not so with the joint-stock banks. Let a man possess a good name in the commercial world for business character and morality, and he may check away for thousands—his only collateral, his promise to pay, his honesty, and known integrity.

Show yourself worthy of the confidence of an Englishman, and there is nothing he will not do for you—your word is his bond. Our bonds, therefore, command his money! Really, they are a wonderful people! What other people would submit to paying an income tax of sixteen pence in the pound, levied in order to meet the expense of a most unprofitable war? England's commerce is on the increase—the nation prospers, and the national debt stands at four thousand millions of dollars! How, then, must it be with America, who can sleep soundly, without national *nightmare* of mammoth notes to pay? If in thirty years we have caught up with the old mother land in commerce, how will it be in 1886? Shall we not leave her far behind? England's orthodox policy with her oldest son made America; her surplus and criminal population organized Australia; in all, three Anglo-Saxon nations,—each commercial, each financial. But the old man watches with anxious eye the progress of his precocious boys—the elder has already passed him, the other is in sight!

Have I made too many figures? For fear of taxing your space, I will rest awhile, although I wanted to talk of France and her railways, and of Russia, and what she wants to do; but must wait another month, and in March more changes may be chronicled; for we are to have another Congress! What a sarcasm— what a commentary on the *peace!* I could laugh, but the peace of the world disturbed is not a subject for merriment.

Steam across the Atlantic was once the exciting topic of the world; now it is the telegraphic cable. Only three hundred and fifty five-thousand-dollar shares! London takes 101; Liverpool, 86; Glasgow, 37; Manchester, 28; other English towns, 10; and the balance, 88, in America :—one-fifth, or 20 per cent., to be paid up; and Mr. Field tells us that on the 4th of July, 1858, England and America—separated on the 4th of July, 1776—are again to be united! Stand back, Columbus! and you, Vespucius, and Ferdinand de Soto, retire! and you, old Miles Standish! You never dreamed that Franklin was to chain the lightning, and that Morse was to extend the chain across the surging Atlantic Ocean! Shakspeare was the only man in early times who thought of putting "a girdle round the earth in forty minutes!" What food for contemplation in the ocean telegraph! The grain market rises in the morning in England, and in the afternoon the ships are filling up in the East River. Cotton advances 1-4 d. in Liverpool at noon, and in New-Orleans, an hour later, thousands of bales change hands.

ARTICLE III.

Milano the Assassin—Verger kills the Archbishop—Former Murders of
   Prelates—Bourse not affected—Parisian Congress—Russia, England,
   and Austria—Switzerland arming—King of Prussia obstinate—The
   firing of a pistol may any day produce a Revolution in Europe—Spain's
   National Debt—Loan of *Mirès*—Geo. Hudson—Espartero—O'Donnell
   —Russia's credit undoubted—Cost of late War—Russian Railways—
   Cost of English and French lines—The Barings introduce the project
   in the London market—Austrian Railways—Austria in a bad way—
   France, and statistics of her Railways—Steam Companies—French
   tonnage—Government speculation—Bank of France—French and
   English Funds—Count De Morny—Persia and China—History of
   Herat—Law of nations the will of the strongest—Canton bombarded
   —Yeh says Nay—History of Canton—Outside barbarians—Com-
   merce against morality — Prospects of opening up the country —
   Money market in England tight—Peace in the West—War in the
   East—The resources of the United States—Revenue and Expenditure
   —Imports and Exports—Banking capital—Gold and Silver coinage
   in America—Ditto in India.

PARIS, FRANCE, *January* 17, 1857.

MY DEAR SIR:—While Milano was being racked
to death under tortures that would have damned even
the Spanish Inquisition, for touching with his bayonet

the sacred ribs of the Neapolitan king, Verger's deep-
laid murder was matured.   Bomba escaped, but the
good Archbishop gave, as the new year opened, his
last benediction.   The one is left to shoot and grind
down his subjects ; while the other, like his prede-
cessor on the barricade in the last revolution, met
his death by violence.   Thomas à Becket, in the Second Henry's time, met a similar fate, (1170 ;) but
Borromeo, Archbishop of Milan, four centuries later,
(1569,) was bullet-proof; and now all France is shocked,
in this third attempt upon a prelate's life, at the success and coolness of the assassin !   The trial takes
place to-day ; the execution will be known when all
is over.   Had he murdered a cardinal, or even the
Pope, it would not have moved the Bourse !   The head
of the Church may fall, but while the Chief of the
State is at his post, the stock exchange heeds not
the crime.   Since the horrible deed, every despotic
monarch in Europe feels less secure ; for it may be
his turn next.   The day of the murder, and the next,
Napoleon did not go to the theatre !

The high and mighty potentates have met, and
parted — but only to meet again.   The conference is
over ; and just nine months from the signing of the
first treaty, another child is born.   All parties are
doing well.   They entered Paris with a flourish of

trumpets ; they separated in good nature. There was
trouble at first : Russia asked England, " When her
fleet was to be withdrawn ?" " When Austria moves
her army," was the cool reply. And, turning to
Austria, " When are you to evacuate the disputed
ground ?" " When England turns her back upon the
Bosphorus." Here, then, was a decided hitch ; but
at last it was all arranged. Russia takes some hundreds of square miles of Moldavian territory for Bolgrad ; so all are satisfied—each with humbugging the
other ! The surveys are to be made ; the line drawn,
so that the " sick man" may get rid of his trouble-
some doctors by the 30th of March. Thus another
Congress, and perhaps a fourth. Better talk than fight.
The treaty is patched up, but we have yet to see its
effects upon the money market.

Another topic — our brave little sister republic that
so firmly has held her Alpine home for centuries—Switzerland, has been arming to meet the invader, and already her firmness has won the admiration of the nations.
As England's titles once included France within her
realms, so did Prussia claim her right of *etiquette*
over Neufchatel ; but the weak and vacillating monarch made a false step when he tried to bully Switzerland. Frederick William, (*Cliquot*, as Punch calls
him), instead of the first Napoleon, is now the Gesler ;

but the people of the mountains are still the children of Tell. They bow to no empty title, and the
nation moves as one man, to cut down those who
would harm their Constitution. Therefore, the King of
Prussia must retire. He must accept the terms or
fight. If he chooses war, France and England are
against him ; if he falls back, he makes himself the
laughing-stock of Europe. Financiers think, with the
diplomatists, that he will choose the latter — hence,
the Bourse keeps on the even tenor of its way.

*These two important questions decided, Europe is
quiet—an almost universal peace. Yes, peace ; but a
breath of wind, a scratch, the firing of a musket,
the death of an emperor, would set the whole fabric
in a blaze. Peace, to be sure, but what a peace !
The world looks on, and wonders what next. Is
Europe really volcanic ! Or, do newspaper writers
croak ? Nous verrons.*

But what of the money market ? You will expect
by the Baltic your usual monthly digest of a looker-
on from Paris, and the Magazine shall not be disappointed ; but to get at the working of the Bourse, I
have to touch on outside topics, and run a race about
the ·world, giving you a *salmagundi* on all leading
countries that bear upon European finance.

Take Spain, once so rich in gold, in agriculture,

and in commerce—Old Spain, who, notwithstanding her poverty and her dotage, owns *one* of the only *two* profitable colonies in the world. Cuba is a nest-egg, and Holland is proud of Java. But what other colonies *pay* their mother country? This gallant old land is split up in cabals and strifes. Her public debt capital of $635,000,000 only yields an annual interest of $10,000,000, and that she cannot pay without calling for a foreign loan. Last month the French banker, M. Mirès, outbid the Spanish capitalists, outbid the Rothschilds, and got the $15,000,000 loan at forty-two—the par one hundred! So much for Spanish credit.

Now there's a famine among the poor; her railways don't even declare dividends, although Geo. Hudson is managing them; and her politics are one thing one day, another the next. Espartero fell before O'Donnell, O'Donnell gave way to Narvaez,* and ambitious men stand outside the door to take his place. The Queen may be the next to lose her power. Spain, geographically, is located between Europe and Africa; and her present condition proves that she is about half-way between civilization and barbarism. So let her go, as, save the last loan, she gives little life to finance.

---

* While these sheets are passing through the press, we hear of the Duke of Valencia's fall.

What of Russia? Is she, too, bankrupt? No, by
no means. England may continue to abuse her, and
she will continue to advance. Formerly she was all
war and rapine; now that she wishes to extend her
commerce, build railways in her lands, and cover her
seas with steamers, England calls her a thief and a
robber, trying to pick the pockets of English capitalists to furnish funds to carry out her enterprises.
How absurd! Look at the truth. Her credit, like
Cæsar's wife, is above suspicion. Rothschild, the Frenchman, places it ahead of the United States. During
the late war, while France added $200,000,000 to her
funded debt, and England about the same; while little Sardinia tacked on $20,000,000, half of which
England guarantees and may have to pay, as is
usually the case with her war loans; while Turkey
is only plunged the deeper in the mud, Russia has
only increased her debt $60,000,000; and, since the
war, has reduced taxation, provided for an extensive
coronation, raised new armies, built new fortifications,
and is ready to march 100,000 men—another Alexander's army—to the assistance of Persia! No; Russia's credit is good, and she will build her railways.
Do you doubt it? The entire track is but 2,600
miles:—

St. Petersburg to Moscow......................miles	670
Kowno Branch.............	60
Moscow to Nijni-Novgorod.........	280
Moscow to Theodosia...................	840
Little Archangel to Libau...........................	750
Total............................	2,600

Count de Morny, says the junior Sir Robert Peel, (in his late extraordinary speech, that has so offended England and Europe,) is a great speculator, and when the Count beat Rothschild, and got the concession for Pereire, he knew that the contract was a good one, that Russia's credit was A 1, and that when the time came, the project would be launched, and as much profit made as there was in the Austrian concession. Notwithstanding cheap land, no government expenses, and serf labor, the roads will cost some $80,000 per mile; in France it costs $105,000; in England $180,000 per mile! The Government guarantee of five per cent., and admission of iron and plant free of duty, assist the enterprise. Although the Board of Management is located in Paris, the President must be a Russian. By-and-by, the Barings will introduce the stock into London, and English foundries, most likely, will make the iron. As the Russian funds held their own all through the war, capitalists will not soon forget such security.

The Austrian concession went off quick, with immense profit to the " *Crédit Mobilier*." While her
public revenue in 1855–6 was but $132,000,000, her
expenditure was $200,000,000. Francis Joseph is no
better a financier than his imperial father. Deficit after
deficit calls for loan after loan, and the National Debt
accumulates, and the National Bank refuses to resume
specie payment. The only science Austria knows is
war; and, to fill her powder magazines, she has contracted with the Egyptian Government for all their
spare saltpetre for five years' time,—1,000 tons per
annum. The reception the Emperor met in Italy was
as cold as Polar ice. Webster told Hulsemann some
plain truths about the beggarly House of Hapsburg.

Since the railway concessions, Russia and Austria
at peace will not materially affect the money market.

Now, then, to France. There is little doubt about
the astonishing progress that France has made in
commerce, manufactures, and agriculture, under the
gigantic credit institutions which have sprung up
during the Empire. Like the building up of new
Paris—(2,524 houses torn down and 5,238 erected
since 1852; the population in 1851 was 1,422,065;
last year it was 1,727,419, an increase of 305,354
in five years)—everything has been forced. Before,
Frenchmen were all war—now, they talk commerce.

Why, from 1823 to 1847, the whole length of French railway concessions was but 2,940 miles, costing some $200,000,000, one-third of which was paid by the State; of which only 1,142 miles were open. During the next four years they increased to 3,095 miles, costing, up to 1851, $100,000,000 more. In June, 1855, they reached 7,185 miles, and at the end of last year, the tables show 10,000 miles, (not all finished,)—some 80 per cent. longer than her canals, and 30 per cent. longer than her public roads. And thus far the cost of all has run up to about $600,000,000. The income on French railways in 1850 was about $17,500,-000, against receipts in 1856 of $54,000,000. On a capital of $301,000,000 the State gives a guarantee of $12,-000,000—important aid, which may account in part for the late heavy dividends. For the 1,920 miles made by the State, they are allowed a share in profits of 3,529 miles. The fusion of companies has been a good move. The original 78 concessions were reduced to 59, and now they are cut down to 24; of which 9 hold nine-tenths of all. Last year 1,600,000 shares paid 16 per cent., and 4 per cent. on 900,000 *unfinished. France has not had her railway panic. Her grand trunk lines pay; but wait till the branches are under way; they will be sure to sap the life-blood of the parent tree. As I observed in my remarks for your. January Number, the money market must open its coffers, for these lines must all be finished.   Other enterprises have also been stimulated to expansion by easy credits.*   A company has just been commenced, with a capital of $4,000,000, to run steamers, *a la* Cunard and Peninsular and Oriental Companies, wherever they have a chance for profit.   Shipping companies are springing into existence as rapidly here as new corporations, under the Limited Liability Act, are in England.   In 1850 the coasting tonnage of France was but 2,069,831 tons; end of 1855, 2,417,430.

The Government seems to initiate all schemes, and lately there is a proposition for a Universal Insurance Company — against fire, flood, and famine — maladies, death, or accident.   In fact, it is to cover every possible contingency.   A Parisian writer in the *Economist* remarks, that a Government which has on its hands the profession of " engineer, miner, road-maker, professor of literature and science, schoolmaster, horse-dealer, farmer, grazier, shepherd, teacher of music and singing, theatrical director, trainer of race-horses, instructor of ballet-girls, etc., etc., need not be ashamed to open an insurance office."   With so many irons in the fire, no wonder money is in demand.   The Bank of France is still draining England of her gold.   Nothing is done less than six per cent., no paper taken over seventy-five days.

The fall on railway and other shares, since last May, arising out of the Bank's refusing to advance on stock, is said to be over $100,000,000 ! Still, the stocks are treble their intrinsic value. The Bank of France requires, say its Managers, more capital.

Note the changes in the French Bank during the last three years ; they show some remarkable facts. At the close of 1854, the Bank of France had eighty-one millions of bullion, and only seventy millions of bills under discount. At the same time in 1855, she had only forty-three millions of bullion, and but eighty-four millions of dollars under discount. Again, in 1856 (this last month's return), with but forty millions of bullion, she has bills melted one hundred and ten millions of dollars. *These few figures tell a strange tale — they need no explanation.* Those who believe in better times on this side, should mark the *facts* given—not my opinions — to show the contrary. England buys Russia's funds, but does not invest in the French. Why ? Simply because her capitalists have not recovered from the fearful confiscation of 1797. The English never forget such things. Old stagers still tell of papering their lodgings with " assignats"—at par in 1789, but five years after down to twenty. Talleyrand bid them off, as the leading stock-jobber, followed by such speculators as Mirabeau and Danton. People now have more confidence in the Government securities. In 1798 there were but 24,796 bondholders ; in 1854, 785,243 ! The accumulations of the savings banks are converted by depositors into *rentes*—three, four-and-a-half, and five per cent. In England, the entire debt is consolidated into a three per cent. Some of the heads of Government have become millionaires by their operations on the Bourse. De Morny (the Emperor's half-brother) could not pay his debts in 1848. Now he is said to be the richest man in the Empire, and last month settled one million on his beautiful bride of eighteen summers, that he brought home with him from the Court of Romanoff. No more to-day on France.

Persia and China attract attention just now. Have you room for another page ? These lands bear upon the money market. War costs millions, and they are both engaged. From Europe, let us turn to Asia—the battle-field has changed. By this time, England and Russia may be approaching each other on Persian ground. Ferukh Khan, the Persian Envoy, has just arrived amid a cloud of retainers and blaze of Oriental display. Napoleon receives him like a prince. Russia inspires the Shah, and England and Persia are at war ! As in the Trojan war, there was a woman in the case—frail, fair, and forty. Diplomacy ended in fighting — so *He*-rat fell to avenge *She*-rat! Your pardon, sir.

A century since, the Affghans took it from the Persians, and now the latter have only taken back their own. They tried to do it in 1815, when Napoleon was under a cloud—and again in 1838, when an English squadron in the Persian Gulf frightened them away, just as the city was about to surrender. The fact is, Herat is the key of Affghanistan, and Affghanistan is the door of India. No wonder England loses color, for India is a jewel in her crown, the value of which she will not appreciate till she lose it. She has not forgotten, however, that the Honorable East India Company spent one hundred millions in that memorable frontier war, and lives innumerable. The will of the strongest, is the law of nations; and if Persia is still stubborn, under Russian councils, England must send out troops, and the demand for a few hundred transports would give a push to the freighting business, and the money market would feel the change.

And China!—music again, and plenty of it! 'Tis the old story, Alexander the Great and the Robber! When you have read Admiral Seymour's despatches, tell me if England has not now a right to the title of Chief of all the Filibusters? Canton bombarded will ring through the States!—but England has no argument this time. Before, in '41, with the Bible in one hand and a bill of smuggled opium in the other, she made her claim. The ten columns of the *Gazette* may be sifted down to a few lines.

The " Caroline" went over the Falls, but Mr. Webster and the elder Baring settled the question. The " Crescent City " and the " Black Warrior " were targets for the Moro's guns, yet we had no war with Spain. Kotza was not given up, Austria was humiliated, but it did not end in war.   But it is far different with the lorcha " Arrow."   When Sir John Bowring found that it was not a British vessel—did not fly the British flag—that the colonial register expired on the 27th September, and the Chinese boarded her to take out the pirates not till the 8th October—when the governor found no Englishman was on board, and the Viceroy's arguments unanswerable,—he changed his tactics—remembered that Canton in 1849 was not opened, as agreed in 1842 and '47—and then decided to make that the issue.   " Open Sesame !" said Admiral Seymour. Sesame declined ! Yeh said *Nay !* And when the Governor-General shut the Canton gate, British cannon soon opened it !   Odessa was spared but Canton, no !   One was strong—the other weak ! Another Sinopean tragedy—almost a Copenhagen !

Canton, then, opened by the Portuguese in 1517 ; visited by the British ships in 1634 ; her direct trade with England dating from 1680, which the East India

Company held till the monopoly was abolished in
1834—Canton, which boldly met the British in 1842,
and has been so long the port of Chinese commerce
—has been bombarded ! The ships in port are ships
of war—the " outside barbarians " are British soldiers !
Trade is stopped—and China, with her imperial canals
—her mammoth highways—her wonderful government
ruling four hundred millions of people—people whose
ancestors understood the use of the mariner's compass,
the art of making gunpowder, glass, and printing—
when our ancestors were a lot of savages — China is
to be again humiliated. The prestige England lost in
Europe last year, and year before, she is likely to regain in Asia !

However, commerce demands it, while morality is
shocked. Commerce is a great leveler, and, of late
years, don't associate much with her early friends.
Throwing right and morals overboard, as they seem to
have been, there are no two opinions about the commercial view. A new field is opening—a new era is
commenced. Ministers at Pekin—foreigners in the interior—all ports open ! Steamers on the China Rivers
—and then, perhaps, railways and telegraphs ! Yes,
perhaps ! but during the period of the war, trade will
be paralyzed. The Americans won't have the English
business under the neutral flag, as before ; for already

American heads, mistaken for English, have been hung on the walls of Canton, and American cannon have battered down some of the forts to revenge it. So America is with England, and France will join! Verily, it looks bad for the Brother of the Sun.

Upon the whole, now is the time to make a strike; commerce and morality are battling for the victory. I should think that the stopping of the machinery would smash some of the engineers, for the China trade is a wide spread credit. Break the spokes in a wheel, and down comes the wagon—take the shoes off and you lame the horse! So will this Canton affair complicate the accounts of the outside barbarians—and hence, Persia and China, as they stand, will keep the money market sleepless.

To come back to England. Money growing tight; bank directors change the rate again—now six and a half per cent., and only 60 days. Turn again, Whittington! Last year they made seven changes—from four and a half, June 26th, to seven per cent. November 13th. The year opened at six, and closed at six and a half. In money matters, as England is to the Continent and all the world, so is the Bank of England to the other banks in the kingdom. She rules the whole.

Peace in the West, but war in the East—so don't

look for an easy money market. The old world is going
to sleep, while the new world has just woke up.
With a national debt of only $30,000,000; with an
income of $77,000,000, to an expenditure $73,000,000,
($13,000,000 of which cancelled the debt); with an
estimated manufacturing and agricultural capital of
$2,600,000,000; with an export table of $323,000,000,
against an import list of $315,000,000, worked upon a
banking capital of $344,000,000; allowed to circulate
$200,000,000 in bank notes; with an overflowing treas-
ury, and unexampled prosperity,—the United States, on
the then inflated surface, ranks first among the nations.
The last reports from the several secretaries have astonished debt-burdened Europe. They don't understand
how we can manage to live on $48,000,000, *fast* (the
last five years average), and when they see a customs
revenue of $64,000,000, they cry "Free Trade!" While
Great Britain takes two-thirds of our entire exports, I
observe that we take in return from her one-half of our
entire imports. It seems that the $50,000,000 that
America loses in trade with Spain, South America, and
China, she makes up out of Great Britain. I note
that from 1793 to 1856, our gold and silver coinage
amounted to $549,341,514; and that the total coin in
the land is now estimated at $100,000,000. India,
during only the last twenty years, has coined over

$300,000,000. Let the Company coin the *mohur* again, give the Indian a pure coin, no alloy, in gold, and the drain in Europe for silver will dry.

Hoping to be in time for February, and that I have not bored you with too many figures, believe me, I am most faithfully,

Yours, &c.

ARTICLE IV.

Great Britain's war with China—Defeat of the British Ministry—Debate in Parliament—Critical state of affairs at Canton—Feverish condition of the Bourse and Stock Exchange—The Bank of England—Discussion of the renewal of its Charter—History of its origin and increase—Commercial retrospect of the last ten years—The system of the Bank of England—The Bank of France—Its leviathan operations during the year 1855, and dividend of twenty-five per cent. —Proposed increase of its capital—Coinage of the French Mint from 1795 to 1855—Effect of the receipts of gold from California and Australia since 1850—Analysis of the condition of the Bank of England—And of the Bank of France—London Joint-Stock Banks and private bankers—Financial condition of Turkey—Establishment of its new National Bank by English capitalists—Prospects of Great Britain's victory over China—Advance in teas, silks, and Chinese goods, and other effects of the Chinese war.

PARIS, FRANCE, *March* 10, 1857.

MY DEAR SIR :—Peace with Persia ! But war, bitter, relentless, revengeful war, with China !

Fehruk Khan, inspired by the Emperor of the French, has negotiated a treaty for the Eastern Shah, while Sir John Bowring, the man of many tongues—England's chief minister east of India—has embarrassed his Government, and jeopardized, not only the heads of his countrymen, but the lives and property of every European in China !

I know not which will startle you the most, the sudden and unexpected defeat of the British Ministry, or the critical state of the question which caused it. Both just at this particular time are the bugbears of the money market.

Lord Palmerston fought like a lion, but all in vain. It was a pitiful sight to see the proud old statesman at bay, trying to ward off the blow, to stem the tide. But the coalition was all-powerful—the plot was well organized, and boldly executed ! As the red-hot shot of Admiral Seymour carried destruction among the houses inside the Canton walls, so the brilliant speeches of the opposition went tearing through the ministerial ranks ! Warren Hastings, with Burke, and Fox, and Sheridan, and Erskine on his track, fared better, three generations since, than the British chief at Hong Kong, with such experienced debaters as Derby, Gladstone, D'Israeli, Cobden, Roebuck, and Lord John Russell, against him ! The walls of the English Commons rung with eloquence, but the oratorical display was all against the Premier. He stood his ground bravely to the last, and when the division came, at half-past two o'clock in the morning, the cheers of the Opposition, repeated by the populace outside, told the Minister that out of the *five hundred and ten votes cast*, he was in a minority of *sixteen!* England was not prepared for it. The Opposition can hardly credit their success, and never before has Parliament been in greater confusion than since the vote of Monday. "Parliament must be dissolved," said the noble Lord on Friday, and he calls upon the House to pass the Mutiny Act, and temporary supplies, before the appeal to the country, where his party feel confident of success. But of China, look at the last news. A young friend of mine left Hong Kong on the 15th of January, and from him and other sources I learn that the state of affairs there is most critical. 'Tis war to the teeth, and not with Christian weapons. Piracy and poison, incendiarism and assassination, are now the Chinese arguments!

The British Admiral had lost his foothold in the Factory Gardens, and six hundred war junks were between his fleet and the open sea! The Celestial emperor confirms the measures of his minister, and general war is proclaimed against the "outside barbarians," whose heads command high prices under royal proclamations! This time the English are fighting with an enraged people, not with a weak government, as in 1842. Every house in flames widens the breach,

every shot that drops among them only seems to
madden the people! When the bakers put the *arsenic*
in the bread, who doubts but the plot was all arranged
to sack the city and massacre all who escaped the
poison? This is our latest news! Is it not, then,
terrible to contemplate what may now be the position
of the foreigners in those seas? What are a handful
of Europeans against a populous nation? Admit the
prowess of the West, but how far can it go against
such fearful odds? The Sepoy regiment which the
Governor of Singapore has sent away to their assistance,
has left in dismay at their defenceless position the
three hundred Europeans in that colony. Having protested against it, they are now at the mercy of the
80,000 Chinese and Malays who have already commenced to show their hostility! Lord Canning can send
no troops from India proper, and but a few hundred from
Ceylon, and the Singapore Sepoys. Sir John Bowring
must depend upon the mother country for assistance,
and notwithstanding the Govermental defeat, five thousand men have orders to embark from England forth-
with. I hope they may arrive in time, but I can but
have my fears for the safety of the little band who are
cut off from everything but the ships in the harbor. If
they escape poisoning, or assassination, they may get
away from the country in merchant ships, but they

must move in time. These are the facts; are my fears well grounded? Judge for yourself. You can well understand that the Chinese war and the fall of the Ministry are the leading topics on the Bourse and the Stock Exchange. Both crowd out all others; both touch the Funds. Both seem to keep the money market in a continual fever, which, coupled with the discussion on the Budget, the removal of the bank charter, the gossip regarding the great international credit company, the continual withdrawal of gold from England, to pay for continental silver, which in its turn passes away to India—four million dollars by this mail—the daily announcement of extensive failures, eight houses alone among the Greeks, whose credit has stood so high, —all tend to unsettle financial affairs, and keep up the present stringency—six per cent. *within*, but twice that *without*, the charmed circle of favored names! Outside the defeat of Ministers, the dissolution of Parliament, and the state of China, the bank charter renewal seems to attract the most attention among financial men.

The Act of 1844 died a natural death during the late war, but Ministers were too busy with Russia to talk finance; hence postponement then brings up the question now, and Bank Directors ask for another ten years' charter. You wish me to talk commerce—I

will; but to do so, I must bring in politics, and
both introduce finance, and when that subject is in
hand, one of its important features is the position of
the National Banks.   With your permission, then, as
I have done in former letters, I propose to take up
briefly some of the figures of the Bank of England,
and compare them with those of the Bank of France,
for these two are the fountains from which all the
others are fed.   The blue-books tell us that some one
hundred and seventy years ago, when England was at
war with France, the former wanted funds, and no
better way was suggested than by establishing a National Bank; so in 1694 the Act of Incorporation was
signed, and the Bank of England commenced operations upon a paid-up capital of *six million dollars,*
every penny of which was lent to the Government,
for the sum of five hundred thousand dollars per annum!   The original loan was small, but the system
worked well; and whenever the Government wanted
help, new amendments were proposed, and from this
small beginning the amount lent to Government is now
seventy-three million dollars, which is its present amount
of stock!   The Bank was started as a Government
aid, and not for trading purposes; and as it was at
first so it is now—the Government's pet.   Before the
Act can be annulled, the above amount must be paid

into the Bank. Other Acts only give certain privileges, while the main Act stands as it did in the seventeenth century. Therefore, Peel's Act of 1844, now before Parliament, may be renewed for another ten years, or not, without affecting its original charter. In 1833 one-fourth of the debt or capital was paid off, leaving *fifty-five million dollars*, which is the amount you always note in the weekly returns. This one-fourth paid by the Government was retained by the bank, say *eighteen millions*, as working capital, but then the "*Rest*" amounts to nearly as much, say *sixteen-and-a-half millions*, which, added to the main stock, gives an entire sum of *eighty-nine millions*, of which fifty-five millions were advanced to the Government, and thirty-four million dollars employed in the active business of the bank. All profits are, however, divided among the holders of the seventy-two millions of stock.

The *Economist* has lately published some most instructive Tables, a most important reference for parliamentary discussion. They run back to 1778, just after our Declaration of Independence, when the whole circulation was but thirty-five millions, and the entire deposits were but twenty-five millions, and stop with the Bank Act of 1844, when the circulation had reached one hundred and five millions, and the deposits had touched sixty millions.

The above returns embrace the period of the twenty-two years' suspension (Pennsylvania did better), and covering a fluctuation in the stock of bullion from three millions to eighty-one millions. The lowest depreciation of the bank note during the Bank's embarrassment was in 1814, just before Wellington turned the day against Bonaparte at Waterloo, when the note dropped twenty-five and one-eighth per cent! But in 1821, about the time of Napoleon's death, a resumption of cash payments brought the bank note to its sovereign value, where it has remained, notwithstanding the fact of the Bank having in the one department but two million two hundred thousand dollars in bullion, against an active circulation of one hundred and one million, on the 23d of October, 1847! Had a few of the ten million of depositors called upon the bank, they would have had to use their Government letter, and shut down the gate, as they did in 1797!

In 1825–'26–'27, the crisis was severest upon bankers; the panic of 1837 covered all classes—prosperity in 1835—inflation in 1836—crash in 1837. In 1847 the merchants were the leading sufferers by the crisis, but as is always the case, the general public suffered more or less. Ten years since, twenty-two firms came down in Calcutta alone for about forty million dollars. Following out the view expressed in my first letter, that these periodical revulsions come round every ten years, what is to prevent the rule from including 1857? Certainly some rather astonishing elements have been introduced since the last break down of credit—among other things the aid of steam and telegraphs has changed exchanges, and money markets of different nations are more sympathetic than formerly in consequence. Railroads, industrial enterprises, and commerce have shot ahead as was never known before, and when, I ask, has the rate of interest ruled so high on the European side as in 1856? When has the world ever dug out of the mines before, six hundred and twenty-five millions gold in seven years? and yet, when has the bullion kept so low throughout the year as in the national banks? At no time since 1842, not omitting 1847, has the bullion department of the Bank of England showed such low figures as the average in 1856. When before, in five years' time, have financiers seen one hundred and seventy-four millions specie pass by the pyramids to the East? When did British exports reach nearly six hundred millions previous to last year? and when has a nation built twenty-five thousand miles of railway within so brief a period as has the United States?

These, then, are some of the changes that have come round since the last severe panic in the money

market, and older heads than mine are puzzled to un-
derstand how they are to affect the prosperity of the
world.

The doubling of the rate of interest may be ac-
counted for by the simple fact of the doubling of the
trade, the navigation, and the commerce of the country. Twelve years ago the figures were just half
what they are to-day; and twelve years hence, if the
same ratio goes on with the one, what should prevent
it from affecting the other—placing the interest at *twelve*
per cent. instead of *six ?* Increase of trade demands
increase of capital; and more capital a higher rate
of interest.

But to return to the Bank of England. The Directors pursue a surer policy than formerly. They regulate the rates of interest and discounts by supply and demand, and not by circulation; and the true position of
the Bank may be shown by noting the amount of the
" public securities," and the bullion in the vaults. Last
Saturday's return gives a trifle less than one hundred
million dollars to the former, and about fifty-one million
to the latter !

The Bank of England has *eleven* branches, each
bank's notes payable at place of issue, but all met in
coin at the parent establishment in London. London
takes two-thirds of the entire issue of notes, leaving but

one-third for the provinces—*i. e.*, of a circulation of one hundred and five million, seventy are issued in London, and thirty-five million at the branch establishments. The Bank pays the government, for this privilege of issue, about one million dollars per annum, and receives a handsome sum in return for managing the public debt. The notes are only legal in England—although current throughout the Kingdom—the Joint Stock Bank Act of 1845 having provided against their legality in Ireland and Scotland.

From England let us turn to France. Just two centuries from the time Queen Elizabeth planted the seed of the Indian Empire, and one hundred and four years after the establishing of the Bank of England, Napoleon founded the Bank of France—commencing in 1800 with a capital of eighteen million, and a reserve fund of two-and-a-half million—in all a working capital of about twenty million dollars. Just for a moment look at its leviathan operations in 1855. During that year the bank discounted nine hundred and forty million dollars. No wonder that the fortunate stockholders grew merry over their annual dinner, when the President announced a dividend of *twenty-five per cent.* In 1845, the number of branch banks was twenty-four, and in 1855, thirty-eight; but you will best see the increase of its operations from 1846 to 1856, by making the figures. Before the fall of the Bourbon dynasty, its discounts were but three hundred and forty-five million; under the Napoleonic rule, nine hundred and forty. In 1846, only eighty-six million were discounted at the branches; in 1855, five hundred and forty-nine million. The business of the Bank of 1852 was even doubled in 1856. In 1855, one hundred million dollars was advanced on railway stock alone !

The French Revolution, it is well known, deadened trade. In 1847, the discounts at the bank were some two hundred and sixty-five million; during the two succeeding years they were fifty-one million and sixty-eight million, respectively—showing the effect of revolutions on commerce. But the operations of late years are of the greatest magnitude. If on so limited a capital they have done so much, what might we expect if the Government increase it, as has been proposed, to fifty million? I doubt whether it will be done, for the International scheme, on a capital of twenty-five million, seems to meet the sanction of the Emperor. To change it, would take much time; 'tis a slow process. First the bank makes the movement, then Council of State, then Legislative body, afterwards the Senate, and then the Government has to make it public, all of which creates delay. A glance at the mint operations tells us that—

From 1795 to 1855, the total amount of gold coined in
France was $573,000,000
Amount coined during same time in silver.......... 917,000,000

Total coined.................... $1,490,000,000

During the last six years, France has coined four
hundred million in gold; but only, for the same time,
forty-five million in silver.

But to cut it finer, take the past two years.
While the mint has turned out one hundred and
eighty-three million of gold coin, she has made but
fifteen million in silver. It is estimated that over two
hundred and fifty million of silver coin has been displaced by the late gold discoveries! The Bank of
France, to-day, has but about half the amount of bullion which was in her vaults in 1850––then, eighty-five
million; now, forty million. It is worthy of note, that
of the two hundred million of specie exported to the
East during the last few years, all the silver went on
past Ceylon, while the gold stopped this side the Red
Sea. In round numbers, why not see how this Bank
stands to-day—what are its obligations?

Commence, if you please, with paid-up capital........ $20,000,000
Take its deposits, private and public, say............. 45,000,000
Now add circulation................................ 120,000,000

On the one hand you have...................... $185,000,000

Against: mercantile paper, bearing always three names, a large amount of which is for small tradesmen, under 100 francs—say for bills discounted, short date......	\$105,000,000
Government securities, all realizable, save 10,000,000....	40,000,000
Bullion in reserve....................................	40,000,000
On the other..........	\$185,000,000

Now to make a rough calculation on the Bank of England. We may compare the two—

First take stock entries.....	\$73,000,000
Add accumulated reserve, or " rest"	16,500,000
Making a capital of.............................	\$89,500,000
But of this sum, 55,000,000 is Government debt—not represented by stock, not transferable, and consequently not available; therefore deduct these dead weight securities	55,000,000
And you have, as the actual capital of the bank, but about	\$34,500,000
Deposits, public and private.....	85,000,000
Notes in circulation, including bank post bills and money orders...................	105,000,000
Say........................	\$190,000,000
Add capital, or Government debt, not including reserve of \$16,500,000..................................	73,000,000
	\$263,000,000
But to get a fair comparison, omit Government debt....	55,000,000
	\$208,000,000

And add "rest" or reserve ....•......... $16,500,000

You have on the one side liabilities amounting to.. $224,500,000

Now what has the bank to meet them?

First : Government securities, including dead weight, not available. $75,000,000

Private securities—notes, bills, &c.................... 97,500,000

Bullion, as shown by last Saturday's return... 52,000,000

$224,500,000

Therefore, throwing out the Government debt and the dead weight securities, the two great banks stand thus : With a capital of thirty-four and a half million, the Bank of England has obligations to the public of one hundred and ninety million dollars ; while the Bank of France, with a capital of twenty million, has obligations amounting to one hundred and sixty-five million dollars—which, it will be seen, is a trifle in favor of the English Bank.

The capital and obligations of these prominent national institutions bear no comparison to the credits of London joint-stock banks. They possess a capital of fifteen million dollars, on the strength of which they have received deposits amounting to one hundred and ninety million, against forty million in 1844. Under the Act of 1844, there were two hundred and eight private bankers, and seventy-two joint-stock banks, established. The authorized issues under the Act were twenty-five million to the private, and seventeen million to the joint stock. Since 1844, the decline of private bankers shows forty-five as having ceased issuing notes, twenty-two of which have stopped payment, and nine joint stock, six of which failed. During the last ten years, seven hundred and thirty-eight million dollars bullion have been imported into England; yet the average amount held by the Bank of England was three million four hundred thousand dollars less than in 1846, notwithstanding the increase of exports from two hundred and eighty-eight millions in 1846, to some six hundred millions in 1856; while France imported, 'from 1849 to 1855—

Bullion.. .	$512,000,000
And exported same time...	300,000,000
Leaving in the country.	$212,000,000

And yet the French bank, at the end of 1856, had about eighteen million less than in 1846. I wish some Adam Smith or Francis Bacon would rise up among us, and explain away the inconsistencies and perplexing questions of the time.

Pardon me for making so many figures—another day I will be less elaborate. One word on Turkey, and a closing remark on China, and I have done. I intended to write more at length on the financial position of the Ottoman Empire, but I find I have not the space. You are aware that the American and Grecian bankers have been disgusted by the Sultan's having given the concession for the new National Bank to English capitalists. Sixty millions is the capital, ten of which must be paid down in cash—the bank to commence operations six months after the signing of the firman. Two thirds of the facilities go to the Government, the other to agriculture and commerce. Capitalists are sanguine of success, and English contractors are swarming through Turkey.

I must say I was not impressed with Constantinople, when there last May. Any port but that for me The growth and decay of the Ottoman power, its rise and fall ; now calm, now surging with dissensions, so strangely historical in Mahomet's career, the first Emperor, past the Koran, past Solyman the Great, down to the present effeminate monarch—Turkey, in all respects, is a most interesting study. Financially, she needs support. This bank is just in time. All the old coin and worthless paper hawking among the Turks, will disappear before the new stamp. The " sick man " needs the doctor, for the harem is suffocated with the extravagant bills of the women. All the

Sultan desires is money—money to keep off the duns at his door.

With a revenue of from $25,000,000 to $30,000,000, say..... $30,000,000

See what is done with it :

Interest on the national debt................... $5,000,000
The Sultan—for his harem, his palaces, and his
      women—takes the modest sum of....... 7,500,000
Leaving for the military and civil list, say..... 17,500,000
                           ————— $30,000,000

In fact this last sum is much cut up, for it is well-known that the Sultan, for the use of the seraglio, is privileged to issue bonds called "shekims," bearing two per cent. interest per month—California rates. During the last six months the Sultan has been short, and has issued five million dollars of these bonds, which you will see adds, for the small item of interest, the enormous sum of one million two hundred and fifty thousand dollars to the State debt. To gain the outside sum, put down as revenue, twice that amount is levied. It first costs at court fifty per cent. to get in the taxes, and then the court alone pockets one-third of all that gets into the treasury—a system of thieving commencing with the slave, and improving in deceit till it reaches the palace. English energy and English capital will give new life to decay-

ing Turkey. As a nation she is strong in her weakness.
The great powers guarantee her nationality, and will
fight over over her grave.

Since writing the foregoing, Parliament has been active on the China question. Lord Palmerston is game
even yet; troops and ambassadors are getting away
with all dispatch. Meanwhile, teas, silks, and all Chinese "notions" will advance. Firms may suspend,
and European heads be strung along the Canton walls,
but, in the end—when England commences in earnest,
when John Bull is fairly aroused, when "Dear Tea"
will be the word to return Lord Palmerston's party to
power, when the fleet walls up the Chinese waters
and stops the machinery of the Imperial Canal—who
can doubt as to who will be the victor? England must
succeed. Opportunely enough, the Persian affair is put
to bed, and a fine army is released for China purposes. The result will stimulate commerce. Human
life, individual property, and public treasuries, will not
be spared to shake the Tartar's dynasty. The East
and the West must have an understanding. England
wants more room for trade, and she sees it along
the China rivers. Those who are familiar with the
China trade will see at once, how embarrassing all
this meanwhile will be to Chinese commerce and Eu-

ropean operations. Ships go a begging, for China has nothing now for them. Commission houses look wishfully at their cotton goods in the Canton *go-downs.* By this time they know how much the Chinese owe them, or rather *how much they owe the Chinamen.* Exchange operations stand still; documentary credits are useless. The East India Company write home to say, that it is killing the opium trade; and the Parsees, who are dropping one hundred and fifty dollars on every chest, must fall back on the India banks; and the India banks have had all they want in the way of losses, through advances on rice and seeds. All wait now for later dates. Other nations, in China, are no better placed than the English. The Americans cannot manage the entire trade as in 1842. That pleasant dream was dispelled when Admiral Armstrong shelled the forts; but now he has withdrawn, on the clause in Yeh's letter, to the Rev. Peter Parker, saying "There's no cause of strife between us;" but no apology was given. The French and Americans indirectly assist the English; but their nations are not so decided what to do. Such is the position of matters in the East; so, between this China question, the dissolution of Parliament, the Russian railways, and the Turkish bank, with a speculative mania commencing again in France, and new operations requiring capital on all sides—money is in demand and tight.

If I have taxed your pages, and your readers' patience, in this letter, I promise to be more agreeable in the next.

ARTICLE V.

PARIS, FRANCE, *April* 1, 1857.

MY DEAR SIR:—The "Tulip Mania" of Holland, the "Mississippi Land Scheme" of France, and the "South Sea Bubble" of England, are landmarks in the history of the Stock Exchange. The journals of those days have recorded the madness of the times. The Arabian Nights' Entertainments are not more romantic, for there is a certain wildness in reckless speculation.

Fraud in high places was the word of the hour;

money in trust vanished with the air; and mercantile morality was hardly known among the pullers of the wires.

Think of paying thousands of pounds for a tulip root, millions for paper land, and tens of millions for ventures in the South Sea! And when this last bubble swallowed up all its rivals, and burst; when, like Alexander, it had nothing more to conquer, the explosion spread misery throughout the Kingdom! The thousand per cent. dividend was a myth, and the rich man was poorer than the pauper!

A century and a half have passed since then; England has rolled up a National Debt that would sweep away 40 per cent. of the entire National domain, and individual and public wealth, to liquidate it; but America, in the meantime, has lived and flourished through three wars, and many "rumors of wars," and placed her fifteenth President in the White House.

Great as is the lapse of years since the Old World was speculation-mad, some of the elements of the present day are not so unlike. Bubble Companies may have a sounder bottom, but little less morality. Schemes as desperate, on a smaller scale, find daily birth; neat circulars, glowing advertisements, "splendid results," meet you everywhere. Speculation marks our day as well as theirs. Forgery, breach of trust, fraud among the leaders, seem to be as prevalent now as then, though not on so grand a plan. Each day the London editors chronicle some new instance of crime. The press of France is voiceless, hence French bubbles are seldom seen floating upon the waters. The water runs too deep—the plans are not worked out. 'Tis true that Charpentier and Grelet took a few hundred thousand dollars out of the Northern Railway, but what of that? And Cousin, Legendre, and Duchesne de Vere managed to cheat the shareholders of the " Docks Napoleon" out of $1,400,000—a refined swindle—but, with this exception, *the bubbles are not quite ripe.* In England, however, we get them every mail. The shameful frauds of the Tipperary and the Royal British Banks, are not yet cold, when crash on crash increases the malady that keeps the money market so sleepless. No wonder shareholders tremble and grow pale under such terrible responsibilities. A dozen bubbles have exploded since I wrote you in February—each worse than its neighbor. The public was disquieted to find that the Directors of the Paris and London Bank had squandered $70,000 in preliminaries before the Bank had opened its doors; still more so, to see the Australian Agricultural Company run through all its capital of

$1,900,000, with nothing to show for it; but what is now their surprise, to see the London and Eastern Joint-Stock Bank in such a mess—only three years old—with a capital of $1,250,000, loaning one Director, Col. Waugh, on his rotten securities, $1,200,000, within $50,000 of its whole stock in trade! How many other leading financiers have taken in the Banks as junior partners? The community is indignant, and well it might be. More misery for shareholders and depositors; more spoils for the lawyers; more distrust; less confidence; a general inquiry of—What next?

The North of Europe Steam Company is also in the papers — $2,500,000 was a respectable capital, but lately one man has relieved them of a handsome sum, and it seems that their last was a bogus dividend! Bogus directors—bogus auditors—no wonder the bubbles burst so rapidly! Redpath coolly takes $1,200,000 out of the Northern Central, (an English Schuylerism,) and gives a portion to his church—the rest to charities! Noblemen shake hands with the $1,500 clerk who could give such dinners, and was so good. Robson was more modest. His frauds had not matured. The Crystal Palace—poor bubble—did not need this last stab to sink it. While these pleasant transactions were taking place in England, Huntington was gaining popularity on forged notes in Wall-street.

The moralist has room for work. Go on the Bourse, and look at the starting eyes of some of the opera-tors—what a life is that of the *Rouge et Noir!* M. Proudhon, the Socialist writer of 1848, has the pen--- "Wild luxury—sumptuous debauchery—vice reveling in gold—prostitution attired in silk—are the consequences of fortunes made without labor!"

The present century cannot record more financial immorality than the journals have announced during the last six months. Formerly you noted one fraud a year—now 'tis every week. When Robert Ashlett robbed the Bank of England, in 1803, of $1,600,000, wild was the excitement; but when Henry Fauntleroy, in 1824, forged for $150,000, he was arrested, tried, convicted, and *hung* in the presence of one hundred thousand persons! When Rowland Stephenson, in 1828, gambled away $1,350,000, and broke his bank, the public was indignant. The shock to public morals was most severe—" 'twas more than half a dozen failures," wrote the *Times* on the 10th of January, 1829.

Such cases were very rare till lately, when the mania breaks out anew. M. Proudhon uses strong language when writing on the Bourse. He says all France is stock mad. No matter the company, it is sure to sell. Gold is the motive power with which Napoleon moves the machinery of his Empire.

Pensioned generals, salaried colonels, well-paid soldiers : gold on all sides—a golden shower. Bonaparte
made his throne, and holds it well. Ministers, bankers, and the Bourse—a goodly company. Notwithstanding the ruinous depreciation in the public fortunes of
France during the Revolution of 1848—a fall of 50
per cent —in spite of short crops, famine, inundation,
and two war years, the outward sign of prosperity
stands more prominent than ever. Mark, I say, the
outward.

In 1833, the entire public fortune of France was
but $4,000,000,000 (the sum of England's unpaid
notes). This amount was represented by—securities,
$3,350,000,000 ; metallic currency, $650,000,000. To-
day, the same returns show an increase of 75 per
cent. ; for the National wealth has rolled up to $7,000,-
000,000 ! Can this be a sound state of finance?

In 1826, there were but 32 companies, with a capital of $11,000,000. Twelve years later, just after the
crisis of 1838, there were 1,039 companies, representing a capital of $350,000,000. Railway shares
alone have increased, since they were first issued, some
$212,000,000! Will this continue ? The *Budget* will
best show the returns. In 1829, just before the Bourbon tried his hand as King, it amounted to $180,-
000,000 ; now it is nearly twice that, and yet taxes are
collected as easily as thirty years ago.

Association is also one of the traits of the present age. A certain joining of forces—a combination of interests—union of capital. Europe is swarming with companies—a prospectus for everything in Christendom—from supplying a theatre with actors to building a church. What an odd idea—putting a church into shares ˋand stock ! But so it is. Where individuals fail, companies lose larger, and bring wider ruin. Government the prop of all ; and when it trembles, down tumbles the house of cards—the credit of the Bourse ! Corporations take the poor man's money, and the nation prospers.

See what association has done for the United States. Our railways never would have been built by individuals. The farmer's real estate advances to make up the loss on stock. Foreign iron must be imported, and able-bodied Irishmen ; which gave employment to a fleet of ships, and mechanics prospered in launching them. The labor itself was a fortune. If a black man will sell under the hammer for a thousand dollars, the several millions of able-bodied workmen brought over from the old country to make our Western roads, at Southern prices, would be worth more than a cotton crop. But we should wait for the re-action.

Association covers a wide field, and rules our time, while individuals rule it. The grand company, after all, follows the beck of the originator. As Palmerston rules England, Napoleon France, Alexander Russia, Biddle ruled the Bank. So one mind in the Board of Directors has everything his own way—one head generally manages the Board. Enterprise, talent, launches the scheme; outsiders throw in the money; dividends are paid for a few years, and then comes another phase of association—companies assisting each other; a wider range of kiting.

Literary clubs, political reunions, public charters, are some of the fruits of association. When you reflect, you find but a few men rule the world; a few men formed the Fremont party, and a few men elected Buchanan! Association of governments gave us war, and afterwards the same association made a peace. I wish they would turn their talents to something useful, such as cutting that Siamese band at Darien, making islands of the two Americas, as France and England propose to do with Africa and Asia, by channeling a road to Suez. The world's commerce demands something new, and if no more continents remain to be discovered, why not divide those we have, and multiply the tracks across the seas? The iron path at Panama was worthy of our nation; another year, that from Alexandria to Cairo will connect at Suez the Mediterranean with the Sea of Pharoah.

Association does it. Trans-Atlantic steam lines, under its influence, are most fashionable. The Emperor approves of it; the Government indorses his acts; the *Crédit Mobilier* has the money; and France, not content with military honors upon the land, is looking oceanward. The French merchants are putting out to sea! I saw few French ships and few French firms, while running round the world the other day, while the English and Americans were everywhere. Napoleon will change all that. He reduces the army, but augments the navy, and has much faith in foreign commerce as a civilizer. When the French steamers open the trade, and the French and German railways are united, the new packets will get the continental trade; and with a good Government grant, and all the French business to support them, the new Trans-Atlantic lines will prove a thorn in the side of the English companies, and will bid fair to rob them of some good freights, and English merchants of some good commissions. France begins to profit by the lessons of her neighbor.

Association, which has done so much for England and America, is making its way into the European world. Germany has organized some fifteen or twenty new credit companies, all flushed with paper, based on nothing tangible. She has to-day some 300,000,000 of paper notes in circulation. Austria has $45,000,000 hard silver in her treasury lying idle; but her depreciated paper may be found in every village, valueless after it passes the frontier. I discovered that by the best of teachers—experience.

Banking on a grand scale is the aim of modern financiers. I like to trace its rise and progress—since the first William founded the Exchequer 800 years ago—since the formation of the "Society of Merchant Adventurers," in 1248—since one of the early bankers, Sir Josiah Child, (whose ships did not return from the East, where they assisted in founding the Indian Empire in 1601, in time to bring the money to meet his notes,) borrowed $200,000 to keep him afloat. Later on, in 1661, this company numbered 3,500 members, but the Government suppressed it in 1689. How easily one can run back and look over each step from the early ages—from barter to bullion, bullion to credit, credit to bills of exchange—from the Anglo-Saxons, who introduced *pence*, to the Normans, who added, *pounds* and *shillings*, and thus established the currency of England—so clumsy and inferior to our Federal money. The Jews were the first private bankers, then the Lombards, and afterwards came the Goldsmiths. Henry III. and the Pope managed their money matters by bills of exchange; and when Spain paid France that heavy subsidy in 1804, the financial movement by bills, on England, through the continental exchanges, was a study. The rate of interest in the olden times ranged high—Cromwell reduced it to six per cent., the bank rate of both France and England to-day; Queen Anne dropped it to five.

Leatham estimates the bills of exchange issued in England in 1839 at $2,642,000,000, $660,000,000 of which were running at one time. The amount now must be something more extensive. The bankers of England manage her entire business. America draws and sells bills at home, but in England the buyer in the country draws on London, and the Americans have to meet the bills before maturity. The exchange is on England. Will not our railway securities and our exports some day make a rate the other way? So long as England levies a toll on the business of the world, pocketing a commission out of everything and everybody, she will give herself no trouble about it. New-York, as the outlet of American commerce, must bring the theory into practice. The electric cable will benefit America more than England.

Just now American bonds drag. England prefers Russian to French funds; loans money to Sardinia, but no more to Spain; makes advances on a miserable Greek bond or Persian obligation; builds the Thames Tunnel, the Tubular Bridge, the Crystal Palace, and the " Great Eastern ;" Turkey gets a loan ; India is not forgotten ; Mexico is befriended ; yet when we are in the market, England thinks of Sydney Smith and Pennsylvania ; talks of repudiation ; mentions California ; and looks sharp (but not sharp enough) at all securities that find their way to the money market. Notwithstanding this, we buy the iron, sell the bonds, pay the dividends, build more roads, and grow rich on England's money.

England is, and always has been, in the hands of her bankers—the cleverest men in the kingdom : such as Francis Child, the banking goldsmith, and " Jingling Georgie," old Herriot, who founded the hospital at Edinburgh. Thomas Coutts died in 1822, (one year after Napoleon,) at eighty-seven. At one time he was the banker of George III. His fortune, of $4,500,000, from his wife, passed to his grand-daughter, Miss Burdett Coutts, the owner of the bank of Coutts & Co., managed through trustees. Then there was Strahan, Paul & Co., established in the seventeenth century, one of the first and most respectable of the old bankers. Their successors, as you are aware, have been transported for fraud and perjury. Jones, Lloyd & Co. were long ago great names, and are still. Mr. Lloyd, the dissenting minister, became the banker, whose offspring became a peer, the present Lord Overstone. This was the firm, says Lawson, in his " History of Banking," that introduced the phrase (not the practice) known among bill-drawers—"Pork on bacon!" The Barings have done their share in holding high the banker's reputation.

"Who rules the banking world?" asked Lord Byron, in Don Juan. "Jew Rothschild, and his fellow Christian Baring!" When the learned student, Meyer Anselm, died at Frankfort, in 1812, his parting advice to his five sons was to hang together. He knew the power of association. In 1808, Nathan Meyer Rothschild settled in Manchester. From buttons he went to banking. He managed investments so well as to gain the entire patronage of the German princes, and since then the house of Rothschild has been the friend of despotic kings. He was really a great man. He not only introduced the practice of the payment of dividends on fo reign loans into England, but he arranged them to be paid in sterling. He loaned to European powers, established rates of exchange on any part of the world, moved bullion and merchandise to suit his wishes, founded houses in the chief continental cities, sent agents to every commercial port, always received the latest intelligence—and so retentive was his memory, he never carried a note-book!

On Tuesdays and Fridays you would always find him at "Rothschild's Pillar" on the Stock Exchange. A broker by the name of Rose was the only man who was bold enough to occupy the stand of the Money King, and he disputed the right but an hour. Rothschild wrote a miserable hand. A Montrose banker once made him wait a week in Scotland, that he might see if his check was cashed in London. On the 28th of July, 1836, a carrier pigeon brought to London from Frankfort this simple dispatch—" *He is dead.*"

The Brothers Rothschild have shown, in their success, the power of association. Their sons will take their place, and with proper management may hold their honors another generation. The private bankers have the best of it lately, for the recent disclosures have shaken confidence in the joint-stock companies. Great competition has introduced great facilities, and overdrawn accounts on bogus securities have proved fatal in several cases. The unlimited liability is sweeping in its effects. The rich shareholder is held for every pound of indebtedness. The Bank of England and the private bankers wage hot war against the joint-stock enterprise. Mr. Gilbart, the distinguished financial writer and talented Manager of the London and Westminster Bank, was the first to break down that protective Act, prohibiting the establishment of any other bank within sixty-five miles of London! In 1834, (the year the East India Company lost their monopoly of the China trade,) he succeeded, and most ably has he governed the bank of which he was the founder. At first the Bank of England refused him a drawing account, and the Clearing House was equally hostile. The wedge once in, the system soon spread over the kingdom.

No *banker* can be elected to the Directory of the Bank of England ; merchant stockholders only are eligible, and no stockholder can have more than four votes. The Bank has just declared a semi-annual dividend of four-and-a-half per cent. The "Rest" now stands at $15,000,000. The net profit for the half year was $3,430,000 ! Few questions are asked at these meetings ; " as secret as a bank director or bank return" has become a proverb. The " sweating-room" could a tale unfold !

It was not my intention, when I commenced this letter, to occupy so much room in running along the page of banking, bubbles, and speculation, but the subject widened as I wrote, and from the " Society of Merchant Adventurers," six centuries since, I have passed from age to age, until I come down to the grandest of all banking projects—the " International Bank of Paris"— the most wonderful speculation of the day !* Stand off, Pereire ! The *Crédit Mobilier* has now a more powerful rival than your old employer, Rothschild ! The

* The unsettled state of the money market killed the project in its infancy.

programme is not disguised. It is a "Société Ano-
nymé," styled "The International Compańy of Commercial Credit ;" responsibility limited to amount of
its shares ; its business : banking, commerce, agency,
in short, everything appertaining to *la question d'ar-
gent*. The difference between this Company and the
Crédit Mobilier is, that the one affects to be, while the
other starts upon the ground that it really is, international. The capital is enormous—twice that of the *Crédit Mobilier*—$24,000,000 to commence with ! Eng-
land and France take a third each—the balance is for
the Continent. With such machinery, the advances may
open with, say $500,000,000. This is indeed a power
—a king among his subjects. What an immense field
for speculation ! What an impetus it will give to
trade ! With no liability but its shares—no check save
a warning from the Government ! All minor banks are
swamped—outsiders will be crushed ! With such power,
they can defy litigation ; rule the judicial bench ; dictate to cabinets ; make war or demand peace ; manage
the world's staples ; spend millions where others dispense
hundreds ; play the despot in commerce ; everywhere
dictating with iron rule !

There are to be twenty-five directors—fifteen French,
six English, and four German. Among some of the
proposed names are M. Armand Donon, (Donon, Aubrey,
Gautier, & Co.,) M. Albert Dufour, (Managing Director

of the German General Bank of Leipsic,) M. Robert Kayser, (Vice-President of the Hamburg North German Bank,) MM. Soul, Arthur, De Haber & Henri, F. L. Marce, (agents for M. David Hausemaine, formerly Prussian Minister of Finance, now Manager of the Berlin Discount Company,) Wm. Gladstone, (Thomson, Donon, & Co., London and St. Petersburg Directors of the Orleans Railway Company,) Mr. Weguelin, (Governor of the Bank of England,) David Solomon, Charles Morrison, Arthur Haukey, and several others; but this list will show the metal of the leaders—in my opinion, if it can get under way—the most powerful bank ever established. Speculation can now flourish, and the wildest schemes need not give up all hope. This great project is to wield immense influence everywhere. So sympathetic is finance, each nation acts upon its neighbor. So with the bank on all about it. This scheme will show the wildness of the times.

The movement of the precious metals still occupies the mind of financial writers. That, and the bank charter debates, keep up the money excitement. M. Michael Chevalier is out in the *Debats* on the bank question. He does not believe in dead-weight securities or loans to States—thinks it causes panic when commerce is in a bad way, and that a national bank should stand on national credit.

Humboldt says that the silver production of America

from Columbus's visit, 1492, to 1803, was estimated at $4,355,428,500; from 1803 to 1848, the period of the new gold Ophirs, $1,270,000,000; add for other countries, say $575,000,000; making a total of $6,200,428,500.

Chevalier puts down the *average* silver production during this century at—in 1800, 37,000,000; in 1840, $35,000,000; in 1850, 45,000,000; of which Mexico gives 60 per cent—West Coast and South America the balance.

The Russian economist Oretshoff, says that he estimates, after having examined Humboldt, Chevalier, and other financial writers, that the total weight of silver in the world may be stated at 500,000,000 pounds, or 250,000 tons; while he puts the gold down at 32,000,000 pounds, or 16,000 tons. Now, if these statements may be relied upon, I don't think we need feel much alarm at seeing some $70,000,000 per annum find its way eastward; for if we produce forty or fifty millions each year, the balance can't be great. Besides, some time it must come back again —'tis only a question of exchange, or balance of trade.

For want of some better cause, the money market is said to be depressed on account of the elections— a poor argument. The present election cries have been, War! or No war! Palmerston! or Derby!

Free Trade against Protection, was the rally for the last two Parliaments ; but this time the practical working of the free trade principle has dissipated the illiberal policy. 'Twas up-hill work for a long time; shipowners stormed, landowners argued, colonies battled against that tide which, taken at its ebb, led on to the repeal of the corn laws, of the navigation laws, and to the equalization of the sugar duties. The siege was long and severe, and the result shows that the repealers were right. Examine the trade tables, and you will see the essence of the argument. Continued bad crops made corn prices range high during the ten years antecedent to 1846, when, under the sliding scale, the annual import was 3,028,000 quarters. But the law of that year came into play in 1849, and then it was that our Western lands turned out the grain for British stomachs. From 1846 to 1856, the annual import of grain, flour, &c., into England was 9,019,000 quarters; which, taking 2,000,000 for increased production, and the 6,000,000 quarters additional import, the British people consume some 8,000,000 quarters more than before the repeal of the corn law ! Yet, strange to say, prices before and after have varied, on the average, but *two shillings* per quarter.

Free trade in sugar has given a great impetus to consumption. The reduction on foreign sugars com-

menced with Peel's Bill of 1844, and the extension
or liberalizing of the Act each year till 1848, consum-
mated the equalization of the sugar duties.   In 1844,
the consumption was 197,471 tons; ten years after,
in 1854, 400,096 tons—free trade had doubled the returns. We may safely take the average now at 400,000
tons, against 200,000 for twenty years antecedent to
the change.   The British colonies have also received a
wonderful stimulus—an increase of 40 per cent in ten
years, say 200,000 tons, then, against 315,000 tons
last year.

But free trade supporters find the strongest argument in the shipping returns—before and after the
Navigation Act of 1850, when America, for the first
time in her life, outwitted John Bull in a treaty!
Protection must explode.   England set the example;
France is trying to follow; Russia has modified her
law, reducing the duty on woolens one-half; and even
Persia is extending her commercial relations, signing
treaties with the chief powers, the United States Minister taking the initiative at Constantinople; Charles S.
Spence was appointed Commissioner by the American
Government, and has received the first "order" ever
given to an American by a Persiah Shah; and now
America has at last shaken off a little of the manufacturers' monopoly.

But before I lose the point, let me show the shipping balances. In 1842, the amount of tonnage entered and cleared at British ports was 7,345,000 tons; in 1849, 11,501,000! After the repeal act, navigation shot ahead of all expectations. The same tables in 1856 showed an increase of 150 per cent. over the old restrictive system, and even 50 per cent. over those previous to 1850; say, in 1856, 17,900,000 tons! Even the shipping of Great Britain has doubled since England pursued the liberal policy: those returns give, both ways, in 1842, 5,415,000 tons; in 1856, 9,770,000 tons.

'Tis a little singular that a Northern Senator should have been in time to save the Tariff Bill. As far as it goes, 'tis a good beginning. The idea once started, the lever will do its work. But is it not strange that, while despotic Europe has taken two steps towards free trade, America contents herself with one? Free trade in raw materials—wool, costing over 20 cents per pound, 25 per cent.; under, *free.* I doubt if you get anything from the Australian shepherds on those terms. Australian prices for greasy wool range from 20 to 26 cents, while finer qualities command from those rates to 60 cents. The freight is from one to two cents per pound.

While on this question, let us see where the wool comes from. Step into the wool stores of the London

Docks, if you wish to understand it, where 200,000 bales are disposed of at the four quarterly sales, where $350,000 is the average amount taken every day for five weeks, the length of each quarterly sale. The opium market of Calcutta presents a tableau of Eastern gamblers difficult to picture, but the wool sales of England are but little less exciting. The quantity of wool from the Australian colonies imported into England in 1833 was 14,948 bales; in 1856, 166,640 bales. Even the gold discoveries have not diminished the supply. The Cape Colony has also shown a great increase. In 1842, the imports were 6,431 bales; in 1850, 50,580 bales. While the South American farmers send us their fifty-pound ballots of alpaca, and make us pay from 50 to 75 cents per pound, the Greek merchants charge us similar rates for the goats' wool of Asia Minor. In 1846, 5,231 bales went into England; in 1856, 13,427 bales of 160 pounds. India and China contributed 45,550 bales, of three cwt. each, last year, against 12,550 in 1851.

These large colonial supplies have entirely broken up that monopoly which the Spanish and Germans held for over a quarter of a century. Now, continental buyers can make better bargains at the English sales. You will see the falling of in Continental supply :—British imports from the Continent, 1836, 61,632 bales; 1846, 52,922 bales; 1856, 18,401 bales,

Bradford alone consumes, it is estimated, one-half the wool production of the British Isles. The returns are not easily obtained. In 1800, it was estimated at 384,000 packs of 240 pounds each; in 1846, McCulloch gives 540,000; and in 1851, it had increased to 820,000 packs. The total imports of colonial and foreign wool into England were, in 1855, 329,205 bales; in 1856, 315,035 bales. Official papers give 1,306 woolen and 493 worsted mills under full steam in 1849, employing, directly and indirectly, more than half a million workmen.

While Yorkshire works day and night in turning out the wool, Lancashire blackens the sky with smoke in putting the cotton into shape. Australia supplies the one—America the other. In 1856, the cotton consumption of Great Britain was 2,257,845 bales; Continental Europe, 1,364,000 bales; United States, 770,239 bales; total 4,392,084 bales. One can hardly credit the returns that mark the increase in this important staple during the last ten years. The import of cotton into England in 1846 is stated at 467,856,274 pounds; in ten years, 1856, it increased to 1,014,495,622 pounds; towards which total the United States contributed 803,563,430 pounds, while India gave but 147,436,266.

Denmark, you are aware, has talked the powers into

signing the convention on the Sound Dues, March 14
England pays $5,625,000. Parliament may not in-
dorse the act of her minister. Russia followed suit—
and the German States, so traditional in their policy—
and even France—all have signed the paper—save the
United States—alone, as may she ever be, in her glory.

Lord Palmerston's revenge is complete. He has gained
much more than he had lost. He is again in power
—again England's ruler. The Manchester party has
fallen? Cobden, Bright, Gibson, and Layard are out
of the ring; a great loss to the British nation, for
there are few abler men in it; but Lord John Russell has taken his seat for London. The English people will always vote for war! Eighty years ago a
Parliament was elected to fight us in the West to
the death—so has it been to-day returned to carry on
the war in the East.

Nothing later from China.

Lord Ellenborough says that the war has clogged
the wheels of the Indian trade; embarrassed Government, which has sunk about $4,000,000 in the 22
per cent. depreciation on opium; upset commerce,
ruined the merchants, and already caused a loss
of $20,000,000 to England. The Honorable Company,
he says, have tried in vain, at four, five, and now
as high as seven per cent., to get their $15,000,000
loan. Who wonders, when in six weeks' time the

Bengal banks advanced their rate of interest from six to fourteen per cent. ?

The local controversy looks like a national war. The Canton lorcha may sink the ship of State, unless the Emperor gives up the fight. The philanthropists, the missionaries, the moralists, are all with their " paper bullets of the brain," battling against the merchants and the war-spirit of England—without effect.

Cushing's treaty of 1844 expires about this time. Let us hope that Mr. Read will take good care of the Americans. The " Empress of China," just seventy-three years since—the year after we signed that national contract with Great Britain—was the pioneer. That voyage was successful, and China since then has given our people good returns. China is a garden—not a desert. Our commerce with her is in the future. Tea we must have, (though we once threw it into Boston harbor,) but at a lower price. Silk also must be imported, for the silk worms are dying in Europe.

During the past four years the decreased supply on this side accounts for increased importations. Since 1837, France alone shows a falling off in the value of silk worms from $23,400,000 that year, to $13,-400,000 the past twelve months.

Shipping on all sides seeks vainly for good employment. Even guano charters are hard to obtain—yesterday on application to the agents, they answered " No." French farmers and French soil want guano; but France, in this case, forgets the farmer, and protects the ship-owner. Seven dollars a ton is levied on all brought in foreign bottoms. French ships don't like guano freights, and as only 30,000 tons head annually towards the Pacific, the Americans get most of the cargoes. Hence, while England consumes her 200,-000 tons per annum, little Belgium her 50,000, France only got 32,000 in 1856, and 19,000 in 1855. In England, the imports, in the face of demand and rise in price from $55 to $65 per ton, have dropped from 305,061 tons in 1855, to 191,501 tons in 1856. Montaigne & Co., for France, like Bareda Brothers, for America, and Gibbs & Co., for Great Britain, make the charters direct, or through their agents, and when they change the rates they seem to give the wink to each other! How natural!

Your readers desire *permanent*, not *transient* articles. Well, you will find some facts crowded into this letter. I will try and be consistent, though I touch on many subjects. I will avoid repetition as much as possible; but keeping no copies, and memory none of the best, you may note some eating of words.

Don't, I beg of you, because I commenced with

some remarks about bubbles, and found some similarity in the present times, suppose for a moment that I think the world is coming to an end! Perhaps now there is more method in the whirl of speculation. Things have changed since Newton saw the apple fall—Watts the kettle boil. Whales are scarce upon the ocean, yet Gas increases with the coal. Railways pass every village, yet the stage-horses continue to find employment. The penny postage gives more revenue than the shilling. Steam has cut the ninety days' passage to New York down to ten. The telegraph makes the talking distance nothing. With one spare shirt we may soon voyage round the world. If such things happen, why shouldn't money be on a pinch? The "Persia" will tell you of the state of affairs. Last week Messrs. J. R. Brown & Co., of London and Sunderland, failed for $1,600,000! Three days since, the old-established house of Green & Co., Paris, closed their doors for a heavy sum—a bad South American account the alleged cause. Depositors are much embarrassed—those traveling in Europe with their credits are cut off from supplies. 'Tis hard for the students. Straws show the course of the wind.

In 1825, seventy Banks failed in six weeks—we have not come to that yet. Credit and business, I am told, are perfectly sound, though high prices for raw material are telling upon the manufacturers of

England.   Credit, like a monument, will stand, if you
don't touch the foundation.   Throw the stones off from
the top of the pyramid of Ghizeh, and you may work
till the last day—commence to undermine, and the
fabric may totter.   Therefore, the failures and the
frauds of the day may only be the topmost stones,
leaving the general body of credit firm as the rock
of Gibraltar.   This simile would be a strong argument
for those who believe in the continuance of prosperity,
if, in the madness of the age, speculators had not
turned the pyramid of credit upside down.

ARTICLE VI.

ROME, *June 1st.*, 1857.

MY DEAR SIR :—From New-York, on the Hudson, to London, on the Thames, is but a twelve days' journey; twelve hours more will take you to Paris, on the Seine, and in as many weeks you may run through France into Italy, and home again by the northern kingdoms; for weeks are days, months are weeks, in the age of steam! My last went from Paris, now I write from Rome. Having nailed the language in France, I wish to try my tongue in Italy, so I took a trip over the Mediterranean Railway, and stopped at *Lyons*, situated where the Saone joins the Rhone, chief of manufacturing cities, with a population of 275,000 people, and 7,000 factories, turning 20,000 looms, in working up silk, cotton, wool, crape, and gold and silver lace, into all the colors of the rainbow, to meet the American and European tastes—for Broadway depends upon Lyons for many of its choicest samples. Americans owe her large sums of money. 'Tis a flourishing town, but dull and heavy in appearance, with houses almost as high as those in Edinburgh, and dark streets and uninviting squares. One day here, and then we rattled on, through many tunnels and banks of solid rocks, to that old Phœnician town—established when Confucius was a baby, some six hundred years before the Christian's religion—Marseilles, first of Levantine seaports, the steam-packet station for the Peninsula, Italy, and the East, where art has assisted nature in making a splendid harbor,

where soap, coral, porcelain, glass, tobacco, and printed goods are manufactured.

Where, too, the successful bidder for the Spanish
loan, M. Mirès, is making docks out of mountains—an
enterprise worthy of Napoleon's reign! Marseilles has
about 185,000 inhabitants, and seems to be almost
entirely a commercial city, and, like Cologne, or a
Chinese port, the filth of the streets about the wharf
is only exceeded by their stink—(an expressive word,
in common use in England). Besides the activity of its
commerce, there is little to interest the tourist.

The more you travel in the country, the more you
see the truth of the oft-repeated remark that Paris is
France. The other cities and towns are drained to
ornament the capital—see Paris and be happy. Leaving Marseilles, we passed the ship-building port of
Toulon, where Barras saw Napoleon's genius for war,
and where ships' anchors, canvas, cordage, and other
shipping materials are made. Sailed by Nice and
several towns at the foot of the mountain ranges, and
one day's steaming showed us the hills where Columbus spent his boyhood's days in mapping out a world!
Genoa, *La Superba*, with a population of 144,000,
a Levantine commerce, and few American ships. But
the most beautiful place in Genoa was the Pallavi-
cino, where a prince has spent millions, with a taste

that startles you with wonder that anything could be made so grand! Yet after all 'tis not so gorgeous as Chatsworth. From Genoa to the commercial port of Tuscany, Leghorn, where there were more American ships landing tobacco, and loading marble, and there was some cotton on the quay. The port is free, and with Americans could be made to flourish—with Italians—never! Commodore Breeze unfurls his flag, and represents the country in the " Congress," while the Susquehanna has just sailed to assist in laying the Atlantic cable. From Leghorn we coasted along to that dirty, miserable hole, Civita Vecchia, the port of Rome—a place full of unclean spirits, a disgrace to the Pope and his dominions. Afterwards to the chief. city of the Two Sicilies, Naples, with 360,000 inhabitants and 300 churches, a splendid library, a classic bay, and, towering high in air, Vesuvius. The volcano is in full blast, and as I gazed upon the *crater*, and jumped aside to save my head from a shower of red-hot lava, I could but contemplate upon the scene, and having wandered over the ruins of Pompeii and Herculaneum, destroyed some eighteen centuries ago by this same mountain, I asked myself what can save Naples when the volcano takes another erratic flight? Who understands it? Why not expect another shaking of the mountain? Were I a Neapolitan, the coming comet most to be feared would be Vesuvius. I saw enough to stifle any desire one might have to buy real estate in these parts! I think a little stream of lava running into the king's palace would be a good thing for Naples. Bomba still chuckles at Lord Palmerston and his miserable attempt to frighten him, and lives shut up in his castle surrounded by spies, hated by all, while his brother, the Prince of Syracuse, drives four in hand among the people, who admire him for his talent and good nature, in such marked contrast to the king. I saw Naples, and here I am at Imperial Rome.

> " While stands the Coliseum, Rome shall stand;
> When falls the Coliseum, Rome shall fall;
> And when Rome falls, the world !"

was the prophecy of the early Saxon pilgrims.

The first two lines I can indorse, but as for the last suggestion, I think the world would stand some time, and be much richer, if Rome were blotted out of existence.

Modern enterprise has at last got in among the ruins of the Cæsars' palaces, for M. Mirès is giving the Pope a railway, and on the 1st of January, 1854, an English Company lighted the streets of the Imperial city with gas, and thus far have realized eight per cent. per annum on the investment. Rome needed lighting bad enough ? Here you have a flood of history, coming down from the foster mother of the Romans—a she-wolf! and genius and science, beggars, bigotry, art, and foreign fashion, all mixed up in unhappy confusion ; old ruins, and a church that was 176 years in building, which took 350 years to finish it, and cost $50,000,000! Romulus and Remus would never have sanctioned such extravagance, for they showed their economy in their wet nurse.

America is well represented here ; our artists have made their mark ; our sculptors are walking up the ladder of fame ; modern talent is crowding hard upon the ancient ; genius lives in all the studios. Bartholomew's statue of Eve will shortly be as famous as Power's Greek Slave. It is only to be known, and the Connecticut sculptor will receive his just reward. But I forget, I am writing for the Magazine, and must talk of *Commerce.*

Commerce in Italy! where is it ? I never heard the word, and will not insult its noble order by associating it with this unhappy land. The Lombards are gone ; the Venetians are not what they once were. There is nothing that deserves the name of commerce in Italy ! Wherever I go I hear nothing but a low, stifled growl. All the way from Naples, along the coast, to Rome, the life-blood seems stamped out. The Neapolitan king lives in a fortress, while the Pope is moving among his subjects. Swiss regiments occupy the dominions of the one, French soldiers guard the gates of the other; while, vulture-like, hovering on the borders with jealous eye, you have an Austrian army. Poor priest-ridden Italy! no unison in her States, no bright future! For the heel of foreign despotism is crushing out her soul—she lives on in the remembrance of her past glory. But now she has nothing but those memories, and her skies. I find no statistics; in fact I have not the energy to search far, for where the day is reduced to twenty hours, where the difficulty of getting into the country is only excelled by trying to get out again, *and a policeman meets you everywhere, what can you expect ?* And thinking that foreign potentates do not throw enough of obstacles in the road of the traveler, our own Government steps in to hold us by the collar, and like the bandit of the country, *demands a dollar* for letting you pass the gate ! What a singular policy ! While an American President is announcing to the debt-burthened nations, that the more-or-less-United States are embarrassed with some thirty millions surplus revenue, an American consul meets you in every foreign land with "*One dollar for your passport !*" While all foreigners are permitted to range

free and untrammeled over our broad domain, our
own citizens, continental-bound, are met, the moment
they touch another State with, "*One dollar, if you please,
for permission to continue your journey.*" While education occupies so much attention throughout our
land, and every facility is given on our own soil to pro-
mote it, the moment we arrive in a foreign kingdom
you find a United States' official to greet you with,
"*One dollar for your passport before you can go on
shore !*" No matter how well provided you may be
with the proper paper from the State Department,
even go to Italy as the bearer of dispatches, and still
it is "*One dollar for your passport.*" Is it not pitiful to
witness a great nation, with liberal institutions and
treasury full to overflowing, sneaking about in foreign
lands to annoy the traveler, by multiplying the chances
of delay, and picking up a dollar here and a dollar
there, for the distinguished privilege of having another,
perhaps the hundredth, signature to your ticket of
leave ? Depend upon it, Secretary Marcy has won no
laurels by this petty consular charge. European Governments seem to take pleasure in throwing stones in
your path. They do as they please—we cannot help
it. Our remedy is to stay at home; or go abroad,
pay the bills, and grumble! Oh, what a luxury!
Let us profit by England's good, but not adopt her

bad, habits; and if salaried consuls with her demand fees, there is no reason why we should fall into the same practice. America is old enough and rich enough to map out a wider and more enlightened policy. Correct me if I am wrong.

To throw you off anything readable, I must step out of Italy into Europe, and out of Europe into England, for, as I said before, you see little that reminds you of a living commerce in these lands—I must look to England for material, and France, and then go out to China.

The general wail through England is, " Hard times ;" and yet thinking men will assure you that everything is sound! (to be sure, the more *hollow* the more *sound*). *You must dig deeper to find the stain. Powers has already lost five blocks of marble on his statue of California, (for Mr. Wm. B. Astor.) The surface was sound and clear, the statues almost finished, when lo! another cut of the chisel, and the figure was ruined. A little more pressure on the money market, and loss of confidence creates dismay.*

The *Crédit Mobilier* is the bane of Europe. Bad example destroys society. Pereire has just issued his fourth annual report. The figures are startling! Profits for the year, $3,000,000! Dividend declared, 23 per cent.! last year it was 40 per cent. Mark some of its operations. Cash transactions $617,000,000! let me enumerate two or three:—

Subscribed to Government loan.......................... $50,000,000
Account current with Bank of France.................. 240,000,000
Contributed towards periodical settlements of the share
　market...................................../.......... 140,000,000
Purchase of stock to support the public fund........... 8,000,000

—offered to subscribe $60,000,000 to aid Bank of France when in a tight place last fall—and all this on a capital of only $12,000,000! And this is the *Crédit Mobilier!* It buys, it sells, is agent and owner by turns, deals in railways from St. Petersburg to Madrid, builds docks, and the grandest hotel the world has ever seen—for where is there a rival to the " Grand Hotel du Louvre," with its 1,000 beds, and furnished like a royal palace? It can never pay, yet always full!

Pereire and the Directors got 10 per cent. on all these sums. Last week down came one of the clique for $4,000,000! M. Thurneyssen has just stepped over to America, leaving some wealthy Poles and others minus that little amount. Last year another Director failed for a similar sum. M. Place's liabilities were $4,500,000. Yet Pereire writes most indignantly to the *Globe*, and the *Globe* retorts with needles.

Pereire has been before the government to advise

upon the extension of the capital of the Bank of France. He disapproves of it; so does his old employer and present rival, Rothschild. How strange they should give the same testimony! "Steam and credit," said Pereire, in his railway speech, "are the revolutionizers of men." All beautiful in theory, says the *Constitutionnel*, but bad, the way he practices it. He has spread widely the passion for gambling. This child of government (*Crédit Mobilier*) has grown too rapidly for its founders—now nothing stops its power— Napoleon even is too deeply involved to control it. Do not the statistics in the report show it? Smaller minds copy the speculations of the Directors. Farmers leave their fields to dabble in the stocks—workmen flood the towns to earn higher wages, and lose their gains in the dazzle of the lottery! Financial affairs in France must cause the Emperor some sleepless nights, for his crown depends upon tranquility on the Bourse; $20,000,000 increase in the capital of the Bank of France will only inflate the more. The government demand $17,000,000 at once on treasury bonds; subscribers pay the money to the Bank, the Bank lends to the government, and by-and-by it may get back again to the people—meanwhile it draws away the cash and adds to the pressure. Is it a loan in disguise? It looks like it. The present Act ex-

pires 31st January, 1867—now 'tis to be prolonged
for thirty years, say worked out in 1897—the old
laws of 22d of April, 1806, and 30th of June, 1840,
will fall into the new charter. The Bank of France
has weathered all storms handsomely. The fifteen
years' war did not break it—1830 came, then 1848,
when government authorized suspension of cash payments—its affairs grew worse in 1849—yet France has
maintained her credit since Napoleon first organized
the Institution. Its transactions are enormous—last
year they add up to $1,115,500,000! The bills melt-
ed were $883,900,000! The net profits for the twelve
months were $6,750,000, and the dividends range from
20 to 25 per cent. on the original value of shares,
say $200. The new stock will be issued at a pre-
mium of $20, or shares $220.

French railways are still productive. The meeting
of the Northern of France the other day showed evi-
dent signs of being noisy—a shareholder asked about
the 5,752 shares and 1,000 bonds stolen by Grelet
and Carpentier. It opened up a painful subject, but
the subject was soon put to bed. Baron James de
Rothschild rose and said, that rather than have impu-
tations cast upon the House of Rothschild, he would
meet the loss himself, (cheers), and he paid for 5,071
shares and 270 bonds then and there! So the Roths-

childs are *one million of dollars* out on that speculation.

The discussion regarding the falling off in population in France has brought out some strange facts. During the five years ending 1856, the increase has been but 256,000; same time ending '46, gave 1,170,-000. In 1790, the population of France amounted to 26,500,000, at which period England and Ireland had but 14,000,000 inhabitants; now mark the comparison—sixty-seven years have wrought a wonderful change. Great Britain has furnished material for America and Australia, yet, notwithstanding the drain, has doubled her home population; while France, who has done little towards peopling her own or other countries, has added but *thirty-five* per cent. to her tables! In 1854 and '55, the deaths exceeded births! 56 out of the 86 departments in France show a palpable falling off in population.

France, under the elder Bourbons, flourished in colonies, in manufactories, in agriculture, and tried to extend her commerce; but war opened the century, and now each year shows a decline in numbers! *After years will give the results of the present reign. To-day we cannot see them—for the Bourse occupies writers and statesmen. France is living a dream-life. One individual carries the nation!—what an Atlas load!*

Napoleon appears still the friend of England. France can never be—a different creed—another language—looser morals—the galling recollections of conquest and defeat—long and bloody battles—have engendered enmity on both sides. But policy binds the lilies round the lion's neck. That wreath of flowers is full of thorns! France revels in her present luxury. Palaces are being built for the rich, but no schools for the poor. Secret societies hold their midnight meetings. The love-paths of the Emperor are full of man-traps and spring-guns. That ravishingly beautiful Castilignoni *may herself be one of the league : yet the Emperor sneers at danger and dictates to the world! He sees deserted fields—a smothered press—literature declining—and the vital spark of education and religion ebbing away; but what does he care ?*

He rules supreme. Victoria goes to Paris at his beck. To one king he says " Do this," and he doeth it ; to another, " Do that," and it is done. To Frederick William, " Sell your birth-right for a mess of potage." To Alexander, " Make peace," and he made it. To the Persian Envoy, " Sign the paper with England," and he put his name to the treaty. To Palmerston, " Leave the King of Naples alone for a while," and the Premier was most obedient. To the Duke of Valencia, " Hold your ground in Spain," and *Narvaez is still the guiding mind of the Cabinet.* To *Switzerland,* "*Accept the terms of the Prussian monarch,"* and *Neufchatel is patched up.* To *the Pope,* "*Fear not, my soldiers shall protect you."* To *England,* "*Go ahead in China."* To *America,* "*Be respectful."* To *the crown-heads of Europe,* "*Come and see me at the Tuileries,"* and *they all accept the invitation.* One *after another bows before this child of fortune—the man of destiny of the nineteenth century!*

While numbers in France decline, the census in England augments :—

In 1828 the population of the United Kingdom was ____ 23,237.853
1842 _____ 27,102,509
1856._____ _____ .____ 29,000,000

The increase the last fourteen years is 100 per cent. less than during the first, but it must be remembered that emigration latterly has thinned the ranks. During the past ten years, 2,800,000 people left the mother country, against 856,392, as the total emigration for the preceding ten.

The annual report of the Postmaster-General records the epistolary correspondence of the kingdom. The extensive arrangements of the department can be estimated by noting that letters are daily sent over 61,000

miles inland;—478,000,000 letters passed through the
Post-office in 1856, being an increase of 22,000,000
over 1855. In 1839 there were but 76,000,000. England averages 20 to each person. London takes 40.

The Board of Trade Returns for the last four months
are worth perusing. Each month the tables grow
larger. Take, for comparison, total exports for the
four months ending—

1st May 1855	....	$134,000,000
"	1856	173,000,0C0
"	1857	194,000,000

Which shows an increase of 12 per cent. over 1856,
and 40 per cent. over 1855. The chief items of increase are worsted stuffs, iron of all kinds, woolen,
linen, and cotton yarn, machinery, and coals. At the
above average the exports of Great Britain this year
will amount to $582,000,000. America exports staples
—England, save iron and coal, the productions of
other lands. She takes raw material, and gives manufactured value. Were he to live upon what he produced
John Bull would soon be a Calvin Edson. Since
1842, British exports, under *free trade*, have increased
145 per cent. America, during the same time, has
increased hers 212 per cent. by *protection*.

The Merchant Shipping Act of 1854 gets hard rubs

on all sides. Chambers of Commerce and Boards of
Trade are indignant. All pronounce it arbitrary and
unjust. They argue with effect that it is absurd to
place the interests of the merchant marine in the hands
of two justices of the peace, who know nothing of
nautical matters. Military misdemeanors are tried by
military officers—the merchants likewise wish to be
judged by their peers.

Guano—how long is it to last? Are the deposits
giving out? These questions occupy attention. Senor
Elias, in his letter to President Echeneque, in 1853,
said that eight years more would work them out. That
survey mentioned two rocks in sight—one 30 feet high,
another, on the northern island, of 10 feet. During
1851-2, he says that 2,085,000 tons were taken away.
A month after the above survey, by order of Admiral
Moresby, Mr. McIntosh examined the islands, and reported a supply of at least nine years. Towards the
close of the same year a commission was appointed
to make an accurate survey :—

They report an estimate of.........tons remaining, 12,376,100
McIntosh's calculation was........................... 8,600,000
While Senor Rivero, in 1846, said................ ...18,250,000

According to their estimates their is still some employment left on the Pacific coast for shipping. 'Tis

a mistake to suppose that the English bondholders have a lien on the guano deposits: their hold is only on the net proceeds of guano consumed in the United Kingdom. Therefore if the new chief, Vivanco, continues to sell for cash at the islands, where are the bondholders! He will not only pocket the cash for the guano, but all the stealings—all the commissions within commissions.

The *Debats* publishes some interesting facts regarding marine losses. Of the 32,000 to 34,000 vessels, of all nations, on the seas—

In 1852 there were lost.......................vessels, 1,850
     1853... 1,610
     1854... 2,120
     1855... 1,982
     1856... 2,124

The majority of accidents were in December and the winter months. Steam adds heavily to the collision risks.

The English Government have respectfully retired before the resentment and brave protest of another colony. Lord Clarendon has annulled the convention with France of 14th January, 1857, in relation to the fisheries of Newfoundland. The colonists were almost in revolt—speeches, letters, and protests, were hurled over the water. The flag went up union down.

France takes pride in her Atlantic fisheries; for 300 years she has been enriched by them. In 1630 England began to supply the Spanish and Italian market, when the French, not liking such competition, introduced the bounty system—five shillings a quintal was a powerful protection. In 1777, 20,000 French seamen were employed upon the coast; but the revolution of 1793 cut off the bounties, and the number of seamen fell away to 3,897. Then the English sprang ahead, and for twenty years they profited by the change. In 1814 England exported $15,000,000 of fish; then came the peace, revival of the bounties, and now the French have some 500 square-rigged vessels and 30,000 seamen, all hard at work, catching, salting, and packing. 'Tis the nursery of the French navy.

The treaty of Utrecht ceded Newfoundland to Great Britain, but the French fishermen were allowed to fish from Cape Bonavesta to Pointe Riche. In 1763 the treaty of Paris gave the islands of St. Pierre and Miquelon to France, but neither treaty permitted her to fortify. The privileges were confirmed by the treaties of Versailles in 1783, (a memorable year to an American,) and of Paris in 1814–15—notwithstanding which the French and British fishermen have been continually warring with each other. It seems that lately France wished another slice, and England gave it conditionally. Newfoundland howled down the proposition, and the colonists' decision is respected. The United Sates some time since got what they desired, but 'twas like pulling an eye-tooth.

Lady Franklin mourns over the dead more than most wives respect the living. Another expedition is heading towards the land immortalized by Kane. Captain McClintock, who, under Sir James Ross, in 1848–9, again under Captain Austin, in 1850–1, and thirdly in 1852–3, in the "Antelope" and "Resolute," made voyages to the Arctic Seas, is about to give another search after the lost husband. He might as well look for the steamer "Pacific." The Government declines further aid—they probably think, with most sensible people, that the "Erebus" and "Terror" are among the things that were.

On the ground of Arctic explorations, there is some reason in the demand for another trial; already much good has arisen from previous expeditions. Among the results were Sir H. Gilbert's codfish discovery at Newfoundland; Davis's West Greenland whale fishery; Hudson's Bay Company's, under Sir John Ross; Baffin's Bay fisheries; Parray, Lancaster Sound, Barrow's Straits, and Prince Regent's Inlet; Beechy and Behring's Straits whale fisheries — where our American whalemen picked up some $8,000,000 worth of oil in two years. All these discoveries are the grounds upon which more money is asked for; but this time Lady Franklin must foot the bills.

The Hudson's Bay Company's charter is before Parliament, and now that the all-important bill for furnishing a house and home for the Princess Royal has passed, giving her $200,000 for a dowry, and an annuity of of $40,000, some legislation will be made on the Bank Act, and other important bills. The charter of Hudson's Bay Company dates back to 1670, and expires in 1859. They have had it their own way for a long time, but now Western Canada says stop the monopoly.

Contrary to my expectations the Russian railways are almost a dead letter. The Barings brought all their Stock Exchange machinery to bear, but the fourth estate was too powerful, and seemed to be moved by an unseen hand. The stock fell flat upon the market. 'Twas no go from the start. Among the arguments against the enterprise were—high price of iron, no remunerative traffic, only military roads, building estimate too low; but strongest and most important, the low rate of interest guaranteed—a trifle less than five per cent. Those in favor said the track would pass through pasture lands—manufacturing, agricultural, and

forest regions—that no tunnels were needed—few
bridges required—sleepers cheap and on the spot, &c.,
&c. That the Prussian lines, opened in 1854, (2,300
miles,) cost but $66,500 per mile—while $88,000 was
the estimate for the Russian. Throughout the kingdom there was a continual cry against them—"Anti-
English," said one and all. To outsiders the speculation looks bad ; but who can tell a banker's secrets?
The question arises : Who moved the press to write
editorial on editorial? Was it a burst of anti-Rus-
sianism? Perhaps. More likely another agent was at
work—but no matter. The shares were issued at the
same time at fixed exchange—in St. Petersburg, 125
silver roubles; Amsterdam, 236 Dutch guilders; Berlin, 134 thalers ; at Paris, 500 francs, and £20 in
London.

The Grand Duke Constantine makes a short stay
in England. The "frank and open-hearted sailor"
likes Paris better. Peter the Great, 140 years ago,
trod the same ground that the Grand Duke Constantine is over now. In May, 1717, the royal ship-car-
penter visited France and England. In May, 1857,
the Russian Admiral seems to have come on a similar
errand. In 1782, the son of Catharine II., the Grand
Duke Paul, came to France. In 1814, Alexander

walked into Paris with Wellington. Now, Constantine is taking observations.

D'Israeli said the other day, that the railways of Spain, Austria, and India, were the fruits of Australian and Californian gold. England built hers before that day, and has constructed 8,500 miles of road at a cost of $1,500,000,000, on which they have some $400,000,000 debt. America's 25,000 miles cost some two-thirds of that amount, and the debt is about the same as the English. The total capital of 136 lines in Great Britain, in 1336, was :

English lines.	$1,260,000,000
Scotch	160,000,000
Irish	80,000,000
The total traffic receipts in 1856, were	93,000,000
The expenses—about 47 per cent.—were	44,000,000

In 1852, Canada had no railways, but now they have 1,500 miles in operation, and 500 more under way. The cost of the Grand Trunk line must have disappointed its originators. The estimate of $15,000,000 seems to have turned out to be $45,000,000, and the cry is still for more.

Just now the India railways are making a great racket. W. P. Andrews is continually before the public. The papers are full of railways in India, and the

scheme has been well pushed.   Question on question—
answer and a new suggestion—now 'tis an editorial—
then in the money article—a never-ending advertise-
ment.   This is the track :

	Miles.	Days.
London to Trieste, a continuous rail, after skipping over the Channel to Marseilles—then road on road, a complete chain to the Adriatic....	1,300	2
Trieste to Seleucia, the old Mediterranean port, by steam.......	1,600	6½
Seleucia to Ja'fer Castle, on the Euphrates, by rail..	100	⅛
Ja'fer Castle to Bussorah, by steam................	715	3½
Bussorah to Kurrachee, by steam..................	1,000	4

Say to India from London, 4,715 miles, in 15 days
8 hours ! This certainly is one of the startling projects of the day.   Like the Atlantic Cable, the Pacific Railway, the Suez Canal, the " Great Eastern "—
this cross-country path to India is an undertaking
that dazzles all minds.   All this requires immense
sums of money—railways must be paid for. If England alone required $1,500,000,000, America $1,000,000,-
000, what will meet the wants of Europe and of Asia ?

The Star of Empire now takes its way Eastward,
instead of Westward.   America is already on the borders of the Pacific, but England is not at Pekin.
The Orient is full of cares to her—mutiny among the
Sepoys is no little cause of anxiety.   In 1806 the

troops refused to go to sea—now 'tis the Enfield rifle cartridge. The 19th is disbanded at Moorshedabad. The 34th are equally mutinous. England's great power there is in the Indian army. A general mutiny, and India will require European regiments. She may be slumbering on a volcano.

All eyes turn to China. England is in earnest now. At first it was an election dodge—now 'tis war. Formosa, which was annexed to China by Khang Hi in 1683, will be the first to fall. The Americans have had some trade there. Afterwards, Chusan, for a military station. England never liked the idea of being isolated at Hong Kong. China managed that well. China is surrounded by royal buccaneers, and all the world want a share of the booty. The troops of England are arriving. Lord Elgin has passed Singapore. The French ambassador is on his way through Egypt, and Mr. Reed is packing up his trunk.

England, France, and America are no mean foes. But the half has not been told. Portugal—yes, little, almost forgotten Portugal—is despatching some 500 troops to Macao. Spain is about to strengthen the Manilla garrison. Austria is going out, and Prussia sends a ship or two, while, long since, Russia had an army on the frontier. Poor China, like a fox in the royal pack, must fight—fight hard, and die. All nations wait to see Asia split asunder—each expecting a share of the spoils.

The war of 1842 was short and fierce. Three thousand English troops, in the face of the north-east monsoon, plunged into the coast ports, and one after another Shanghai, Amoy, Chusan, Ningpo, and Chapoo, fell, and British officers dictated peace—200 miles up the Yang-tse-Kiang; and when the document was signed, our Admiral quietly walked into the camp and asked the favor of a treaty. It was granted, and since then, look at the extent of the American trade. Shall there be Commissioners at Pekin? Up to this time the Celestials have bagged the question. In 1260 Nicholas and Marco Polo tried it, and in 1295 Marco Polo alone; but "No!" was 'the reply. The Jesuitical Portuguese at Macao, in 1573, were not more fortunate. The Dutch, in 1655–'95, also failed, and in 1720 the Russian mission fared no better. Lord Macartney was shamefully treated in 1795, and Lord Amherst was kicked out in 1816.

All these attempts to establish Ministers at the Chinese capital were introduced by liberal presents. The Emperor received them as tributes, and shut the door upon his foreign slaves! Cannon balls and bombs are now the tributes offered. Promises will not answer, and hard knocks must open the door. All former at.

tempts were commercial—all failures. This is political, and nations are determined. The Rebels are joining hands and cause with the Imperialists, and the Chinese will fight and die. Yeh's orders are still to "Push the devils into the sea!" Even Alum, (good name for a baker), and his band of poisoners, are pronounced *not guilty*.

The Chinese illustrate the horrors of war. Wherever they are settled, insurrections are taking place—at Penang—at Singapore; but more dreadful than all, in Borneo. That wonderful man, Sir James Brook, adds another thrilling chapter to his marvelous history. He eloquently paints the midnight attack, the surprise, the barbarous slaughter of innocent women and beautiful children, the defeat, and the rescue. Dark was the deed—awful the judgment! Headed by the Dyaks and Malays, the Chinese Kungsi were butchered like cattle. The few wretches who escaped the Europeans' revenge are starving in the jungle. The suddenness of the blow, the rapidity of the punishment, seems more like Eastern story. Rajah Brook's wild life in an island sea would furnish material for a dozen works of fiction. He possesses that Cortez and Pizarro fire which wakes up the heroic and the brave. Walker, in Central America, is striving to gain a similar reputation. The Rajah has again established his power, but he has still his traducers in England. Hume persecuted him till his death, and minor scribblers grumbled; yet he has proved himself a great man. Such men should lead armies. Where is there a similar history?

Supremacy, dominion, lust for power, are the China-men's dreams. 'Tis constitutional hate — and Asiatic hate is poison.

With such intelligence arriving every mail, no won-der the money market continues in such a feverish state. *Those who have notes to pay believe in better times*—some say that high money will be permanent; others prove that it must be temporary. The *Times* pronounces for high interest for several years—and who disputes the *Times?* Nobody; unless on " Railways and Revolvers in Georgia !" D'Israeli sees a great fall in the rate for money " looming in the future." I don't—I wish I could. Business matters still wear a sombre aspect. The cotton trade is working short— woolen factors are gloomy—people meet at Smithfield and cry for work. Frost is creeping among the vine-yards of France—she has turned importer instead of exporter. At Lancaster the mills are running forty hours per week. Exports are increasing—imports de-clining. The world at large owes England—England owes the banks—the banks hold the deposits of the people, and cannot stand a run—money, as before; now, six-and-a-half at bank—the last was the forty-sixth change in rate since Peel's Bill of 1844—all this, and still consols at 94 ! I cannot see why they should not fall to 75. The English people like that dear debt —it holds them in solemn unity. Everybody buys consols—dowager ladies—East Indian pensioners—old people dying and leaving money in trust to buy them—all tends to absorb the funds—all artificial props : without them, down they go ! Three per cent. was once a good investment, when the rate was one-and-three-quarters— not as now at seven per cent. This absorption of consols is the salvation of the English Government. London saps the kingdom. America is the only fire-proof Government afloat !

The terms *dear* and *cheap*, as applied to money, are much more to the point than *scarce* and *plenty*. When was there so much money as now ? and yet they say it is *searce*, instead of saying it is *dear*. Railway shares average four per cent. ; consols three-and-a-quarter ; money forced up to six-and-a-half at Bank of England ; while joint-stock banks declare dividends all the way from 10 to 20 per cent. ! The money-lender swallows up the borrower ; the bank eats up the trader ; new loan societies are springing up daily ; the State lends consols at three per cent., and borrows money at seven ! England is a mere house for the precious metals—simply a common carrier for the world.

Australian accounts are bad ; shippers looked at the

$70,000,000 gold, not at population.; and as in 1853 and 1854, the markets are overdone again !

There is a money panic in Austria ; the workmen there are tired of receiving paper money—they demand metal ; and the Government has refused to sanction new *share* enterprises. The Austrian Bourse will explode some fine morning.

All through the railway mania, 1842 to 1849, interest ruled from two to eight per cent.—bullion fluctuated from $4,500,000 in 1842, to $33,000,000, in 1847. This was before the gold. For a quarter of a century previous the amount never varied $5,000,000 ! In railway times the drain was inside of England's borders—now it goes abroad. England pays more for the raw material ; prices have been continually advancing ; cotton, wool, and luxuries are higher ; tea, since 1850, has advanced 100 per cent. in price in China ; and now England only gets half as much for her money as formerly—*she paying cash and giving credit.*

Having no national bank, many think that America will escape a national crisis. But England, ruled by the Bank of England, is in great danger. This institution has passed through the fiercest fires in its life-time.

The rumored invasion of the Pretender, in 1707, created a run ; again there was another rush in 1745 ; and when Napoleon was preparing to land on British soil in 1797, the bank suspended. The panic of 1825 reduced its cash to $250,000. The lowest price that its stock has touched was 91—the highest 299 ; while dividends have been declared from 4 to 21 per cent. Think of consols (only three per cents) at 94, and money at 6½ per cent. ! Joint-stock banks allow 5½ per cent. on deposits, and loan at 8 per cent., taking consols for security ! Consols at 93 and 94, while French *rentes* (bearing same interest) are 69 ! Twenty-five per cent. difference ! Such is the solidity of the English Government !

England imports annually about $140,000,000 bullion —yet 'tis all drained away. February 20, 1844, there were $81,000,000 in the vaults of the Bank—to-day, some $45,000,000 ; while exports walk rapidly on from year to year, and the circulation of notes now is about the same as then. *Therefore, look at the credit of the kingdom—one thousand millions of dollars in paper afloat at one time ! Think of the financiering—the renewals ! Modern inventions economize capital—one steam-engine is worth a thousand men and half as many horses. Exchanges—clearing-houses—pass amounts from hand to hand with increasing facility. Since General Jackson's day new machinery has been invented—new wheels are turning. Through these inventions one million notes and bullion will go as far as two millions did twenty years ago ago. A single sixpence at a whist-table will pass from one to another in the room, and answer the purpose of cancelling twenty accounts—such is the beauty of exchange.* Dear money falls on the consumer—not the trader—like a high tariff. What is it to the merchant whether he pays 6 or 12 per cent. ? He will charge the difference to his customer. " Cheap money gives you the world's commerce ; make it dear and you will lose it"—said Rothschild before the Government committee.

How singular that Ireland and Scotland, both under the same Parliament, should have a different currency from England—and yet only twelve hours apart.

Duncan argues in favor of paper currency. He says that it broke Napoleon at Leipsic when the Allied Powers raised the wind by issuing notes ; that paper money enabled Frederick to raise Prussia from misery to opulence ; that paper money built Scotland, where for one hundred and fifty years it has proved a blessing. He, however, does not mention the little history connected with our Continental paper money—with French assignats, and the depreciated notes of Austria and of Russia ! Miller says, that from 1797 to 1844, some five hundred Banks failed in England, while but six stopped in Scotland !

The Chancellor of the Exchequer announced in Parliament, on the Savings Bank Bill, that at the close of 1856 there were no less than 1,339,00,0 depositors, to whom the Banks owed $174,000,000 ! During the year 1,409,000, amounting to $38,000,000, in sums of about $25, and 793,000 withdrawals, amounting to $40,000,000, in sums averaging $50. This statement shows the magnitude of the Savings Banks' operations.

I spoke of dull markets in Melbourne—note these figures : Imports from 10th Janury to 7th March, 1857, two months, $18,000,000; exports, $12,000,000; giving an average annual excess of imports over exports of nearly $36,000,000 ! The colony continues to pour out gold, and will. During 1856, the production of Victoria was one hundred and forty-seven tons weight— twenty-four tons more than the previous year; 3,533,- 527 ozs., at 80s., equal to $70,000,000 :—almost equal to the famous year 1852, when we got 4,247,152 ozs., at 70s., equal to $74,000,000.

The cotton supply creates much comment—like Lord Napier's New-York speech—the European papers do not understand it. The *Constitutionnel* sneeringly writes, " that the bonds of friendship that are being celebrated are not chains of flowers, but simply twists of cotton that supply the Manchester market."

You will have later dates than I can send from Italy ; but from this distance the money market appears no better. The cord tightens—not yet snapped ; the bowl fills—not yet overflown. I do not write to

*point out hidden rocks in still waters, but to the
actual breakers which we see on our lee. The storm
once over we may hope for better prospects.*

The mammoth wonder of the century, the Great
Eastern, progresses slowly towards completion. Think
of this leviathan—notice her dimensions—length 692
feet; breadth, 83 feet, and 120 over paddle-boxes;
8,000 tons of iron consumed in the 30,000 plates
which compose her hull. She is 23,000 tons, or 18,000
tons larger than the largest ship afloat; with six
masts—such masts!—ten anchors—and such anchors!
twenty long-boats, and two seventy-ton propellers! She
accommodates 4,000 passengers, and could, upon a
pinch, take 10,000 troops! They say she will be
launched in August, and that you will see her at
Portland in October. Three hundred and sixty-five
years before, a sailor from this same land crossed the
ocean in a cockle-shell of a boat—for the Mayflower
of 1620 was not much else. All the world wonders,
while Europe looks at the critical state of the nations, all of which are volcanic!

The Papal Government moves with Mohammedan
Turkey against Christian Greece—the Pope's tempo-
ral power smothers Italian liberty—Hellenic Russia
against Catholic Poland—despotic Austria trampling under foot the national rights of Italy—perjured Bour-

bons against the pledged liberties of their people ! The European monarchs promised their subjects everything to conquer Napoleon—when conquered, they laughed, and performed not. Now all the world waits for another chapter. The balls still rattle harmlessly against the shirt of mail of the only man in Europe who can stem the tide of Revolution. Napoleon dead, and anarchy again. All this bears upon the money market. Who wonders at hard times ?

ARTICLE VII.

VENICE, *June* 15*th*, 1857.

MY DEAR SIR:—What a quaint old city is Venice!
So odd, so singular in construction, so unlike all other
places. China is most eccentric; all Eastern nations
turn upside down our Western notions; while in
Australia the animal and vegetable kingdoms compete
in changing nature from right to left. But here, in
Venice, you will find another chapter, equally peculiar—where the land is water; the streets are canals;
its carriages are boats; its horses are men; its hotels
are palaces! The poor fugitives from Attila's conquest
were hard pushed for a township when they selected

these seventy-two islands for a site. Commerce did it. Nothing else could have driven such piles and placed such stones, in building up this " glorious city in the sea ;" where four thousand gondolas, in dark, funereal garb, steal noiselessly along the one hundred and forty-six canals that branch out of the main stream, and creep so silently round the corners of the moss-greened walls, and under the three hundred and six bridges that cross and recross the city everywhere. How beautifully Rogers paints it! and Byron, too. But, without a spark of poetry, and accustomed to the noisy din of great cities, where carts, and carriages, and horses, and busy humanity make the welkin ring with industry, I could not live in Venice. And yet you see the foot-prints of a once grand commerce—once the commerce of the world! She possessed it for a time, grew rich, built marble palaces in the ocean, became indolent in prosperity, and lost it. Holland, Spain, and Portugal picked it up, and they, too, have carelessly let the jewel, that gave luster to their reigns, slip away, and now they are all dying out together. England found it, and filled her treasuries. America watched; worked hard; slept little; discovered the secret, and now comes the struggle—America or England. Who doubts the result? Already we are some hundred thousand tons of shipping in advance of those who taught us the road to fame!

Venice was all powerful in the days of the Lombards, now she lives but in books. A few small ships are on the stocks, and boats in numbers; for, besides the fishing smacks, Venice has some 30,000 tons of shipping in the coasting trade. Lately the channel near the Malamocco Pass has been deepened, and now you can take in fifteen feet of water, but you must have a pilot. Although Venice is a free port, it does not thrive under the Austrian's despotism; besides, Trieste draws away all Government patronage, and pockets all the profits.

Save the few cargoes of fish, and the iron and coal that return in payment, England and Venice have little sympathy. The Grecian, Dalmatian, and Austrian connections are much more important. Some four or five thousand people find employment in her glass works, in making mirrors, artificial gems and beads and pearls, gold and silver work, velvets, and some few silks and laces. The sugar refineries and spermaceti works also assist in endeavoring to galvanize life in this extraordinary city, where a population of one hundred and six thousand people look back with ancestral pride to the glory of the Doges, who, in wedding the sea, dazzled Europe by the gorgeousness of the pageant!

Artesian wells supply tolerably good drinking water,

and everything eatable must come from off the neigh-boring islands. The railway bridge was expensive, but how superior to making the distance in a gondola! You may ride on the rail all the way to Milan, save a short shake in the diligence. The house of Titian, the "Bridge of Sighs," and the palaces built a thou-sand years ago, all fade before the brilliancy of the the San Marco—the only place in Venice where the stranger is reminded of a living city; for here the band at evening draws the rich and the poor. Else-where, you may look from the windows of the palaces, from the squares, from the bridges and the boats, and nothing reminds you of other lands—nor horse, nor ox, nor ass, nor anything like cities not built in water, meets your wondering gaze! But of all strange sights there's naught so marked as the animal instinct of the city pigeon.

As Rome was saved by the cackling geese, so Venice was warned of the enemy by a pigeon from the main. 'Twas centuries ago, yet the Venetians have not forgotten it, and to-day the bird is as sacred as a family picture. Government protected them; in-dividuals fed them; and at two o'clock, on the strik-ing of the old town bell, you see them flocking from all quarters to the San Marco, where they are sure to find (only at that hour and minute) their expected food. Small as was the spectacle, I enjoyed it much, for it portrays the instinct of nature.

When in Venice, take your credits and circular letters to an English banker, for the Italians here do not seem to have improved in civility since Shylock talked ducats and daggers with Antonio on the Rialto.

Thirty-six hours diligencing from Rome (where I mailed a package for the "Magazine," on Southern Italy and Western Europe) brought us to Florence, the city so delightfully situated, so beloved by strangers as well as Italians. It takes one hundred hours with the *vetturini*, and a day less in a post-carriage, but the courier's conveyance even beats the diligence.

You will find railways at Forence branching out to several cities—to Leghorn, at three hours' ride through a most fertile, picturesque country—to Pisa, where the old tower still bends apparently with age —to Lucca, for sea bathing—to Sienna, Empoli, and Pistori—quite a net-work of rail. Florence numbers a population exceeding that of Venice by some ten thousand persons. They have quite an English colony here, and a dozen or more American families. Here Jarvis employs his pen, and Powers, for nineteen years, his chisel; while Livingston's ambition is driving all the way from four in hand to twelve!

Of all Italian cities, give me Florence for a home.

Healthy, not expensive, delightfully situated, rich in natural beauty if not in historical association, within a two-hours ride of Fiesole, and boasting the most beautiful forest drive in the world—the Cascine. The Grand Duke and all the Royal family give tone to the evening drive; but I little thought, when seeing them on the parade, that so soon the Grand Duchess was to lay in the tomb of the princes.

The hotels on the Arno are the most patronized; and for two-thirds what it costs in England or America, you may pass a year most agreeably in Florence.

The Italian journals are as speechless as those of France, else I would not here record the terrible calamity that has clothed in mourning the city of Leghorn. Thank God I was absent from the theatre that night; but those present have told me of the catastrophe. The house was crowded—the play, the "Taking of Sebastopol." The first acts went off well; battery after battery exploded; and the thrilling spectacle made the theatre ring with applause All eyes were turned to see them take the Malakoff. At last 'twas stormed. The soldiers rush in—then the explosion— amid the wildest cheers. At that moment a spark caught the scenes—they blazed—the audience thought it a part of the play, and cheered the louder, the scene was so natural! Alas! it was too perfect.

Another moment they saw their mistake—a wild cry of terror drowned the applause. Higher and higher it rose, maddening the spectators with fright. Five minutes more and the fire was extinguished; but the audience, like a herd of frightened buffaloes, like a panic-stricken army, like a flock of sheep before the wolves, like passengers from a sinking ship, losing all thought but for self-preservation, rushed from their seats. The shrieks of women, the shrill cry of children, the hoarse voices of the men, all struggling for life, presented a scene indescribable. Some threw themselves from the boxes into the pit, killing themselves and crushing those beneath them! No judgment—no forethought; out of the windows—over the *loges*—stamping each other to death! The sentinels were ordered to stop the passage with bayonets. A few of the flying crowd were run through and through, then the soldiers with the rest were mutilated with the feet of hundreds!

I look in vain in the Italian journals; the Tuscan Minister says forty killed, one hundred wounded. The next day I expected more particulars—I found none, and asked the reason. The Government forbade it, was the reply—such things excite the people these revolutionary times. The Grand Duke has gone down, but you have heard all it is intended you shall ever know. But my banker, Fenzi, has shown me a private letter. It paints the horrors of the accident, and closes the letter—*one hundred* already dead, and *five hundred* wounded. Worse than the Black Hole at Calcutta, or the fire at Richmond—more mortality than is recorded off the battle-field—or a Coolie passenger ship!

We arrived at Bologna just in time to see the Pope leading off the great festival of *Corpus Domini.* We drove through one of the twelve large gates, and it appeared as though the entire seventy-two thousand people in the city were out to meet his Holiness. The town is old, dirty, and full of churches, priests, and convents. In 1848, the Bolognese made the Pope tremble—now he is not the most beloved of saints. What an odd idea—for the Austrian general in command to get up a little insurrection, and quell it, to amuse the Pontiff!

Just now he is flooded with petitions. The government officers want increased pay—the people pray for reduced taxes. These continual demands trouble the Pope. He pardons individual cases, but declines to give a general amnesty. He is particularly anxious to please the Bolognese, for they have furnished Rome with six Popes and more than a hundred Cardinals! We rode through Mantua, where Napoleon's marshal, Serrurier, starved the Austrian general, Wurmser, into capitulating, but not till (like General Williams at Kars) the old soldier had eaten all his horses and cattle. Here we took the railway to Verona, an old Italian city of sixty-five thousand people, where you will find ruins more perfect than at Rome ; and three hours later we took the omnibus (a boat) for our hotel on the grand canal.

From north to south, the Italian States, save San Marino, are governed by absolute monarchs ; eight of them in all, with nothing in common but their religion. Their laws, their customs, their currency, their very language, are different. There is no unity of action in the land—no energy—no life—and I doubt if one ruler for all the States would give contentment to a people that cease to think for themselves. Foreign despots give their orders, and foreign armies execute them.

You may bribe the custom-house ; you may fee the beggars ; you may sneer at the priesthood, and swear at the boatmen ; England may threaten, France dictate, and Austria interfere ; and Italy will move on, with an occasional revolution bursting out, like the fire-fly, only to be darker after the blaze ; the stabbing of a king, the burning of a palace, the shooting of a garrison, and the breaking of a prison door ; but as for independence, self-government, liberal institutions— it will be a long time, I fear, before the Lilliputian emperors follow in the footsteps of the Sardinian king.

Italy, like Turkey, must share the fate of Poland, and some time be divided among the vultures that may ever be seen hovering over and around a dying nation.

From Italy we go to Austria, and I will write a page or two from the capital.

ARTICLE VIII.

VIENNA, *July 25th*, 1857.

MY DEAR SIR :—Trieste, like Venice, is a free port.
Planted just under a range of mountains at the head of

the Adriatic, it grows in prosperity, and some day will rise to importance, for it is the only outlet on the south for the commerce of Austria and Germany.

When the Emperor Charles VI., in 1719, removed all port charges, the population was but four thousand, now 'tis eighty-one thousand, made up of all nations—merchants from every land, Saxon, Swiss, English, French, Bavarians, Swabians, Rhinelanders, Greeks, Romans, Neapolitans, and Levanters—are all represented by their respective consuls. I believe there are but one or two Americans, although I counted eleven American ships turning out tobacco and cotton, under the guns of the frigate "Congress," on her way to Constantinople. Some sixty or seventy American ships bring cargoes yearly to Trieste, and find some employment in return.

Here is the depot of the Austrian Lloyd's, the steam line that keeps pace with the French and English companies. Many of the steamers were built in Scotland. Freiherr Von Bruck was the founder of the enterprise, which has been one of the most successful in Austrian commerce. Last year the imports and exports of the port, in round numbers, ran up to $50,000,000, and when Austria branches out to India and China, as she is desirous of doing, Trieste is well situated to increase her trade. The inner harbor will accommodate but fifty ships, but outside there is room to anchor a navy. The canal in the city is very handy; you can tip the goods from the boats into the doors of the warehouses. As I before remarked, Trieste contains all the many-featured, many-costumed merchants of the Levant. In such a Babel of tongues, Elihu Burrett would almost require a dragoman.

England, Brazil, the isles of the Mediterranean, and Alexandria, supply the commerce, Great Britain, as usual, taking the lead; but New-Orleans does considerable in cotton and tobacco. Saltpetre, gunpowder, salt, and tobacco, continue government monopolies. Trieste boasts a Tribunal of Commerce, a School of Navigation, and Imperial Dockyards. The Mole is some sixty feet in width, and extends from the end of the town some twenty-two hundred feet into the Adriatic, entirely built of stone—a splendid piece of masonry. Trieste is to the Austrian Lloyd's what Marseilles is to the Imperial Mail Line, and South-ampton to the Peninsular and Oriental Company.

The Greeks, as usual, are the most active among the merchants. With houses in New Orleans and Man-chester, they manage cotton and cotton goods, regulate exchanges, and grow rich. M. Chiozza's soap factory is worth a visit; 'tis the largest in the Empire. Griot and Chiozza live in palaces built with soap! Carciotti commenced with a bale of Yankee cotton, and died leaving millions.

Eleven hours diligencing over cultivated mountains and sterile plains, rocky, desolate hills and fertile valleys, brought us to Laiback. A month later you can go by rail; as it is, I made the journey last year from Trieste to Liverpool in less than a hundred hours. When the road is opened, the express will run through to Trieste from here in eighteen hours, a distance of 336 miles. Our baggage was checked through, but over twenty pounds weight is extra. The highlands overhanging Trieste, with the active bustle of a seaport city at their base, looking out along the Dalmatian and Italian coasts, present a scene unsurpassed for natural beauty—wildness and sublimity everywhere around. The table-land along the post road is as barren as the Indian hills, and the rocks about the old castle of Lueg are honeycombed with caves like those at Inkermann. Not far distant, nature opens a mammoth cave, the most wonderful grotto in Europe, that at Adelsburg, and close at hand you step down some 757 steps, hewn out of solid rock, into the quicksilver mines of Idria, one hundred and forty fathoms deep. These celebrated mines have proved nearly as rich as those of Almada, in Spain. Six hundred tons a year could be produced, but the Austrian Government restrict it to one hundred and fifty, most of which is consumed by the American gold and silver mines. It finds its way over the Atlantic in cast-iron bottles, while bags of skin, steeped in alum, take the balance to Vienna.

The twenty thousand people that compose the population at Laiback, are anticipating joyful times when the Emperor goes down next month to inaugurate the opening of the railway.

From Laiback to Gratz, our track seemed to be a continual cutting of rock, a road where tunnels and viaducts were the chief characteristics. From Gratz to Vienna, the scenery opens with a classic grandeur—towering cliffs, sharp defiles, deep cuttings through the mountains of rock, abrupt precipices, interspersed with artificial forests, and ripening fields of grain, foretelling a good harvest in Austria.

At Serumering the tunnel is cut 4,600 feet through a solid rock, 2,893 feet above the ocean—the highest railway in the world. The turnpike road is 400 feet above this!

The precipices of Weinzettelwand have had three tunnels cut through them. Then comes more engineering; the viaducts of Gampelgraben and Jagergraben, the Klam tunnel, rivers crossed, deep gullies bridged, mountains undermined, splendid forest trees in the distance—all bespeaking human skill—almost, yes, quite, the subjugation of nature.   Nothing in England or France can compare with this stupendous work.   Who says that Austria has no enterprise?

I arrived in Vienna at a memorable period in its history, just in time to witness what no person now living will probably ever see again—the celebration of the Centennial Anniversary of the High Order of Maria Theresa, the highest order in the world, given only to emperors, or the army and navy, for deeds of daring courage This is the first féte day, and all Austria has been called upon to make the occasion an era in the Empire's history.   Vienna is packed with strangers ; hotels, Government buildings, palaces, and private dwellings, are glittering with uniforms, every nook and corner occupied.   The military are here by special order, and their presence fills the city, while the sight-seers must camp outside.   'Tis a gala day in Austria, occurring but once in many generatians, and the preparations are made accordingly.

I was fortunate in receiving invitations where the doors were closed to civilians.   First, I looked down from the saloons of the minister of war, on the midnight serenade of the bands of the Empire—three hundred and fifty instruments, a torchlight procession, numbering as many hundred thousand spectators.

The square was jammed with humanity, a Boston Common scene at the fireworks, on the Fourth. The martial music filled the air, and you heard the notes for miles outside.

The next day, the review of the Austrian army. I dare not mention the number of troops; but infantry, cavalry, artillery, covered a space that tired the sight, presenting a military spectacle indescribable. The magnitude of Napoleon's regiments under exercise at Paris, astonished me. I was awed into silence when witnessing the tactics of six immense armies—real, earnest, fighting armies, on the grave-yard plains of the Crimea. I have seen Russell's vivid description of the Coronation of Alexander at Moscow—but this review, you must remember, takes place but once in a hundred years.

'Twas the grandest spectacle ever seen in Vienna, and in the apparent loyalty of the army, bespoke the absolutism of this remarkable Empire : remarkable for its antiquity, going back centuries before Rodolph of Hapsburg, even to the Cæsars; for Marcus Aurelius died on the old Roman station of Vidobono; remarkable for having crushed to death all revolution, all hope of liberty ; remarkable for the wealth and haughty pride of its nobles ; remarkable for the number of times it has been conquered and regained its nationality, and for having the credit of being the poorest, the most despotic, the most despised of European monarchies.

The Emperor, surrounded by a staff of officers two hundred strong, the chief of the kingdom, received with dignity the acclamations of the dense mass of soldiers, whose cheers were echoed back by the people. That day the knights of the Order were entertained at the Emperor's banquet, and the celebration closed with the glorious pageant at the theatre.

Again I am a witness to another, the last act in this splendid drama. I was early there and saw the pride of the Austrian nobility as they arrived. The house was crowded; the boxes five tiers high, each seat occupied by a noble or knight of the Order. Save the diplomatic corps, the door was shut to the civil world.

The invitations came from the imperial palace; they could not be bought or sold. Not one spare seat, and thousands sent away disappointed. The wealthiest dignitaries of the land were there—distinguished statesmen, grey-headed generals, the hope and pride of the aristocracy, came in their coroneted carriages; all the Esterhazys and Metternichs of Austria were there, each endeavoring to outshine the others in the richness of their dress, the brilliancy of their diamonds, and the number of their decorations. Hungarian chiefs, in that beautiful hussar dress, and Bohemian jagers, and the uniforms of all the princes, gave a scenic effect to the house.

The imperial box contained all the living members of the grand and kingly house of Hapsburg; the Emperor's mother, the boy Emperor, almost beardless—his young and beautiful Empress, her sisters, brothers—all the royal family, blazing with diamonds and the choicest gems.

The evening's entertainment was something entirely original. The programme was decidedly novel. First came a recitation in German, by a star actress; she described the gradual rise of the kingdom from infancy, and then stepping aside, clouds appear passing and repassing, and, opening in the centre, you are astonished to see the Empress Maria Theresa and her court, as she appeared when she established the Order one hundred years ago—the same dress, the same statesmen—represented to life.   The scene changes. Another recitation: she describes one of the early battles; the audience are wrought up with enthusiasm —we hear the sound of battle; the clashing of arms, the thunders of the real artillery, the shrieks of dying soldiers, the wild strains of martial music, the rattling of musketry, the trumpet-toned voice of command; the spectators are crazed with the exciting sounds, when the curtain rises, and there you have a battle-field.

Hundreds of men and officers in all and every attitude, advancing, retreating, dying, dead ; horses plunging into action, regiments at the cannon's mouth, bayonets, the cut, the thrust, the cry of the last moment before eternity—it was a tableau never to be forgotten. Each actor, at least three hundred on the stage, motionless, spell-bound, and for five minutes the dropping of a wafer would have been heard, the silence throughout the house was so intense. The scenic effect was such, you looked down over the living actors for miles upon camps and marching armies, and when the curtain fell, a wild cheer, doubling, trebling in intensity, rose from the theatre, each man rising to his feet, with face turned towards the youthful Emperor, who, standing, bowed his obligations for such a demonstration of loyalty. No man, a witness of that spectacle, can doubt the centralizing power of the house of Hapsburg.

Again a change came over the spirit of the scene. More declamation, and the stage once more is filled with actors ; this time the picture represents the leaders of the Austrian army—an officer in every uniform, as they appear, holding high the flag of victory. Nothing could equal the imposing appearance of these tableaux. And after them came a military play—camp life, all the actors soldiers. During the performance, seve-

ral times, when allusion was made to the royal family, all rose to their feet, and deafening cheers, oft-times
repeated, announced the unmistakable feeling of the
Austrian leaders. I saw the Emperor rise on three
separate occasions to make his acknowledgments, and
as I gazed I could but think of the absolute power of
that boyish mind.

At each dropping of the curtain, refreshments were
passed round on silver salvers. As before observed,
the house contained the flour—and carefully sifted too
—of the Austrian chiefs. No strangers were present
save a Russian general or two, and Lord Seaton and
Admiral Moresby, who were decorated for some brave
deed during the long war—I believe, the saving of the
Emperor's life. Only three Englishmen have the order.
I saw no other foreigner. Yes, there was one. I
must not forget to mention the courtesy of the Emperor to an American officer. At the review, Commodore Breeze, of the Levant squadron, was standing
on the platform, when a staff officer approached and
asked if he did not recognize the uniform of the American navy. The gallant captain made himself known;
the officer at once informed him that he came by
command of the Emperor, who knew the naval dress,
to invite him to the anniversary celebration. The compliment was passed in the presence of the staff, them-

selves forming almost a regiment. Webster and the
Austrian Minister were less friendly than the Emperor
and the American Commodore.

I have dwelt longer upon this imposing celebration,
because it forms a centennial link in Austrian history.
One hundred years must pass before it can be repeated, and Austria meanwhile may live through a thousand
changes. Down in the dark, cold vaults, under the
Church of the Capuchins, I counted seventy-one metal
coffins, where are embalmed the departed members of
the Hapsburg family—all Imperial dust, save of one,
a governess, the humble instructress of Maria Theresa,
whose memory lives afresh on the birth of every century. One subject among a colony of kings—seventy-
one in all, from the year before Miles Standish dropped his anchor off the Plymouth shore, when the Emperor Matthias was deposited here, down to the small
plain coffin placed in the tomb the other day—for you
are aware that death has but just entered the Imperial
palace, and borne away the infant princess ; the flowers
are still fresh upon the tomb, and the sadness of the
Empress throws a gloom over and about the palace.
Two steps away from this little child, in the shadow
of the sarcophagus of the late Emperor, I saw the
mortal remains of her who so poorly supplied the place
of Josephine—Maria Louisa, Empress of the French,

and by her side, near to the Emperor Francis, who loved him so well, is Napoleon II., the Duke of Reichstadt. What would not the present Emperor of France give to place the son of Napoleon beside the ashes of his father, in the tomb of the Invalides! But who cares for the mother?—that mother who disgraced the name of Empress, who forsook her husband in adversity, to marry again, and that husband Napoleon Bonaparte! It may add another page to the eventful history of this wonderful family, when France wars with Austria to regain the body of his child.

Don't be surprised to find me recording a brighter opinion of the Austrians than you have been in the habit of observing. The truth is, when I passed through the Empire thirteen months since, I was stamped, checked, signed, viséd, up one side and down the other, from the moment I touched the border of the Adriatic until I had left the frontier—a continuous, never-ceasing, vexatious espionage—sufficient to justify the traveler in forming erroneous opinions of the country, government, and people! Now all is changed. Austria has just abolished the inland passport system! Yes, don't be astonished; there is no mistake about it; the fiat has gone forth, and thus far I have scarcely seen a policeman in the land! I heard of it, and gave no credit—I read, and believed not—I observe,

and am convinced. Austria has, indeed, set a praise-
worthy example to passport Europe ! The change, so
sudden, so complete, gives a different aspect to the
country, a different odor to the atmosphere. Before, I
observed only despotism and ignorance—but now, coming as I have from beggared Italy, where police and
custom-house mark every man a thief and smuggler,
where priestcraft stalks forth at all hours and in every
place, and mendicants, mutilated, sickening, loathsome
beggars, fairly taint the air with their filth and wretch-
edness—coming, therefore, out of the Italian States into
the Austrian dominions, this simple change in the passport system gives brighter colors to all one sees.

Before, to my bandaged sight, vice seemed predominant
—now the country appears in a fairer light. Instead
of misery and squalid poverty, I find happiness and
contentment. The farms seem better cultivated, the
streets better paved, better swept, and the people appear better clothed, better housed, better fed, than any-
where in Europe ! With the removal of their spies,
the scales drop off, and that Austria, notorious for beating women in public squares ; that nation, despised by
the Saxon, contemptible for having wrung the heart's
blood out of Hungary—this same Austria now com-
mands my praise ! Traveling like a prisoner, I did
not observe the magnificence of her hospitals—where

the lame, the halt, and the blind are furnished with
the comforts of home by Government—the best on the
Continent. The Lying-in Hospital may encourage immorality, yet its arrangements are most perfect, for the
rich as well as the poor. Here the new-born babe may
commence its guileless life, live and die, and know not
whether its mother was a princess or a beggar!

The system of National education has been long
recommended. Generations before England awoke to
its importance, Austria established schools and colleges, and in her peculiar way taught religion and general knowledge to her people. Miss Dix will tell you
of their prisons, and your own eyes may satisfy you
of the unlimited extent of their arsenal, the richness
of their paintings, and the classic beauty of the mas-
ter-works of Canova which adorn the capital. The
hotels are well kept, but the charges are high. The
private galleries and private palaces are the pride of
the nobles. The collection of coins is the best in Europe, and scientific men seek and obtain encouragement in Austria. All these things I notice now, but
saw them not before. But having said this much
on the one side, I will add a line on the other.

The total abolition of the passport system conveys
one painful thought; need I tell you that it is—the
death of Republicanism! So strong is the Emperor,

he can afford to be liberal. You want no better proof that "liberty, fraternity, equality"—the Magyar's not the Frenchman's doctrine—are gone for the present. Absolutism is the word of command. 'Twas a bold and daring thing, the Emperor's visit to Milan and Venice, but it was politic. He went, he saw, and returns a conquerer! Bolder still in going into Hungary! There, too, his mission appears successful. His daughter's death, and the celebration of the Order of Maria Theresa, have brought him to Vienna, but he will go back to his independent subjects in Hungary. Kossuth may still weep over his fatherland! But Kossuth's day is close at hand.

Politically, a temporary quiet is observable. New agencies are working—new engines turning the wheels of their social system. I will mention two, the *Crédit Mobilier* and the Concordat! The Government, through these two agencies, works upon the minds of the people. The former has demoralized and unhinged the healthy working of trade. Sprung into life in an evil hour, *like its huge pattern in the French capital, the Crédit Mobilier of Austria has inflated land and all kinds of property. The population is as speculation mad as in France; "Money! make it honestly if you can, but at any rate make it," is the creed of the Austrian Bourse! A few bankers and noble-*

*men, who sneered at trade heretofore, as the Hindoo
sickens at pork, will become enriched, but thousands
will be wrecked when the hot air of inflated credit
begins to escape! When the bubble breaks, down
tumbles the miserable fabric built upon the sand.* The
Government displays little financial ability, yet no
nation possesses such talent for diplomacy.

Sixty million dollars deficit last year, and this will
show a wider gap, for the revenue is falling off, and
Government expenses increasing. Each new loan only
goes to cover present difficulty. The future is a blank,
the past is forgotten. "Sufficient for the day is the
evil thereof;" who careth for the morrow? The Bank
Directors still sleep upon their forty-five to fifty millions of silver, and still continue to issue their miserable trashy paper, which requires care to prevent it
from falling to pieces in your hand. Out of the kingdom lead is a better medium—it possesses more value.
The National treasury is exhausted to pay the army,
and, like the Government of France, all the pet projects of the Emperor must be paid by the *Crédit Mobilier.*

The Government becomes like that of Japan, a
gigantic commercial firm, were the chief partner is the
Emperor himself; Vienna is his warehouse, and he becomes enriched by the money of strangers. From nurs-

ing an illegitimate child to covering the empire with railways, from building the arsenal (like the Louvre at Paris, a disguised fortress for some expected turn of fortune,) to speculating in a newspaper—the cabinet takes the lead, and the emperor has the credit of guarding and protecting his subjects. The policy of the day is to govern the people in disguise. Stocks, shares, money, credit, work one way—religion, education, charity, another. Exorbitant prices, extravagant living, unbridled dissipation, result from gambling in credit; this occupies the mind of the wealthy, while the Jesuits, who swarm throughout the land, furnish mind and thought for the poor. The Jesuitical doctrines are gaining rapidly in Europe, and Austria makes spies of the priests. Whisper your private thoughts in the ear of the Jesuit, and the ready tool reports the secret to the Government, and fattens on credulity! This is the working of the Concordat.

By these means the Emperor rules the country without the people understanding the machinery. He remembers well when the Turks broke the chains across the Danube—when Napoleon battered down the walls —but more vividly than anything in the past, he remembers with fear and trembling, 1848, when the streets of Vienna run red with civil war! His Hungarian subjects pretend loyalty, but they despise the

Kaiser. The George Law muskets and the Kossuth saddles, may some time be useful. But to-day the emperor is all-powerful; his army is overwhelming. His strength lies in that and in the priesthood. Opinion, independence, thought, are strange-sounding words in these despotic lands—centralization, supremacy—no other words will answer. To his subjects he says, "Obey or die!" They listen, observe the order, live, and appear as happy as a bridal party! The Emperor faces the lion, and has walked among the revolutionists of 1848, and now he has returned to lay the cypress on the tomb of his child, to worship the memory of his ancestors, and celebrate that day which will return again long after his mortal remains are laid in the tomb of the Hapsburgs. The second anniversary comes round not till 1957.

Out of the 471,442 people in Vienna, 442,207, the census tells me, are Catholics. This will give you an idea of the material for Jesuitical education.

In running through the empire, I have talked with the most enlightened men upon my track, and the foregoing are the conclusions which I have formed. Our minister here, Mr. Jackson, of Georgia, who is homeward bound, has given me much reliable information on the empire, and I think will bear

me out in many of the opinions which I have advanced.

Americans in America see Europe through England.
We live, move and have our being, on continental affairs,
through the "glasses of the London journals!" Baron
Haynau is kicked out of Barclay & Perkins's brewery;
the English papers record it, we copy with comments,
and send them back the yell. England formerly abused
Austria—we echo her opinions. Hungary sent a cry
for liberty through the British Isles—'twas natural for
us to be sympathetic. Ingraham demands Kotza—we
were pleased at our national victory. On European
affairs, generally, England takes snuff, and we sneeze!
Just now a new element is working. The dulcet tones
of Lord Palmerston have been heard in the Sardinian
court—"Watch Austria—a dangerous enemy!" whispers
the Premier—another dispatch is put in the hands of
the Emperor Joseph—" Keep an eye on Sardinia, Count
Cavour is ambitious for his king." And thus the "tory
chief of a radical cabinet," "the old, old bird," puts one
monarch against the other, keeping Europe always in
a ferment. During the Russian war Austria played a
capital game : her cards were all trumps. Nicholas, for-
tunately for Austria, sleeps with his fathers, else he
would have a small account to settle—without doubt he
was the greatest mind of the first half of the 19th cen-

tury, the emperor of emperors, and history will write him down a chief!

This letter and that from Venice will not burthen you with figures, for Italy and Austria furnish poor material for commercial correspondence.

ARTICLE IX.

LONDON, *Sept.* 28, 1857.

MY DEAR SIR :—While at St. Petersburg last month, I received a copy of the London *Times*, containing an able article from your journal, sympathizing with

England on the Indian insurrection. The *Times* gave a leader partially accepting the proffered aid, and the editorial in question, you are aware, went the rounds of the European press. Since the opening of the Indian question, I have expressed similar opinions. I feel that you are right—England thinks so—while Continental Europe say that you are wrong. Why? Because every despotic monarch despises the free mind of the race from which we sprang.

To-day, India absorbs all other topics. You have introduced me too often to your readers not to find space for an outsider's opinion on England and her Eastern possessions. To commence—let me observe that John Bull looks sad to-day; that good-natured face appears more careworn—mark the crow's feet about the eyes. There are more wrinkles on his brow; more gray hairs, less elasticity of spirits. Really our grand old Saxon father begins to look for a cheering word from his eldest boy. He shall have a thousand; but the truth is he is too proud to accept our sympathy. A few months later that feeling will wear away, and Brother Jonathan will be treated with that dignity which the child of a proud old English sire has a right to demand.

I am glad to see America extending her hand to England in this terrible affair in Hindostan. The Sepoy mutiny! Mutiny did I say? Call it insurrection, revolution, anarchy! the fiercest, the wildest, the most terrific in the annals of the world.

Young Bengal is aroused—young India is red with the blood of Englishmen.

It is just two hundred and fifty-eight years since the Anglo-Indian tree was planted.

Macaulay says the bells that rang out the knell of 1599 rang in the Charter to George, Earl of Carlisle, with his two hundred and fifteen merchants, knights, and aldermen. Sir Thomas Smith was the Governor, and the cash capital was but one hundred and fifty thousand dollars.

That bigoted old fanatic, the first James, the patron of our Protestant Bible, in 1604, 1610, 1613, and 1618, extended the charter; but that stern old reformer, who told his men to put their trust in God and keep their powder dry, did for the Company what he afterwards did for Charles the First. Oliver Cromwell upset the entire monopoly, as General Jackson did old Biddle's Bank. Two years later, they got under way again, with a cash capital of three million six hundred thousand dollars. That gay bird, Charles the Second, clinched all former charters; then came the princely dividends. Just a century before our Declaration of Independence, (1776,) the company got more privileges, and in 1683 their political power commenced. Ours sprang into life just one hundred years later. Delhi was the seat of the Mogul's power. " Delhi must be undermined ! " said they, a hundred years ago. " Delhi must fall !" is the feeling of England to-day. But without American aid India may stand another generation.

Immense dividends brought powerful rivals. In 1693 and 1695 a new company was formed, called " the English Company trading to the East Indies." In 1702 both companies joined hands, under the firm of "the United Company of Merchants trading to the East Indies." More power was granted in 1726. At this time Madras, Bengal and Bombay obtained an existence as corporations.

From eight per cent. in 1698, to three per cent. in 1743, they became lenders to Government.

The charter was extended in 1880.

Pitt's India bill of 1784 established the Board of Control, which still rules the company. Vernon Smith, like Walker in Kansas, wishes he was out of it.

The Act of 1794 extended the charter till the close of the war of 1814, just before Alexander and Wellington rode into Paris together.

In 1834, the East India Company's monopoly was broken for ever, but the owners of stock were secured a dividend of ten and a half per cent., the Government reserving power to reduce the capital stock of the Company, after the 30th of April, 1874, fifty per cent., or one hundred pounds for every two hundred. From present appearances, this proviso will be of little service. The Honorable East India Company will have ceased to be *Honorable* long before that day.

On the 20th of August, the Government was continued in trust for the Crown, and the next year the Board of Control made other arrangements. This then gives you an abridged history of that great Power that is being shaken to the centre. Young Bengal is in earnest.

During the last half century the Indian records give the details of eight mutinies in the Indian army. But what were they compared to this?

When a son of Tippoo Sahib was to be placed on the throne of Mysore, India was startled by the mutiny of Vellore. That was in 1806. Two hundred soldiers were killed and wounded. Such mortality is now taking place perhaps every hour.

The Madras army were up in arms in 1809, and in 1811 Colonel Munroe blew some sixty men into the air. This was the time when the Rajah of Travancore and the Madras native officers conspired. There was another mutiny about the time that Napeleon was on his way to St. Helena, (a little incident by the by, not forgotten by the Emperor of the French.) When the "Bengal Java Light Battalion" were kept too long away from home in 1815, they occasioned the Honorable Company some anxiety by their insubordination.

During the Burmese war in 1824 (the year before the panic,) the Barrackpore regiments refused to go to Burmah, because no cattle were sent to transport their baggage. Again, in 1843, the Madras Sixth Cavalry wanted more pay before they would march on Scindh.

Six years since, the Bengal troops at Barrackpore, mutinied against going to Burmah during the late war.

The Sepoy several times has refused to go across the Indus; or, as he expresses it, upon the "Kala Pawnee," and has objected to work in trenches. But all these petty mutinies amount to nothing compared to the horrible atrocities of to-day.

Having gone over the page of Indian history, giving a passing word to the several insubordinations among the Sepoys, let me take up scene by scene, act by act, the terrible drama being enacted while I write, where nations are the audience.

The same year that Austria celebrated the centennial anniversary of the Order of Maria Theresa, England rejoiced over the centennial anniversary of the battle of Plassey.

Lord Clive in 1757—Lord Canning in 1857 : the former won the laurels of a soldier and a statesman—

the latter has gained thus far neither the one nor the other. England lost America, but at the same time she planted the seed of her Indian Empire—that Empire which totters to-day and must fall on the morrow, unless England accepts the proffered sympathy of America.

England to-day is blind to the dangers that surround her Oriental dominion. To-morrow she may wake from her lethargic slumbers.

THE TIMES ARE CHANGING, but she declines to change her system. Red tape brought disgrace upon her Crimean army—red tape will stultify her action in the East. The fact is, she refuses to open her eyes to the danger, and this policy she has adopted from the first· You can trace it to a day. Mark this observation, and tell me if she does not sleep when the world requires that she should be awake.

On the centennial anniversary of the battle of Plassey, the *Times* and other journals ushered in the new-born year with the sounding of drums and the clashing of timbrels. The *Times* wrote a splendid leader (they always do). Mark, said the writer, our universal Empire. Look at India, from the Punjaub to the Carnatic—from Bombay to Burmah—from Madras to Meerut —from Ajmeer to Calcutta:—throughout our entire dominion contentment reigns supreme—an almost uni-

versal peace.   At the same time there was a cloud
rising in the East not bigger than your hand, spread-
ing larger and larger—a summer cloud concealing the
thunderbolt that destroys a nation.

While this " leader" was in the hands of the printer, a
plot was matured to massacre every man, woman, and
child in Hindostan.   Every European was to die.   The
King of Oude had some twenty thousand men outside
of Calcutta as laborers, mechanics, and servants.   Those
twenty thousand men were trained soldiers, brought
there in disguise to murder every European in Calcutta.   The plan was to turn the frowning guns of
Fort William on the shipping and sink it in the Hoogly,
so that no white man could escape, and then as the
cake was passed from hand to hand, the slaughter was
to commence.

In due course of mail the intelligence arrived of the
Nineteenth regiment having mutinied at Barrackpore.
They refused to use the Enfield rifle cartridge.   Of course
they were disbanded.   The thirty-fourth followed suit.
The news in England created no uneasiness, save with
Lord Ellenborough, who saw therein the handwriting
on the wall.   His eloquent warnings are recorded on
the register of the House of Lords.

England saw the mutiny and waited for later news.
It came.   Eight thousand men had revolted.   England

turned red—then pale—then laughed, (but like Riche-
lieu, she shuddered as she laughed,) and finally breathed
a note of sorrow. They waited for another mail. It
arrived. The telegraph told them thirty thousand men
had "disappeared." England shook off her drowsi-
ness, and said "Let there be no discontent;" and up
went the funds. Another despatch—" The Bengal army
has ceased to exist. General Anson was dead." Still
another rise in the funds. England said, "Well, we
begin to see daylight." All an Englishman wishes to
know is the worst. "Show us the dark side and we
will soon make it bright. Another mail will have put
the mutiny down." Yet thirty thousand men were
shipped away in July and August—some in steamers
—some in sailing ships—M'Kay's clippers—the "Lightning," "Champion of the Seas," and "James Banes,"
were the only Americans that got a charter. They
took out some 2,600 men, at one hundred and twenty-
five dollars each—a good business for the owners.
American clippers are already on the way. American
officers, stung by the atrocities at Cawnpore, are im-
patient to revenge them. American soldiers are ready
to follow. When a Saxon woman is outraged England
and America are one.

The most intense excitement was created throughout
the kingdom. The Journals said, "We will soon put

it down. Madras and Bombay stand firm. Delhi must fall."

Still later intelligence.

Delhi not taken. General Barnard dead. Reid succeeds. Cawnpore in danger. The telegraph told but half the story, but the excitement was terrible to the looker-on. The community lived on hope.

Another arrival—Fourteen days later.

Delhi still in the hands of the rebels, who are flocking in from all about the country. General Reid dead, and one thousand Englishmen, women and children, slaughtered—mutilated—butchered at Cawnpore. The brave General Wheeler fought like an Englishman—fought hard and well—but the enemy were too powerful. The garrison was to be saved, the papers signed; and when the Europeans passed out, there came a volume of smoke, and the "red artillery" flashed across the river. Brave men, beautiful women, and a regiment of children were shot down. English mothers and English daughters were reserved for a more terrible fate—outraged before their husbands, their fathers, and their brothers. Nena Sahib the fiend—the assassin —the Marat—the Robespierre of the bloody deed. Curse his memory. All this; and yet history makes the Black Hole of Calcutta more terrible!

The funds now commence to droop. Indian families

are dressed in mourning. Indian merchants are trembling for their credit. The India House have ordered ten thousand more men, for August and September. Forty thousand soldiers before the 1st of September. More news. Delhi still holds out. The rebels making sorties like the Russians at Sebastopol. Lucknow in danger. General Lawrence dead—as brave a man as ever wore a sword, as sound a statesman as ever administered the affairs of a country. The Bombay army is up; the Punjaub is rising. Cholera is in the camps. Bad as was the despatch—worse still were the details. The funds still droop. The Indian massacres are in everybody's mouth—*even an English newspaper gets out an extra on the occasion.* The journals are full of letters—letters that at one moment chill the heart with horror, and at the next fire it with indignation—letters recording brave exploits. Think of young Willoughby: he placed the torch in the magazine, and a thousand Indians were hurled into their Hindoo world. A woman, the wife of an officer, shoots six Sepoys—all the while loading the guns for her husband; and then, rather than see his wife outraged, her husband shoots her, and with a prayer upon his lips, blows out his own brains.

Letters—full of misery, full of dread despair—to mothers, to families at home; letters that make the blood run cold—their details so sadden the heart.

~Once more the mail is in—news this time to the end of August.

The army before Delhi besieged instead of besieging. General Havelock fought great odds, and has beaten in every battle. Havelock, the bravest man in India. " Cry Havelock ! and let slip the dogs of war !" says *Punch.* Lucknow growing weaker.

The army before Delhi in great danger. Agra hopes to hold out. Two hundred troops ambushed and killed at Arrah. Five hundred fell at Delhi. Lord Canning disarms his body guard. The Madras army is up. The Sepoys refuse to go to Calcutta.

Lord Elgin has arrived from China. The China troops are all at Calcutta—four thousand men. So China is put to bed for a while.

Lord Elgin and Sir Colin Campbell not on good terms with Lord Canning. No harmony in the councils. General Grant nobody.

The Gwalior Contingent of thirty-two thousand men with the rebels. Distrust, discontent, and gloom throughout the Indian Empire.

King of Delhi on the throne of the Moguls. King of Oude a state prisoner in Fort William. Queen of Oude had an audience with the Queen of England *after the mutiny broke out.* Sir Colin Campbell on the sick list. Canning growing more and more unpopular. The wisdom of the father was not inherited by the son.

Anxiety in England increasing.

The Sepoy army everywhere warring with those who gave them salt.

No Lord Clive. No Warren Hastings. No Wellington. No general but Havelock, and he surrounded by three Sepoy armies, and yet he has but a thousand men. I dread to hear the tidings of another mail.

Nena Sahib, who has been killed several times by telegraph and the London journals, is marching on Lucknow at the head of an army of 30,000 men.

This is the latest news. I have given it to you in despatches, as correctly as my memory served. Is it not terrible?

Mail after mail will record massacre after massacre. Lucknow, Agra, Havelock's gallant band, and the army at Delhi, are in great danger—the danger increasing every hour. Would to God that every man, woman, and child—every free-born Saxon—were safe on board the ships in the river, for I tremble for their fate.

This is the position of India to-day—anarchy and murder from north to south, east to west! The Sepoy soldier is wiping out the stains of a hundred years of oppression; his religion moves him to murder; fanaticism makes him torture his victims. No Spanish Inquisition—no North American savage—no Ladrone pirate ever committed deeds so dark. History gives no record

of such wholesale atrocity! Children tossed from bayonet to bayonet, women mutilated—passed from harem
to harem—paraded naked through the streets—and then
handed by the Sepoys over to the rabble.

Young girls—young wives—young mothers—great God!
my heart sickens! I will write no more. I shout
with Tupper, " Shoot them down! those who shame their
Creator by their infamy!" The author of " Proverbial
Philosophy" demands " vengeance of Hell upon the Indian race."

America to the rescue! England must have our
help, or her power is waning rapidly.

The Mohammedan festival of Eed passed, the 2d of
August, without bloodshed. The Mohurren, thank God,
had also gone by. But other religious days are rapidly
running on.

General Grant has gone to Madras. General Lloyd,
at Dinapoor, like General Hewitt at Meerut, is to be
court-martialed. Both were imbeciles. The latter has
been fifty-three years in India. If you understand the
enervating influence of the Indian climate, you can imagine what amount of energy this old man could have
had.

How, then, are matters to-day? I have examined
the subject, and understand what I am writing. I differ from the English press; their nationality blinds their
judgment.

Forty thousand men were said to be in India—European soldiers—when the mutiny broke out, and yet they could not save Cawnpore or take Delhi. In my opinion, thirty thousand is nearer the truth—however, in round numbers make it forty.

Then the Chinese army of five thousand—and say, from Ceylon, Mauritius, Australia, and the Cape, five thousand more—will make an army of fifty thousand men. Add the troops sent round the Cape from England, forty thousand more. Here, then, you have an army of ninety thousand men.

The English army got away from England in July, August, and September ; they would arrive in India in November and December—all before January. But be it remembered that the European population of India is at the mercy of an enraged Sepoy army of three hundred thousand men (save a few straggling regiments), in a country containing one hundred and sixty millions of Indians who hate the Saxon's rule—from the latest dates to the end of November—from two to three months before the army can reach the East. Be not, then, surprised at anything you hear. England knows not the danger ; if she does, she dares not tell it to her people. America alone can save to the Saxon race the Indian Empire.

Now for a little analogy. When standing on the

heights of Inkerman and Balaklava, I looked down upon five gigantic armies. The allies could be seen on every side. There was that splendidly equipped Sardinian army; there were the Turks, the Piedmontese, and fifty thousand Englishmen just arrived, fresh for war; and then I saw Napoleon's soldiers. Five armies, composing—the journals say—some three hundred thousand men. And yet the Crimean vineyards and the Crimean hills seemed almost uninhabited—the camps so far apart, the armies covering so little ground. Now, I ask you, if over a quarter million of men make so little show on the Crimean battle-ground, what will ninety thousand soldiers make in Hindostan, when the one, compared to the other, is in about the proportion of my finger nail to my whole hand?

It must also be remembered that there are four hundred thousand drilled soldiers in the pay of independent native princes and rajahs, who have thus far remained neutral. Scindh and Holkar, hitherto, have been true but they cannot be trusted.

The climate destroys the European soldier right and left. When I was in Calcutta in March, I was carried in a palanquin—no man walks where labor is so cheap and the sun so scorching. George Ashburner placed a dozen servants to do my bidding; and my suite of apartments were like a hotel, there were so many.

The great difficulty is the distances.   Take Wild's
map of India. I bought one at once, and have studied
it carefully. The moment the telegraph announced the
mutiny of a military station, I drew an ink mark
about it; and, with the Indian Empire represented on
my table, I have made myself acquainted with the
subjects on which I write. The distances are great,
and no railways of importance completed, save 120
miles out of Calcutta, 50 miles out of Madras, and
but fifty miles out of Bombay. No railways, and
military roads none the best. Bullock drays get on
but two miles an hour, night and day work. It takes
some three weeks from Calcutta to Delhi; by the
river steamers on the Ganges and the Jumna, it will
take you four weeks; therefore, after the troops arrived at Calcutta, a month is gone before Delhi can
be reached. Hence, for a long time, our Indian cousins
are left at the mercy of the most savage barbarians
the world has ever witnessed.

When the army arrives, mark the distances: 976
miles from Calcutta to Delhi; 774 miles from Bombay
to Madras; 1,182 miles from Madras to Cawnpore; 839
miles from Agra to Calcutta; 1,301 miles from Calcutta
to Bombay: 1,103 miles from Delhi to Seringapatam
(memorable for being the place where Wellington, for
the first time, turned his back on an enemy); 1,167

miles from Allahabad to Pondicherry (where France
has just landed a regiment of soldiers—only a little, very little spot upon the horizon); Bhooj to Dina-
pore, 1,748 miles; 1,475 miles from Darnhar to
Patna.

These figures will give you a better idea of what
an English army has to encounter, than a volume of
argument. England refuses to look the danger in the
face. She says it is purely a military mutiny. It is
not so alone. Has she so soon forgotten that after
the massacre at Meerut and Cawnpore, the women
were turned over to the rabble in the bazaar, who
stripped them, walked them naked (Lady Godiva rode)
through the city, and then outraged, mutilated, and
tortured them to death? The picture is too horrible for
contemplation. The people are Asiatics; their religion is
fanaticism; their wrongs are household words. Shoot
them down—there is no other way—but it must be
with the assistance of the Americans. The Saxon's
government is better than their own.

England says they are short of percussion caps.
Has she forgotten that a Hindoo received the prize for
the manufacture of percussion caps at the great Exhibition in London?

England says that they are short of powder. Has
she forgotten that Delhi has been made a Cronstadt,

a Sebastopol, by the East India Company during the last half century, and that Hindostan furnishes more saltpetre than all the world beside? And yet, when the mutiny broke out, not a European soldier was inside the walls!

England says that there are no leaders. Where's the King of Oude, the King of Delhi, and that fiend incarnate, Nena Sahib?

England says they are short of funds. Where are the hundreds of millions of silver that have been shipped there, disturbing the currency of the world?

Was it not a ruling mind that waited for the breaking out of the Persian war before they struck their colors?

Was it not a ruling mind that took advantage of England's attention in China before they raised the red flag of mutiny?

Was it not a ruling mind that selected the centennial anniversary of the battle of Plassey for the general insurrection?

Was it not a ruling mind that chose Delhi, the centre of the Mogul Empire, as a rendezvous?

Was it not a ruling mind that made the question a question of religion?—and, most important, was it not a ruling mind that postponed the evil day until the world had been drained of silver—silver which is hoarded throughout the Indian Empire, disarranging the exchanges of the West? Are all of these things the result of accident?

Tippoo Sahib of the Carnatic—Tippoo Sahib of Seringapatam—the Indian King who corresponded with Napoleon when in Egypt, regarding the invasion of India— Tippoo Sahib's doctrine was this, to use the sense of his own words:—" We do not understand these English soldiers. Their scientific warfare; their military tactics; their discipline; their arms and equipments; their courage—all are too powerful for the Indian race. We must learn their art of warfare; we will work for them; they will arm us and teach us, and when we are sufficiently strong, our time will come." Well has the system worked. Regiment after regiment, till the Sepoy army numbers some three hundred thousand men—men who have shot down their European officers like cattle—officers who, for a generation, have grown around and amongst them.

It is absurd to say that they are not good soldiers. There is one of two things—either the Sepoy has not the material to make him a soldier, or the British officers who taught them were not good teachers. Before the mutiny the first point would have been answered by pointing to the medals that the Sepoy wears for battles won and brave deeds accomplished. I saw medals on most of the Bengal soldiers.

The tragedy of Cawnpore requires to be portrayed by the historian, the poet, and the orator, before England and the world can feel its startling horrors. The Black Hole of Calcutta—an accidental tragedy—chills us when we look it in the face; but what was that to this? Another mail may bring us similar deeds from Agra, from Lucknow, and even from Calcutta. What can seven thousand Europeans do with a hostile city—with a population of four hundred thousand people?

I pity every white man, woman, and child in India.

There is another disagreeable feature—the financial question.

The East India Company is burdened with debt. Shall I make a few figures? For the year ending 1855 and 1856, the gross revenue of the Indian Empire was one hundred and forty-four millions of dollars.

```
Opium contributed..............................  $24,000,000
Land taxes .....................................   89,000,000
The salt monopoly......  .......................   12,000,000
While stamps, Post-Office, &c., gave............   19,000,000
```

It cost to collect this sum nearly one-third—say $33,000,000—leaving a net revenue of $111,000,000.

Against which there is an expenditure of $115,000,000,

showing a deficit last year of nearly $5,000,000 to be added to the debt of India.

Already it runs up to, including interest, sinking fund,
    home funded, &c.... .... $310,000,000

(Our corn crop is more than that.)

Add to that debt, expenses of 40,000 men, passage to
    India and back, expenses up the country, equip-
    ments, pay, &c.—say $5,000 per man—for three
    years' work 200,000,000

      Total*... $510,000.000

—which must be added to the national debt of England before 1860, already in round numbers amounting to $4,000,000,000, or five dollars to each man, woman, and child that compose the eight hundred millions of human beings in the world.

The interest on that debt per annum will pay the entire expenses of the United States Government for three years.

Throughout the Indian Empire the revenue is stopped, the machinery has broken, the system has worked itself out. No receipts—but payments daily; nothing

---

* Lord Ellenborough says that it will take 15,000 men per annum to keep the army up to 40,000.

coming in—everything going out; treasuries being robbed on the one side, while Christians are being butchered
on the other. The Indian commerce is paralyzed—the
Indian banks are undermined. When there are wars
and rumors of wars the banker and the merchant
must bid good-bye to kiting. The Calcutta merchants
are in about the same position with their fellows in
other portions of the globe—they have worked the
oracle of expansive credit till it will work no more.
The day of reckoning is close at hand.

Commercially it is bad enough, financially it is worse
but politically it is the very worst of all, and yet
England is unconscious of the danger. She lives on,
regardless of others' fate and of her own; she believes
that she will conquer India; she believed also that
she would conquer Russia. Russia still lives. England, to-day, financially, is in the same position as
India was, politically, before the breaking out of the
mutiny. She sleeps on a volcano.

With doubt and dread I wait for later intelligence
but I fear the telegraphic despatch will be written in
drops of blood. Bad news is close at hand; if not
by the next mail, it cannot be far away.

I am sure the Americans will not allow their old
mother land to lose her Indian empire. This time
it is no infringement of treaties; and if I understand

the signs of the times, next winter you will have more volunteers than you can feed.

When England asks our help let us give it, and history will paint in glowing colors the age when the American eagle and the British lion, rushing to the rescue of the Saxon race, pounced with a blood-red vengeance upon the Bengal tiger, as he was gnawing at the breast of a Saxon woman, and tearing in pieces a Saxon babe.

SPECULATIONS,
CALCULATIONS, RECOMMENDATIONS,
ETC., ETC.

The World, the Flesh, and the Devil—1837 and 1857—The Past, the
Present, and the Future—Western Lands—Chicago represents " *Land
Mania*" Latter-day Millionaire—Railways of Illinois illustrate Railway Mania—Ohio Life and Trust Company—Railway Reforms recommended—Floating Debt—*The times are changing*—*Loco*-motives at
a discount—Illinois Central—Depreciation in all speculative property
—The Disease requires a powerful Remedy—Hard Currency—Specie
Imports and Exports—Coinage at United States Mint—Bank Statis-
tics—James Buchanan's warning—History of Paper Money—Credit
based on Faith—Hard Currency Countries—Bacon and Adam Smith
ahead of their time, but behind ours—Protection—Free Trade—
Economy—The Father and his Family—The West Rich—Credit—
Obligations to Europe are paid by two years' economy—How Ame-
rica sold Bonds in England—Repudiation condemned by America—
Secretary of Treasury's *mis*calculations—Corn crops over-estimated—
Farmers better sell—England owes America for grain—Andrews'
Statistics of Produce—Cotton not the only interest in the country—
Hay crop larger than Cotton crop—South no richer than the North
—Credit and Labor as cheap in America as England—Industrial
productions.

" The World, the Flesh, and the Devil," was the
pithy text of an old Calvinistic preacher, who, like the

Rev. Dr. Beecher, had the odd habit of calling plain things by their Christian names.

" I propose," said he, " to pass rapidly through the world, touch lightly on the flesh, and hasten on to the Devil."

In publishing " YOUNG AMERICA ABROAD," I passed rapidly through the world ; in publishing " YOUNG AMERICA AT HOME," I have touched lightly on the flesh ; and, in writing this concluding chapter, I shall endeavor to avoid the last alternative of the minister, by telling the truth, with the hope of shaming the Devil.

Having croaked for twelve months, you may be surprised to find me croaking still.

My introductory remarks endeavor to prove that our Banking and Commercial sages are some ways behind the times, in comparing this financial picture with that of former days. If the mind of the Bank Director who weathered the storm of former panics, had expanded at the same rate as his Banking operations, he would not now be fancying a resemblance between things which twenty years had rendered totally dissimilar.

The upsetting of a stage coach at that time might have broken an arm or two ; but when the Express train runs off the bridge, it carries misery to many a happy home.

The master of an onion sloop between Cape Cod and

Boston, during the last war, might well feel astonished when wrecked in mid-ocean in the clipper "Great Republic."

The times have changed since that day, and ARE CHANGING STILL.

Are the merchants of New-York aware that some fourteen hundred banks have suspended payment throughout these United States ?

Have they also realized the fact that some fourteen hundred firms and corporations have failed ?   If so, where, I ask, is the clear sky which they have discovered in the financial and commercial horizon ?   Would to God that my vision could descry so bright a promise !

But let the past go by.   Yet if they close their eyes to the disaster of the present, how can I expect them to join me in speculating on the future ?   With due regard, however, to their opinions, I intend to do so and from Wall-street, after taking a bird's-eye view of our own country, I propose to step into the Old World to mark the changes *now in progress.*

This financial storm has no parallel in the history of commerce.   I heard the muttering of the gale in Europe ; I now see in the "Suspension" of the Banks its middle stage ; but the great trees will stand till the tempest increases to the tornado.

These are some of its workings:

ALL SPECULATIVE PROPERTY must drop, from day to day, all the way from forty to sixty per cent. Land and railways, stocks, houses, ships, cotton, and sugar are feeling the terrible effect of depreciation.

Speculative Western lands must come down from the sky. FIFTEEN HUNDRED PER CENT. ADVANCE is too high a jump to make in the price of a house-lot in eighteen months ; eighteen years would hardly warrant it.

Chicago in the New World has done what the *Crédit Mobilier* has accomplished in the Old: set everybody crazy with their immense fortunes made in lands, their magnificent warehouses, and their grand trunk railways.

The Prairie City is full of paper millionaires.

I can best illustrate the madness of the age by introducing here one land operation in the West. This will give a fair idea of the LAND MANIA.

Some Western merchant is desirous of investing some of the money *which he owes to the East*, believing that he can turn a few thousands before the dry goods note comes due. If not, he can easily get his paper renewed. He buys a lot, raises money on mortgage, and sells to another, *who owes for goods bought in New-York* The lot changes hands nine times.

These are the figures:

First purchase	....	$1,000	....First mortgage	....	$500
Second "	....	1,500	....Second "	....	750
Third "	....	2,000	....Third "	....	1,000
Fourth "	....	3,000	...Fourth "	....	1,500
Fifth "	....	4,500	....Fifth "	....	2,000
Sixth "	....	7,000	....Sixth "	....	3,250
Seventh "	....	10,000	....Seventh "	....	4,500
Eighth "	....	12,500	....Eighth "	....	5,000
Ninth "	....	15,000	....Ninth "	......	6,500

The ninth time it changes hands the owner raises $6,500 on the original $1,000 purchase, valued before the crisis at $15,000! The sales all made in a year and a half—*the land in no way improved.*

Brigham Young represents the "Latter Day Saint," but it took a French poet to describe the "Latter Day Millionaire:"[*]

> "*Monday*, I started my land operations;
> *Tuesday*, owed millions, by all calculations;
> *Wednesday*, my "brown-stone" palace began;
> *Thursday*, I drove out a spanking new span;
> *Friday*, I gave a magnificent ball;
> *Saturday*, smashed—with just nothing at all."

—(At least nothing that the creditors could get at.)

It reminds me of the Australian land mania of 1853. Here is an inflation of fifteen hundred per cent.; and yet Mr. Appleton says that there is little cause for the panic but the *sugar speculation!*

---

[*] Mackay's "Popular Delusions."—Law's Mississippi Land Scheme, 1719-'20.

Take another interest—Railways. Having mentioned Chicago, I may as well take the State which Chicago represents, to illustrate THE RAILWAY MANIA.

The Western States are cross-barred with railroads. They branch out of Indianapolis and Chicago like the veins in one's hand. Examine the map—it's a curiosity. Illinois is the State before me ; observe the lines :

	Miles.
Chicago and St. Louis	220
Chicago and Rock Island	229
Chicago and Milwaukee	45
Galena and Chicago Union	259
Great Western Illinois	148
Illinois Central	704
Illinois and Wisconsin	91
Terre Haute and Alton	215
Chicago, Burlington and Quincy	138
Peoria and Oquawka	152
Ohio and Mississippi	147
Michigan Central	10
Michigan Southern	12
Belleville and Illinoistown	15
Joliet Cut-off	44
Fox River Valley	42
Northern Cross	100
Total	2571

Two thousand five hundred and seventy-one miles of rail in a State of only about one million and a

half of people!—costing, at an estimate of thirty
thousand dollars per mile, some seventy-seven millions,
or about forty dollars to each man, woman, and child
in the State. This ought to convince "unbelievers"
that the West has ridden a free horse to death.

Henry V. Poor gives in the *American Railway
Journal* (see Appendix) a statement of all the lines
in operation in the United States. The number of
miles completed on the 1st of January, 1857, was
twenty-four thousand, two hundred and ninety, costing
between nine and ten hundred millions of dollars
(about the sum left among the Eastern tribes by
the Allies during the Crimean war).

To show how rapidly we have been using up England's money, I will give here the annual increase
since January 1st, 1848, the year the Emperor of
the French realized one of his "Napoleonic ideas."

	Number of miles R.R. in the U. S.	Increase over preceding year.
1848	5,265	—
1849	6,195	930
1850	7,350	1,253
1851	8,856	1,408
1852	10,878	2,022
1853	13,315	2,437
1854	15,511	2,196
1855	19,438	3,927
1856	21,440	2,002
1857	24,290	2,850

Nearly three thousand miles during the past year! Progressing at this rate, we would have had fifty thousand miles of railway completed in 1867. But, Presto! the Ohio Life and Trust Company exploded, upsetting every speculative hobby in the country. That company proved to be the corner brick of a ten-story house, built with very bad mortar, by very bad workmen, on a very rotten foundation.

Many of the roads are wanted to carry on the legitimate business of the country, but to make them pay, sweeping reforms are necessary.

Raise prices. Don't make the capital stock twice the cost of the road. Reduce expenditure. Don't expend too much on fancy engines. Cut off the runners. Never allow five different agents belonging to the same company to hang the same placard up in the same room. Don't pay one hundred thousand dollars a year for advertising. Live within your means. Keep out of debt. Bury all "dead heads." Don't pay Presidents $25,000 salaries. Don't borrow money to pay dividends that were never earned. Don't let speculators have anything to do with the management. Let those who own stock and live along the line of road manage their own property. Let stockholders attend the meetings. Don't send proxies, but go yourselves. When there, speak out; don't be gagged by "cut and dried" resolutions. Ask for the accounts; examine well the details, especially of "construction account." You have certainly a right to inquire about investing your own money. Don't be afraid of great men; you have as much right to talk as they. Make yourself thoroughly acquainted with the subject, and, when loaded, fire. *An American respects a man who dares to express his mind.*

Two hundred millions of railway paper under protest, with a floating debt of some sixteen millions unprovided for, is too serious a matter to widows and orphans for stockholders to go to sleep over.

THE TIMES ARE CHANGING. Men must work, not play. Churches to-day are more popular than clubs. Health, industry, integrity are worth more to-day than railway shares. *Loco*-motives may conduct the national train in the "glorious summer" of prosperity, but they run off the track when the "winter of our discontent" blocks up the road with the snows of adversity.

The LAND MANIA and the RAILWAY MANIA IN ILLINOIS will be land-marks in the history of the age. She possesses the largest railway in the world, which railway squeezed out of the government a *little* land, which land is mortgaged for a good deal of money. A railroad through such a country, (not quite as densely populated as Belgium,) not entirely paid for, and which can never be run to pay, cannot be worth more than a hundred per cent. premium on its shares! Illinois illustrates the rash speculations of the Western States.

Other interests have also been pushed to their utmost tension by inflated credit; but the two interests mentioned will be sufficient to endorse my argument, that every kind of property must fall, day by day— down—lower and lower—till it finds a substantial value. Nothing can raise it but inflation again, and who is so bold as to recommence that?

"Expand, expand!" said the financial sages to the banks. They did expand—and burst! Speculation has carried prices to a dizzy height. They must find a level. Expansion placed them in the air; contraction brings them to the ground again.

Let the merchants make up their minds to look the enemy in the face, and not pursue the *ignis fatuus* idea that a let-up is close at hand to dispel the nightmare of a hard winter.

THE TIMES ARE CHANGING. The nature of the disease requires a powerful remedy. What is that remedy? Hard currency. Rodin, in the "Wandering Jew," resorted to the tortures of a galvanic battery before he rid himself of the cholera.

Hard currency will mend the steam engine; nothing else can. At any rate, we must try it for awhile]

The Bank of England issue no notes under $25. The Bank of France issue none under $20, (although lately a smaller note has been recommended). In America no note should circulate under $10. This would soon bring the American eagles out of the old stockings in the farm houses.

Cushing compliments the ladies, and uses metaphor when speaking on the crisis. Banks, more statesmanlike, gives figures. "In round numbers," said he, at Faneuil Hall, "the records show $300,000,000 of specie in the country." If so, there you have hard currency by the wholesale.

Andrew's valuable work gives the following table:

Importations of Bullion into the United States from 1821 to 1852.........................	$274,407,398
Exportations of Bullion from the United States during the same period.............	265,529,935
Leaving in the country the amount of........	$8,877,463

And this small amount comprised the product of two California years.

Our Imports of Bullion in 1837 were...........	$10,516,414
While our Exports that year were but......... .	4,540,465
Our Imports of Bullion in 1857 amounted to....	12,461,199
Our Exports from our mines show the sum of...	70,000,000

Which completely turns the tables.

This table will show the

Amount of Coinage at the Mint, and Amount left the Country during the past Seven Years :

	Coinage at the U. S. Mint.	Amount exported.
1850	$33,847,838	$ 2,894,202
1851	63,388,889	24,019,160
1852	57,845,597	37,169,091
1853	64,291,477	23,285,493
1854	60,713,865	34,438,713
1855	44,060,302	52,587,531
1856	64,283,963	41,557,853
1857...(six months)...	26,794,782	69,949,133

RECAPITULATION.

Amount of Coinage since 1850, in round numbers, $415,000,000

Amount of Exports,........................   286,000,000

Excess of Coinage over Exports $129,000,000

Estimated Amount of Coin previously in the country, 171,000,000

$300,000,000

Giving an average of about *Ten Dollars* each to the twenty-eight millions of people in the country.

Hunt gives the entire coinage of the United States since the time of the first director, David Rittenhouse, to the close of last year, at the several mints, as follows :

Mints.	Commencement of Coinage.	Amounts.
Philadelphia	1793	$391,730,571
San Francisco	1854	59,369,473
New-Orleans	1838	59,423,415
Charlotte	1838	4,384,694
Dahlonega	1838	5,792,841
Assay Office, New-York	1854	42,732,712

Total amount of specie that bears our national
stamp.. $563,433,706

TABLE,

Showing Number of Banks—Their Capital Stocks—Amount of Notes in Circulation—Specie in their Vaults, and Indebtedness of the People to the Banks, during the respective Years of the Three Great Financial Revulsions of 1837, 1847, and 1857.

	Number of Banks.	Capital Stock.	Bank Notes in Circulation.	Specie in Vaults.	Indebtedness of People to Banks.
1837	788	$290,772,091	$149,185,800	$37,915,540	$525,115,702
1847	716	208,070,622	105,519,766	35,182,616	810,282,945
1857	1,415	370,834,274	214,778,822	58,349,838	684,456,837

Mark one feature :—While the Banks have nearly doubled their capital, the specie in their vaults shows no proportionate increase.

California and Australia saved the Banks from breaking before; but there was no new gold field to postpone the evil day this time.

These tables will furnish food for the reflecting mind. I give them to show that we have specie enough for a hard currency.

Bear in mind, that of the $6,000,000,000 of gold and silver in Europe and America previous to 1831, only $2,400,000,000 was used as currency.

The issue to-day is: *hard money and cheap labor—* or *paper currency and dear labor*. The prudent merchant can have but one opinion. Franklin was before the age with his lightning-rod, but behind it when he recommended paper money. Washington was in favor of hard money; Jackson would have no other, much to the disgust of Biddle; and James Buchanan is of the same opinion. The President, with prophetic foresight, foreshadowed in his speech in the Senate on the Sub-Treasury Bill, the crisis that is upon us.

"When," said he, "the collapse comes, *as come it must*, it casts laborers out of employment, crushes manufacturers and merchants, and ruins thousands of honest and industrious citizens."

Paper money and protection on the one side, against *hard money and free trade* on the other. Protection has exploded; so have the Banks, with their paper currency.

"Free Trade and Hard Money!" will be the cry of the people—and the people are the *sovereigns* of this land.

Count de Tendilla introduced paper money into the world about eight years before Columbus found America. When besieged by the Moors, in the Alhambra Palace, in 1484, his gold gave out, and he paid his soldiers in written bits of paper, which he afterwards redeemed. Printing soon came into vogue.

Paper money was not known to the Virginia planters and Puritan farmers. *Barter* was their currency. In the Treasury Room of the Winter Palace at St. Petersburg, I saw the progress of barter through all stages of the precious metals, from the time of Rurick and of Alfred, to the silver rouble of to-day. The North American Indian used wampum. In 1690, Massachusetts issued her first paper money to pay for the conquest of Quebec. (Four years later, the Bank of England was organized. Two years afterwards it suspended payment; and one hundred years later, it stopped again.) South Carolina made her first issue in 1702, to pay for her piratical expedition against St. Augustine. New-Hampshire and Rhode Island issued notes the same year. North Carolina, Connecticut, New-York, and New-Jersey got their "paper mills" agoing in 1713, to pay for the Indian War. But Pennsylvania held out till 1722; Maryland till 1733, and Virginia till 1755.

It worked very well till it was overdone. The immense issues of the Revolution killed the child. The first period of paper money, after barter, run out in seventy-five years. The explosion ruined everybody concerned. The second was equally disastrous; and the third, coming down from Continental money past the U. S. Bank to the present suspension throughout the country, I hope will prove more satisfactory to the holders of notes.

"Cæsar had his Brutus, Charles the First his Cromwell, and George the Third," said Patrick Henry, "may profit by their example."

This brief summary will show that it requires paper money to carry out any gigantic enterprise, and that in due time the faithful agent, having accomplished its work, suddenly explodes. "All those passengers that hav'nt paid their fare need'nt—because we're bound to pass that ar steamer or bust."—(Albert Smith's "Americanisms.")

HARD CURRENCY is what we want to restore confidence. Credit is based on faith, but to-day there is no faith.

The Banks issue notes payable on demand. You call for the money which you have lent the Banks, and lo! you cannot get it.

Justice Marshall says, "We dodge round the clause in the Constitution prohibiting 'Bills of Credit' by issuing 'Bank Notes.'"

We may say with Law that our "paper mills are nothing but sand banks to wreck the National ship."

The advocate for paper money will no doubt say that speculations may be made as wildly on hard currency as paper money, and mention California and Australia as examples. True, but those lands were far from the marts of commerce. Give us an instance nearer home. Cuba was much sounder before her Banks than after their establishment!

We want a currency that will take a man from Portland to Pensacola; from St. Louis to St. Augustine; from New-York to New-Orleans; from Connecticut to California. Some National currency, based on *hard money.*

Who will mark out the plan?

THE TIMES ARE CHANGING.—This crisis should bring out some new financial men, for those who have been leading us during the last generation do not appear to bring their minds up to anything more extensive than 1837.

Is there not such a thing as wisdom going to seed?

Even Francis Bacon would be lost in this age of steam, while Adam Smith might not have been equal to the management of the Illinois Central Railway? We must wait for another Albert Gallatin, and even he, I fear, would be lost in our day.

I think, however, we can all agree to settle down on hard money and free trade. The free traders say to the protectionists, "You have had your day for a long time ; it is our turn now. Give us a trial, and, if we don't succeed with direct taxation, then try protection again.

The shoe trade is protected, yet it is as bad as any other. Shipping is protected, yet ship-owners are anything but rich. Cotton and woolen mills are protected, yet they are all breaking up. The iron interest is protected, but the iron-masters are not making fortunes. Ask the people to choose, and free trade will ring throughout the land.

With free trade comes *hard currency*. We have had enough of expansion.

Another point. ECONOMY *must be the order of the day*. Economy at Washington—economy in the State —economy in the city—economy in the country, the corporation and the individual—everybody will economize in every thing.

I don't intend to buy another hat this year. I

have about twelve months' clothes on hand, and have paid my tailor's bill. I have an extra shirt and two or three pair of boots. I never smoke; I never chew; I never drink; and, since leaving Australia, have never driven fast horses. Going down town I walk, and save six cents. Instead of buying three papers every morning, I buy one, and get the boy to change it for another. (The *London Times* generally passes up one street and down the next before it goes to the owner in the country.) I have been in New-York several days and have not bought a thing, not even a ticket to the theater. In fact, I am only doing what everybody else is doing throughout the country. Economy—rigid, uncompromising economy on all sides.

The times are changing. I would rather have the wealth of the poor than the poverty of the rich. Health, industry, and honesty are at a premium to-day. Economy in the palace—economy in the hovel. Go up and down Broadway, you see no purchasers.

The father says: "Wife, I have lost nearly everything; we must economize. We must give up the carriage, the horses, the dogs, the coachman and the servant girls. Julia can wear the same bonnet another season. Carrie must not buy that new dress now. Bella had better return that French mantle. Willie must dispose of those beautiful furs. Charlie must make his old clothes answer to the end of the year. Frank must sell his horse; and, wife, if you won't buy anything for twelve months, I won't."

And the good wife cheers the husband, and the husband is happy to see how willingly his family conform to his change of circumstances. This is characteristic of the American mind. An American family may change from prosperity to adversity in a single day, but the family prayer goes up from the family altar, and the family kiss goes round the family circle as before—each cheering the other with the celestial nectar of sympathy.

The young will assist the old, and the old will no longer *sneer* at the young.

Most of us have supplies a year in advance. The city is full of stores—the stores are full of goods.

The same remarks apply to the country as well as the town. Stocks are large from north to south, from east to west—easy credits tend to enlarge stocks.

The man who can save a dollar will do so. Every individual will follow Micawber's advice to Wilkins, to "live within his means."

Hence, economy in every State—economy in every family—and this economy will carry out my argument, that prices of all speculative property must drop to their natural level. For, where all are sellers, who will there be to purchase? Fashion rules our land;

and as it will be now the fashion to curtail expenses, who will dare to be extravagant?

But even Free Trade, Hard Currency, Cheap Labor, and Economy, will not speedily dispel the cloud. THE TIMES ARE CHANGING.

The commercial world to-day is an " inverted pyramid" —all are watching it, but who can tell on which side it is to fall?

The West bears the same relation to the East, that America does to England. The West has the East's money—America has England's. *The West is therefore rich on what she owes.*

The same argument applies, in part, to America. Credit insinuates itself into every interest, like the mixing of liquids or the blending of colors. Trace it.

America owes England; bankers owe the holders of the notes; merchants owe banks; country merchants owe city merchants; *farmers owe country merchants, and will not sell their grain;* and nobody has any money; consequently, nearly everybody fails. At this rate, universal liquidation will become a mutual understanding.

Sampson, of the London *Times*, one of the cleverest financial writers in Europe, estimates American indebtedness to England, on securities, public and private, at $400,000,000

The *Economist*, an established authority, takes the same view.

In round numbers, we may add: Indi-
vidual Debts and Debts of Incorporated
Companies, Balance of Trade—say, for
Iron, Hardware, Dry Goods, Borrowed
Money, and all indebtedness outside of
the above securities,   . $160,000,000

Showing a sum of   .   . $560,000,000
All of which is due Europe during the next few years.

Large as is this sum—and I have made the amount
large, so as to be sure and cover—our general cry of
Economy will balance it in two years' time.

Let 28,000,000 people economize $10 per
annum, which can be easily done, you
have the sum of   .   . $280,000,000
Two years of such economy, and you
save   .   .   . $560,000,000
—The whole amount of our foreign obligations.

That is one side of the question. England will get
a portion of her money—not all. The United States
will pay. Individual States will pay. Repudiation
would be howled down by the people. The American
people at heart are honest, though predisposed to insolvency. England need not fear that any State will
dishonor itself. Even California will pay every penny.

The people rule this country, and the people will bear
taxes before dishonor. Those States that hung fire
in Sydney Smith's time have never been able to hold
their head as high as their honest neighbors.

Arkansas, Florida, Mississippi, and Michigan must
pay every dollar before their sister States will invite
them home to tea.

The entire debt is but . .	$17,000,000
While the interest has run up to	20,000,000

Only $37,000,000 to a population in the four States
of 1,500,000. Now why don't the people take the
matter out of the hands of politicians. Let each man
open his pocket-book, take out two dollars and-a-half,
pay the debt, and be respectable ? The sum is a bagatelle when you bring the amount down to the individual—(chew one less plug of tobacco a week, and
the thing is done.)

Public opinion is a tyrant, but in a case like this
the tyrant is a man of honor. One of the rising
poets of England is now in this country, and in his
pocket is Sydney Smith's original letter to the Penn-
sylvanians. 'Tis a scorcher—but no Englishman will
ever again have occasion to write such a scathing
philippic. We will pay what we owe.

The railway debts and individual obligations will
not show such returns as the State and the Nation.

England may make up her mind to lose a good portion of these. As a bank manager leads a young man into reckless speculation by giving him extensive accommodation—so has John Bull dazzled the good sense of Jonathan by showing him too much gold. The bank manager comes out a loser—so will John.

'Tis a notorious fact that an Englishman, to get two per cent. extra interest, would sell anything but his national glory.   Three per cent. was the height of his ambition—vide consols. Knowing this, we went to England with our six, seven, and eight per cent. bonds, which bonds we sold *low*—" very cheap, for cash,"—taking iron at *high* prices for payment. Remembering his favorite consols, and forgetting the warning of Wellington, who told him that " high interest was a sure indication of bad security"—they bought the bonds—and, speaking *ironically*, the *iron* masters have got their *iron* safes full of *iron* bonds, which bonds, by the by, just now are anything but *iron.*

Many of our bonds we have forced upon the English capitalist; much of his iron he has forced upon us.   We had agents in England : he had agents in America—each trying to overbuy or undersell the other. We asked for six months credit. He gave us twelve. He has led us into temptation. We, easily persuaded, have been tempted, and, not being Josephs, did not resist as we ought to have done. In his avarice to grasp the interest, he loses sight entirely of the principal. While beating the bush the bird steps out. The old story of the spigot and the bunghole. Had our bonds, like his leases, been for ninety-nine years —we might, like Hudson, have managed to pay the dividends—and we mean even now to pay them, if we can. Any way, as we have in some cases paid him enough interest to cancel the principal, we must now try and make a fair compromise.

I fancy that an American in London just now is by no means a nosegay in the nostrils of an Englishman.*

THE TIMES ARE CHANGING.

Importations will fall away. Our Secretary of Treasury, instead of having *thirty* millions *in,* will discover that he is about forty millions *out.*

'Tis hardly a year since Secretary Guthrie made his calculations for the fiscal year as follows :

---

* "I never meet a Pennsylvanian at a London dinner without feeling a disposition to seize and divide him ; to allot his beaver to one sufferer, and his coat to another ; to appropriate his pocket handkerchief to the orphan, and to comfort the widow with his" (the word *breeches* was written, but is erased), "silver watch, Broadway rings, and the London Guide which he always carries in his pocket. How such a man can set himself down at an English table without feeling that he owes two or three pounds to every man in the company, I am at a loss to conceive."—SYDNEY SMITH'S *Letters* (Nov. 3d, 1843,) *to the* "*Drab-colored men of Pennsylvania.*"—*From the original MSS.*

Balance in Treasury, July 1, 1857, .	$22,300,000
Estimated revenue for fiscal year end-	
ing July 1, 1858, . .	73,000,000
	$95,000,000
Against which, Government made ap-	
propriations for about . .	$80,000,000

At *economy* prices we have not far from a year's stock of luxuries and necessities in this country. We are overcrowded with goods. The city stores are filled from cellar to garret. The public warehouses are wait-ing to take the duties on some *thirty millions* of bonded goods, which in these economical times are not wanted. Government having tried to stem the crisis (by emptying the Treasury in canceling their debt) dis-covers all at once, that, like Copperfield trying to sleep with one eye open, " it can't be done." The money has walked out of the sub-treasury. It declines to return. Therefore the *corn* is all off the COBB.

No land sales. Importations comparatively nothing. Treasury emptied by paying off debt—before due—at premium rates. Extravagance in every department. These are some of the ills which financial flesh is heir to. So look out, Mr. Cobb, and don't protest Govern-ment drafts, as was the case fifteen years ago, on the plea of N. S. F !

Importations will fall off at least one half, for two reasons   first, economy will make our stocks last a long while ; second, Europeans will demand cash, or payment of old debts before they trust us for more. " An eye for an eye, a tooth for a tooth," is their law. The Romans punished insolvency with death. And the Germans hold a debt over a man for forty years. While American laws (vide Bank Suspension) protect the debtor, European laws protect the creditor.   In England, a man who fails seldom again rises above low-water mark.   In America, where ninety-five out of the hundred come down, everybody floats in on the flood.

An American stops once in five years and pays fifty cents on the dollar; while an Englishman breaks once in ten and pays nothing.   American yachts take the " cups" upon the water, and American horses take the " stakes" upon the land. So, in the case which I have given, (I regret to say,) our cousins are beaten two to one.

The reduction in imports will embarrass our exchequer, and most likely the Secretary will make up the revenue deficiency by an issue of treasury notes. Thirty millions will be about the mark.

Our exports in 1836 (the year before the crisis) were $128,600,000, against $190,000,000 imports. In 1840 the returns give $132,000,000, against $107,000,000, showing an increase of $4,000,000 in exports, and a *decrease* of $83,000,000 in imports.

This gives a falling off in imports of nearly fifty per cent. *the third year after the crisis.* Secretary Cobb must make his estimates with great care, or he will come out worse than Neckar did in France. If he gets off with less than a forty million loan before 1st January, 1859, he will indeed be fortunate.

Our exports in 1856 were $327,000,000, against $315,000,000 imports.

Imports for the financial year ending 1st July, 1857, $360,890,141 (which included $12,461,799 specie, re-exported goods, $14,905,509), leaving some $333,532,833 for home consumption.

Exports, cotton,	. . .	$132,000,000
Manufactures,	. . .	126,000,000
Agricultural and all other produce,	.	70,000,000
		$328,000,000

In 1860 our exports will bid fair to double our imports; but in this age of changes 'tis hardly safe to make estimates.

In 1837 we imported wheat, but had no California to furnish gold in payment. Now we are exporters of grain, and receivers of some forty millions of gold from our own soil; yet we have to send this gold away to pay for the silks and gewgaws of Europe, which trash adds nothing to the wealth of the country.

THE TIMES ARE CHANGING.

Retrenchment is the order of the day. Banks are down; railways are nowhere; manufactures are in very poor health; buildings don't pay. By-and-by a palace will not rent so high as a prison. Provisions must drop; cotton will probably touch six cents. (The world is full of cotton goods. I have found them everywhere, from the half-yard round a Hindoo to the entire sheet worn by the Turk.) Ships must go lower; land will only be valuable for what it produces; labor, like everything else, will be much cheaper. Everything in the country, from a lady's dress to the Government estimates, has been inflated.

Some of our journals are harping upon our splendid crops. I believe that the crops are about as much over-estimated as other things have been. They talk of bringing the crops forward, as if the export of grain would cancel our foreign obligations.

Figures don't lie. Study this table; I see nothing therein to warrant such a hue and cry about. Our entire exportation of grain would hardly pay for the ribbons and laces which are annually imported. (We are an extravagant people.)

Export of Breadstuffs to Great Britain and Ireland from all parts.

Total from Sept. 1,			Barrels Flour.	Barrels C. Meal.	Bushels Wheat.	Bushels Corn.
1856 to	Sept. 1,	1857	849,600	685	7,479,401	4,746,278
1855	"	1856	1,641,265	6,816	7,956,406	6,731,161
1854	"	1855	175,209	4,768	324,427	6,679,138
1853	"	1854	1,846,920	41,726	6,038,003	6,049,371
1852	"	1853	1,600,449	100	4,823,519	1,425,278
1851	"	1852	1,427,442	1,680	2,728,442	1,487,398
1850	"	1851	1,559,584	5,620	1,496,355	2,205,601
1849	"	1850	474,757	6,411	461,276	4,753,358
1848	"	1849	1,137,556	82,900	1,140,194	12,685,260
1847	"	1848	182,583	108,534	241,309	4,390,226
1846	"	1847	3,155,844	844,187	4,000,359	17,157,659
	Total, eleven years		14,051,209	1,103,427	36,689,691	68,310,728

This gives an average (estimating the flour and meal at four bushels to the barrel) of about 15,000,000 bushels per annum; or, at a dollar a bushel, $15,-000,000, which would about half pay for the Illinois Central Railroad. As some extensive shipments of breadstuffs went to the Continent last year, I give the

Exports from the United States during the last Four Years.

				Barrels Flour.	Barrels C. Meal.	Bushels Wheat.	Bushels Corn.
Sept. 1, 1856, to Sept. 1, 1857 ...				483,344	2,875,653	543,590	216,162
"	1855,	"	1856 ...	748,408	2,610,079	282,083	1,975,478
"	1854,	"	1855 ...	7,763	4,972	308,428	35,569
"	1853,	"	1854 ...	791,028	1,904,893	90,556	318,882

Another line of figures will show that even bread-stuffs have a margin for depreciation. The farmers, if they take my advice, will sell; all hands will be at the plough next year.

A Comparative Table of Prices on 1st September for the last Ten Years.

	State Flour.	Red Wheat.	White Wheat.	Rye.	Ind. Corn
1857 ...	$5 75 a 6 35	1 40 a 1 52	1 55 a 1 78	93 a 95	84 a 93
1856 ...	5 90 a 6 50	1 50 a 1 54	1 62 a 1 65	88 a 90	60 a 70
1855 ...	7 50 a 8 75	1 75 a 1 85	1 90 a 1 93	1 00 a 1 10	87 a 88
1854 ...	9 75 a 10 00	1 60 a 1 88	1 90 a 2 10	1 20 a 1 22	86 a 88
1853 ...	5 75 a 6 00	1 15 a 1 23	1 35 a 1 42	90 a 98	75 a 78
1852 ...	4 31 a 4 56	70 a 95	1 00 a 1 10	80 a 81	71 a 72
1851 ...	3 87 a 4 00	60 a 65	90 a 1 05	67 a 68	57 a 58
1850 ...	4 25 a 4 50	80 a 90	90 a 1 13	69 a 70	61 a 62
1849 ...	5 25 a 5 50	90 a 1 10	1 10 a 1 28	59 a 60	60 a 63
1848 ...	5 94 a 6 00	1 00 a 1 05	1 18 a 1 30	73 a 74	62 a 72

Why should'nt the estimate of crops be as much exaggerated as is every other interest in the country? Those interested had better overhaul their statistics. 'Twould be no laughable matter to discover that, after bragging so much, we possessed so little.

The shipments of grain from Chicago to 31st October, 1856, were 19,496,022 bushels, while to the 17th October, 1857, only 13,751,438 bushels have gone forward.

The Banks did not suspend till the 14th October,

therefore the disorganization of exchanges will not account for a falling off of some 5,000,000 bushels at that port alone. Depend upon ᶜₑ it, the grain crop this year has expanded only in imagination.

If America has 20,000,000 bushels to spare before 1st September, 1858, it will be 5,000,000 more than the usual average (and about 10,000,000 more than I estimate). But taking the brightest view of it, the entire sum would only about pay for the Michigan Southern Railroad.

Let the bankers leave the farmers to manage their own affairs. The crops will find their way to market by the stern law of supply and demand. When prices warrant, the grain will come. Suppose we had the crops in New-York—what then? European advices don't warrant shipments. Since the first shipment of Indian corn—since Iglehart made the present of Indian meal to the Queen—since James McHenry organized the trade, and introduced American corn and American provisions to the British public—from the first operation to the last shipment, America has lost money by the speculation. Who will dispute it? I have made out too many invoices—examined too many account sales, to be led away by the shipment of grain on English quotations, with the expectation of profit. One year it may pay; the next 'tis a losing game; but, at any rate, the prices quoted by the late mail give little encouragement to a shipper.

The farmers had better sell, or next year they will realize less money.

The crops in Continental Europe were never better. Passing through France, Italy, Germany, (a thousand miles in the interior of Russia,) Sweden, Norway, Denmark, and Holland, good crops met my gaze on all sides.

In Great Britain, the wheat crop is splendid ; all other crops are bad.

The fact is, after we have fed our own population, we must depend upon a European famine for the sale of any surplus grain we may raise, over and above our 15,000,000 bushels, which we annually ship to Great Britain, and generally at a loss to the shipper.

The statistics prove that notwithstanding our activity in shipping grain during the Irish famine, the entire quantity only amounted to about nine days' consumption to the people of the United Kingdom.

Shipments from the West to New-York, and from New-York to Europe, are generally made to regulate exchanges, with the hope of profit.

The farmers had better sell, or they will find to their cost, that, at the end of the year, they are poor in purse, although they think themselves rich in grain.

Andrews, (page 619,) gives the pro-
duction of 1852, of Wheat,   . 143,000,000 bush.
Indian Corn, ... 652,000,000 "
Oats and Rye, ... 176,000,000 "

How much more has been grown during the past
year of "unexampled prosperity?"

That year, our agricultural products amounted to
$1,752,563,042.

From Corn, the king of the West, I turn to Cotton,
the king of the South.

Do the Southerners suppose for a moment that they
can resist the course of the storm? They have but
experienced the puff that precedes the hurricane. THE
TIMES ARE CHANGING.

The South should wait till the "Arabia" touches
the shores of England with the news of the bank
suspensions, before they issue any Southern manifes-
toes, that they are rich while the North is poor.

Our cotton twists around the British Lion are iron
bands.   Cobden, a quarter of a century ago, told the
English people that America possessed the power that
would eventually ruin the British nation.

In 1832, (about the time that the Iron Duke got his
windows broken by the Reform mob,) the United States

exported but 322,215,122 pounds of cotton, amounting
to - - - - - $ 31,724,682
Three years later the export increased to
387,358,992 pounds, amounting to - 64,961,302
In 1852, (Andrews,) it rose to 1,290,000,-
000, pounds, amounting to - - 129,000,000
Last year to 1,351,431,801 lbs. valued at 128,382,351

Planters and factors estimate the present
crop, in round numbers, at 3,000,000
bales, at 400 lbs. the bale. 1,200,000,-
000 lbs. at 16 cents, (the anticipated
price, before the crisis,) would be - 192,000,000
But at 8 cents, which I think is too high an
estimate, the crop would only amount to 96,000,000

When the Southerners realize the fact that they
must sell their cotton (as well as negroes) for about
half of last year's prices, notwithstanding the loss of
the Indian crop, they will be less confident.

England has been forcing her manufactured goods
upon all nations. But now—

THE TIMES ARE CHANGING. America has been the
producer—she is to be the manufacturer, and that,
too, under free trade. *Money* and *labor* were the
rivals that we have had to contend with. Labor must
drop towards English rates, and money will be cheaper

in America than in any part of the world. For a long period England has taken the cotton from our plantations to the sea-board,—from the sea-board to Liverpool,—from Liverpool over a British rail to Manchester—where British factories turn out the goods which she sends back to us in a British steamer—pays us a high duty, and sells us our own staple at prices lower than our own manufacturers.

Secretary Walker, in his Treasury Report of 1845, said that the cotton crop yielded then but $72,000,000, while the manufactured fabric produced some $500,000,000—the balance of which all goes to foreign merchants, foreign bankers, foreign factories, and foreign laborers.

Credit—steam—were the agents. The Arabia's arrival will shake the former to its centre, and a loss of credit reduces the value of steam. America will profit by that experience.

The Southerners make the most of their *cotton.* The Northerners are as proud of the crop as their Southern neighbors. Yet there is something besides cotton in these United States.

California produces a *third* of a cotton crop every year in *hard gold.* While the cotton of the South amounts to hardly a *third* of the *corn crop* of the North.

In 1852 the corn crop amounted to . $391,000,000
The cotton crop was but . . 129,000,000

We produce another staple in this land—a staple for cattle to feed upon—that we stack in the open air, and tread under our feet as if it were of no value. I mean the *hay crop*, which amounted in 1852 to $190,000,000. Some *sixty millions* more than the entire cotton crop of the South ; and yet who reflects upon it ? The North talks less about its hay, corn, and wheat together, than the South regarding its cotton.

There is still another interest greater than cotton, or corn, or hay.

In 1852 the total value of the *industrial productions* of the United States amounted to $2,932,762,042.

PURSUIT

OF KNOWLEDGE UNDER DIFFICULTIES.
INTERROGATIONS.

HAVING just arrived from Europe, I feel like John Bunyan, that I am in pursuit of knowledge under difficulties. Many new words have been coined—many new customs introduced—some of which I do not understand. Therefore not daring to make assertions on so short an acquaintance, what possible harm can there be in asking a few good-natured questions? Afterwards I will open a chapter on Europe, and then return once more to America.

If the banks had on the 2d May $108,000,000 liabilities, and only $12,000,000 specie, was it not prudent to reduce their obligations to $76,000,000 on 3d of October?

Why did the banks allow themselves to be bloated up with diseased corporation paper?

Is it true that the banks first broke the railways, and, in trying to break the merchants, broke themselves.

Is the suspension of specie payment a *remedy* for our financial disorder, or only a make-shift expedient?

Was the banking dentist surprised, when drawing Jonathan's financial tooth, to find the whole set false? Shouldn't he have recognized his own teeth?

Have the banks humbugged their customers by lending them their own deposits?

On which principle of law or morality have the judges decided that a bank may *bend* under "suspension," and only *break* under failure?

If I hold a bank note, is the bank indebted to me for a loan of gold, or am I indebted to the bank for giving me an engraving with a signature?

Are the judges personally acquainted with the presidents of the banks?

Would they, if invited, take a cigar and a seat in the bank parlor for half an hour?

Have they any paper under discount? Any deposits? Any bank stock?

Is it true that the President and Cashier constitute the *bona fide* Board of Directors ?

Are the bankers really more respectful to a man in a seedy coat than they were before the suspension ?

Is it true that you can now talk with a Bank President, instead of being coolly turned over to an assistant cashier as formerly ?

Do the old, the most respectable, the *rich* and high-toned Bank Boards still think that the grain grows down in Front Street ?

Do the " kid glove party " still supply a sufficient quantity of " bang-up gilt-edged " paper ?

Do the banks ever discount accommodation notes ? Have the " paper mills " also suspended ?

Were the bags in the window of the Wall Street Savings Bank, marked U. S. M., filled with real gold ?

If so, why did not the Directors remove the card just under them, of " *Offices to let : inquire within*" ?

How much gold did Mr. Leavitt have in the vault when he proclaimed to the " excited populace " that, " sink or swim—live or die—survive or perish," the American Exchange Bank would pay out every dollar ?

Did the old banks really think they could break all the new ones, and yet save themselves ?

What did Mr. Gallatin and Mr. Tilestone mean when, *a few hours before the banks burst*, they issued that " celebrated circular " from the Clearing House, guaranteeing the " MAINTENANCE OF SPECIE PAYMENTS," and asserting that " NO FURTHER CONTRACTION WAS NECESSARY " to accomplish said object ?

Do the banks, by expanding beyond a prudent line, and then suddenly contracting, occasion periodical panics ?

Does our inflated credit system drive our hard-earned coin out of the land, to pay for useless trash which our extravagant habits have ordered from abroad ?

Do the Boston Savings Banks still loan on *three good names ?*

Has anything been paid in the Massachusetts Legislature for " Log Rolling," to obtain an increase of bank capital during the last few years ?

Are their *prayers* likely to be answered when they *pray* again, next session, for a similar purpose ?

Is the Stevens and Appleton correspondence considered dignified ?

Or, in other words, which was the most high-toned, the " New-York insolence," or the " Boston presumption" ?

Since the Suspension, don't bill-holders consider their paper *rather hard currency?*

Have any of the merchants taken in any of the Banks (in confidence) as junior partners?

Has our Banking system entirely nullified the clause in the Constitution that provides that "gold and silver" shall be "the only legal tender?"

Will any one doubt that *the times are changing* when it is known that Western Banks, having lost all confidence in Eastern Bankers, apply to their lawyers to receive and disburse their funds?

Ought we not to claim damages under a "Breach of Promise," for seducing our gold out of our pockets with a "promise to pay" it back again?

Would not "Sperma-*city*" have been a better name than "Island City" to illustrate "lighting the candle at both ends"? for is it not a gro-cer fraud?

If Cotton Spindle, Kite & Co. have a million assets over liabilities, are they considered failed? Should they not be "*suspended*" for asking for a renewal?

Why are Calcutta goods being shipped to England, where, on arrival, the price will be about one-half the original invoice?

Why are American provisions coming back from England by almost every steamer?

Do the shippers expect to *save their bacon* by this new process of kiting ?

Can friction be prevented by packing "pork on bacon" ?

What advantage is derived by sending cotton from New-Orleans to England by way of Lowell, in Massachusetts ?

Are solvent merchants liable to be tripped up by providing for both sides of the Bill Book ?

Are "Flying Kite" and "Raising the Wind" good names for clipper ships ?

Does sugar increase in weight as it falls in value ?

What is the meaning of the historical term, "*solid* men of Boston" ?

What does the *Wise* Governor of Virginia ask to-day for a couple of hundred fat ones ?

Are the lawyers really making money ?

Are the preachers "reading up" to find *texts* suitable for the crisis ?

Have the expenses of the ladies expanded in the same proportion as their dresses ?

Has "Flora McFlimsey" really "nothing to wear ?

Has "Fitz-Frivol" really "nothing to do ?"

Was Dr. Johnson right in asserting that Credit was only a premium on the Imagination ?

YOUNG AMERICA IN WALL-STREET.

Would ladies buy diamonds at Tiffany's, and silks at Stewart's, if they had to *count* out the hard dollars on the counter?

Will the fashionable lady six months hence insist upon dressing her child like an *ostrich*, and herself like an inverted champaigne glass?

Does Brown still arrange these " white kid " parties?

Will not the crisis be the means of putting the everlasting discussion of negro slavery to bed for a while?

Who will be our next President?

Don't you think that Fremont had better remain on his "Butterfly estate" 'till after the next election?

Did you approve of the Members of Congress *raising their own wages* last session?

If so, don't you think it would be a good idea to raise the salaries of our foreign ministers, so that they can represent the United States as they should be represented?

Do Members of Congress who spit on the floor *expect-to-rate* as gentlemen?

Do you believe that anything but the *postage on protested bills* will keep the Post Office Revenue up to $7,000,000 per annum?

If you had been some time in a foreign land, would

you not have supposed that the "Adriatic," like the "Flying Dutchman," was a phantom ship?

Do you not think that Cunard ought to have a testimonial from the American people for carrying our mails some twenty years, without ever *missing fire*, even in the coldest weather?

Don't you think our railways would be better managed, if the Directors lived on the line of road, and the President kept out of Wall-street?

Don't you think it would be a good move to sink Wall-street; explode the Brokers' Board; and kill every "Bull" and "Bear" in the country?

Do you think that the President of the Erie Railroad ought to receive the same salary as the President of the United States?

Do you agree with *Punch*, that, in case of a railway accident, *absence of body* is better than *presence of mind?*

Do you think the *Tribune* ought to rap a man over the knuckles for being *too national* at a Fourth of July dinner, in a foreign land, when asked to respond to the sentiment, "Our Country?"

What good does it do to quarrel with the w.rld

Do you think Mrs. Cunningham is getting up another bogus baby?

Were you not surprised when it was announced that the New-York *Independent* had "suspended" (its List of Failures) ?

Will not that "Pillow" require a clean "case" since that last sixty-four pounder ?

If the General's *breaches* "are as soft as Downy Pillows are," may we not consider him bomb-proof ?

"What is the price of putty, since that "extra judicial decision ?"

Will you accept my apology for having tired you with so many questions ?

I had written thus far, when Messrs. Pudney & Russell's "devil" entered my room for more "copy," so I close this page "with the assurances of my highest consideration," and a promise to open another on the morrow.

AMERICAN CONTEMPLATIONS AND EUROPEAN CONVERSATIONS.

THE Crisis—Two sides to every question—The Wail of the Tempest
—Crosses the Ocean—Joint Stock Banks of England—"Arabia's"
arrival a spark in the tinder box—"South Sea Bubble" and
Western Lands—Panic of 1825—Specie Exportation—Anglo-Ame-
rican Houses in 1837—Their Escape—Long Credits—An Illustra-
tion—The Result—A China Operation—India owes Manchester—
England has trusted all the World, and the World is Bankrupt
—Indian Loan—Where the Gold and Silver go to—All Nations
demanding Specie at Bank of England—Goose with the Golden
Egg—Native receives, but seldom pays away, a Sovereign—Western
States owe Eastern—Bank of England Statements in 1847 and 1857
—Russell's Letter stops the Panic—English Railway Mania—*Crédit
Mobilier*—Law's Land Scheme—"Popular Delusions"—Louis Na-
poleon as a Financier—His eventful History—The Bourse—Louis
Philippe Dethroned—Conspirators—Revolution of 1789 and 1848—
A Dozen Applicants for the Throne of France—Louis Napoleon has
no partner—Italy Dying—Bonaparte wishes to send the Pope to
Jerusalem—Germany is Republican—King of Prussia on the brink
of the Grave—Oscar, King of Sweden, not expected to Live—Tur-
key no account—The Constantinople Farce at Osborne—Union of
Principalities—Russia the Strongest Government in Europe—Conversation with the Grand Duke Constantine—His Character—Russia
despises England—Nijni-Novgorod, a wonderful Fair—Distrust in
Europe—Napoleon scents the Fray—Pereire—Napoleon, the Uncle—

Since Adam was a schoolboy there have always been two sides to every question. The present crisis, however, seems to be an exception. "All the world and the rest of mankind" think (?) the worst has passed. I don't; and, as free discussion is open to every American on every subject, I propose to take the opposite side of the apparently prevailing opinion, and give my reasons why I think the immediate future is about as black as a thunder cloud.

Fair play is a jewel—so is consistency; and, while I simply ask for the former, I will try and practice the latter.

The cause that will not allow a peep at both sides of the argument must be poor indeed.

I will write as good sense as I can, and shall feel contented if I succeed in making it "common." Anyway, I ought not to be *gibbeted* for daring to express an opinion; and yet *suspension* is too common to excite remark.

In the last few pages I have been a listener, now I intend to talk, and "no questions asked." I may again look at the past, to show its bearings on the present; but now I propose to take a speculative view of the future.

Let us commence by following the trail of the suspension of the New-York banks. Note well the course of the gale.

The East on the West—the West on the North—the North on the South—the South back again on the East—the gale increasing to a tempest, sweeping every bank from its path—the tempest quickening to a typhoon, till it reaches the sea-board, crosses the ocean, strikes down the great Anglo-American houses, pressing the Banks of England and France to follow the example of fourteen hundred banks in this country, and makes the throne of Bonaparte totter to its bloody base.   Then, like a huge tidal wave, the reaction washes again our shores, surging, tearing, swamping everything in its way—crosses and recrosses the Atlantic—carrying disaster with the moaning of every tide.

One hundred and sixty millions of dollars are on deposit in the joint stock banks of England on call. The "Arabia" would reach England about the 25th October, with the news of our misfortunes.   Each succeeding mail records the failure of a hundred banks.

You can imagine the effect. Depositors get frightened. One man rushes to a bank. The disease will be as contagious there as it has been here. If one bank closes—down they all must tumble.

The finances of England are more rotten than ours appear to be. Her speculations are almost as wild as those of former times. 'Tis only one hundred and thirty-eight years since the " South Sea bubble " exploded. The capital stock was but one hundred and ninety millions of dollars. (The joint stock banks have nearly as much on deposit.) That bubble was got up to pay off the national debt. Walpole battled against the scheme, but without avail. The stock rose *one thousand per cent.* (Land in Chicago has advanced, in some instances, *fifteen hundred per cent.*) The people of England were bubble-mad. All kinds of projects were under way in 1720.

There was one :

" To make deal boards out of saw-dust."

Linklater, in the Court of Bankruptcy, asked Humphrey Brown, who had swindled the Royal British Bank out of four hundred thousand dollars, whether he had experimented in that way ?

Another company was formed,

" For importing walnut trees from Virginia."

(I doubt if Eli Thayer's emigration project in the same State will give any better result.)

But one sharper astonished London, by advertising:

" A Company for carrying on an undertaking of great advantage, but nobody to know what it is."

That day his office was crowded, and he could but be surprised himself to find at night ten thousand dollars paid in. He pocketed the money, and bolted for the Continent.

(Colonel Waugh, last year, stole twelve hundred thousand dollars from the London and Eastern Joint Stock Bank, and, as usual, went over to France for his health.)

> " The head-long fools plunge into South Sea water
> But the sly long heads wade in with caution arter."

The poet, Gay, was ruined by the bubble.

In 1825, England was again ripe for speculating in all kinds of Joint Stock enterprises. The nation was nearly bankrupt. The Bank was on the brink of ruin, when a Director found a box of small notes. $23,000,000 were issued, and back came the gold ; but the panic was most disastrous.

(America, the same year, caught the Joint Stock fever.

As it was in the South Sea scheme, for every project, ten times the capital was at once subscribed.)

Take an instance or two:

	Capital Required.	Amt. subscribed.
For the New-York Water Works,	$2,000,000	$10,000,000
For the Blackstone Canal, at Providence,	500,000	1,500,000
For the Morris Canal Banking Company,	1,000,000	20,000,000

'Twas the same with the Bank of Southwalk, and a score of other schemes.

In July, 1826, down they began to tumble. Paper money caused the excessive importations, and, as always has been, and always must be, drove the specie out of the country.

The exports of silver for the fiscal year ending 30th September, 1825, were $8,600,000

Imports same time, .   .   .   6,000,000

Showing a loss to the country of $2,600,000 for foreign luxuries that we did not need.

In 1837 the English capitalists were put on their metal by their American losses. Wilde, Wiggin, and Wilson had a large share of the American trade. Nobody suspected them—yet when the mails arrived without remittances they succumbed to the times.

The " Round Robin" from the merchants of Liverpool, and the assistance of the Bank of England
kept Brown, Shipley & Co. on there feet, and Lord
Ashburton came to the timely aid of Baring Brothers
& Co. This was about the time that George Pea-
body came down from Manchester, and commenced
his career in London.

Rothschilds were too powerful to trouble themselves
with so small a place as America. (Just after this,
Vincent Nolte practiced his cotton swindling speculation upon the New-Orleans merchants.)

'Tis to be hoped that these great houses will weather
the storm. But when I consider the import and export trade between England and America, amounting
to some five hundred millions of dollars, most of
which passes directly or indirectly through the hands
of a few firms, I can but feel that the breaking of
the American machinery would be apt to disarrange
the British engine.

The Atlantic is bridged with credits ; and nothing
is so precarious as the system of living on exchanges.

If one steamer's arrival without the needful, upsets
a small house, how many mails will it take to bring
down a large one ?

The English merchant and the English banker anticipate the good, but are never prepared for the bad times.

Never in the whole history of commerce have credits been so expanded as now. Metaphysics is not so difficult a study. The science of financiering is perfect.

Take an operation of a merchant not a hundred miles from Broadway.

(I was initiated into the mysteries in the smoking room of Meurice's Hotel, at Paris. George Hudson at same time introduced me to the English railway system.)

An importer of good standing, who has paid cash before—always prompt, good customer, &c., &c.—calls upon the manufacturer at Lyons. Not wishing to pay for goods at once, he says to seller, " Sixty days after you have made the shipment from Havre, draw upon your banker at four months, and I will send out a credit of mine to pay the bills at maturity." All right. The contract is signed.

The importer in due time sends to *his* banker a letter of credit at four months, payable in London, which the banker discounts, and pays the manufacturer's bills. Therefore, ten months after the goods were bought at Lyons, the four months acceptances must be met. The importer goes to his New-York banker, and gives his acceptance at sixty days, for a sixty day bill on England, which he remits to his London banker to pay the Paris draft.

Recapitulation.

No drafts made till sixty days after shipment from Havre... 2 months.
Manufacturer draws on his banker at..................... 4 "
Importer sends his agent letter of credit to pay manufacturer's draft... 4 "
Buys acceptance in New-York to meet bill in England.... 2 "
Bill sixty days.. 2 "
(Course of mail fifteen days each way.)   —
                  Total..................... 14 "

Here you have an old-fashioned cash transaction, worked out to a twelve months credit, over and above the time the bills are on the ocean; each party receiving a slice of the commissions, and the Fifth Avenue consumer, or the landed proprietor in the fashionable watering place of Cairo (located at the junction of the Mississippi and Ohio river for the express purpose of finding a good terminus for the Illinois Central Railway), *gets credit for the whole*,—when, Presto! the Ohio *Life* and *Trust* Company shows that when people appear to have the most *life*, they are least to be *trusted!* And, to trace the operation to a conclusion, the *creditors* of the London banker are surprised to find that there's a difference between banker's paper and hard currency!

This simple transaction between a New-York merchant and a Lyons manufacturer, may appear complicated, but 'tis the simplest thing imaginable. The system covers the world.

Apply the same analysis to every other interest, and you will realize the signification of a "long credit." Now, if you can fly the kite so high in the North Atlantic, contemplate for a moment what the shrewd financier can accomplish in India, China, and Australia! No well-organized house on those seas pretend to manage their "extensive operations" without a dozen partners, in about as many firms, in different parts of the world.

Canton on Calcutta—Calcutta on Shanghai—Shanghai on Batavia—Batavia on Melbourne—Melbourne on Colombo—then Glasgow, and Manchester:—till at last it strikes the banker in London between the eyes, who is obliged to go over to the Bank of England to get their "promises to pay" (in the absence of sovereigns), and should the Bank of England happen to be short the whole pile of bricks tumbles in together.

Accustomed to the simple kiting operations of State Street, of course I bored the "Eastern Nabobs" with inquiries about their wonderful system.

"My good fellow, you accept our hospitality; now take my advice and don't ask too many questions." There was invariably a quiet smile with the reply, which spoke volumes ; but nevertheless I looked, I listened, I talked, and came to the philosophic conclusion that there was " something rotten" in many States besides Denmark.

As I have had a word to say upon most of the banking institutions of the world, it may be well to add a page on the condition of financial affairs at the Australian gold fields. The "Royal Charter" brings latest dates; and, as 1857, in some respects, at Melbourne, may resemble 1854, so far as over stocked markets and extensive failures are concerned, I will take up the bank statements of the respective years.

Abstract of the Average Liabilities and Assets of the Banking Companies in Victoria, Australia.

For the Quarter ending June 30th, 1854.		Ending June 30th, 1857.	
Liabilities.		*Liabilities.*	
		Deposits not b'ring int.	$25,000,000
		Bearing interest,......	4,700,000
Deposits not bearing interest,	$30,000,000	....	$29,700,000
Notes in circulation,.......	11,000,000	.. ..	11,500,000
Bills in circulation,.........	300,000	....	500,000
Balances due to other banks,	6,000,000	....	4,300,000
Reserved fund, profit and loss account,.................	300,000	....	
Total liabilities,........	$47,600,000	....	$46,000,000

Assets, (same quarter.)		Assets, (same quarter.)	
Coin	$14,000,000		$11,500,000
Bullion	3,000,000		2,600,000
Landed property	500,000		1,400,000
Notes and bills of other banks	1,500,000		800,000
Balances due fr'm other banks	4,300,000		5,000,000
Notes and bills discounted and all other debts due to the banks	31,200,000		37,000,000
Government securities,	1,500,000		2,000,000
Total assets	$50,000,000		$60,000,000

June 30th, 1854.		June 30th, 1857.	
Capital paid in	$15,000,000		$26,000,000
Amount of dividend	1,500,000		1,600,000
Amount of reserved profits after declaring dividend	2,600,000		6,000 000

Like every other place, the markets of Australia have been forced—over-done.

All kinds of stocks, save breadstuffs, are already far above the consuming powers of the people, and still shipments to an immense amount are on the way from England.

Most of the English, Australian and other foreign shipments, for some time past, have been made simply to keep the kiting wheels on the turn. Shipper buys on credit; gets advance from banker, and with said advance pays some old note that *cannot be renewed*

again. Ship charters have often been made in the same
way. Take up ship; pay as little as possible in cash;
fill up with passengers (all which is cash in hand);
get advance on freight list; make shipments and get
advance on them, and draw sight-bills on Australia
against anticipated homeward freight. Each of these
transactions fills up the cash-box and pays old obligations that cannot be worked any finer. On the other
side—buy your stores on six months, which means
twelve; buy your water casks on twelve months,
which means eighteen; don't give the crew any advance if you can help it; and, in short, receive everything possible, but pay away nothing. Then overdraw
your bank-account little by little, till it amounts to
about $150,000, and after that you are safe. You
have got the manager fast. So long as the bank holds
out, the merchant is all right; because the bank, like
the fox in the trap, will tell every body that the merchant is A number one.

Humphrey Brown, of the Royal British, and Colonel
Waugh, of the London and Eastern, are instances of
what I intend to describe.

The Australian banks are sound—much sounder than
either those in America, England or France—yet you
will readily see that, with sixty millions of liabilities
and but fourteen millions of specie, they are not in

a position to stand a run.   But Australia is too far off for that.

India alone owes Manchester some $30,000,000— (while London owes India twice that)—dependent upon cotton, opium, and indigo.   Those staples are killed by the Indian revolution, so Manchester is a loser.   The " Persia," with dates to 17th October, announces the arrival of the unwelcome messenger of *distrust* in Glasgow, Manchester, and Lyons.   England, having overdone her foreign trade by crowding every land with her manufactured goods, all sold on credit, will not fully realize her mistake till the " Arabia" arrives with our explosion.

Manchester has now no foreign market—and credit gone—she is without money : hence Southern planters will realize but about one-half their expected price for cotton.   Carlyle somewhere says that the only way to keep the Manchester spindles on the turn is by spinning cotton a farthing a yard cheaper than the rest of the world.   Manchester has a large amount of capital locked up in manufactured goods, which to-day would not return the first cost for the raw material.   Expanded credit creates demand : contract it, demand falls off; and down go prices.

England has let her money go, not only beyond her fingers' end, but beyond her finger nails.

The English public will shortly be called upon for seventy-five millions of dollars to carry on the Indian war—for the Honorable Company have tried in vain to raise the wind in Hindostan, although they have raised a whirlwind among the Sepoys.

India, like China, can produce just as much as the world happens to require.

Indian exports, from $20,000,000 in 1837, have quadrupled to $85,000,000 in 1857.

From $40,000,000 twenty years ago, Indian productions have grown to $125,000,000 per annum now.

The Indians, in 1846, were contented with draining away $14,000,000 a year in silver; latterly, they require between sixty and seventy millions.

All the gold of California and Australia, and all the silver from Mexico and South America, flows into England, but does it remain there? By no means. All the world are after it. France buys millions every month. Austria gets it when she can. Russia received some of it (from England, by the way of France, towards the railways). India and China take about six millions per month. And now the Eastern trade is breaking up, the Honorable Company will require, monthly, about the same amount, to pay and feed eighty thousand British troops.

All the world are standing at the door of the Bank

of England, with a banker's check for gold ; and the
Bank of England has only fifty millions to meet some
one hundred and ninety millions of liabilities. America,
too, with characteristic presumption, (forgetting her immense European obligations,) expects the lion's share.

'Tis "the unkindest cut of all," for America to ask
England to pay for crops which have been mortgaged
to twice their valuation. Of course, I speak of the
balance of trade and American securities, amounting to
half a billion dollars, not of individual advances on the
cotton crop.

Draw away a few millions more, and America will
kill the goose with the golden egg. The "Persia,"
coming in with sovereigns, meets the "Asia," going
out with eagles! What new spoke is this in the
financial wheel ? America may receive another million
or two, but then she must prepare to pay it back—
with tens for every unit. What financier can break
the golden law of trade ?

During the last ten years, a *thousand millions* of
gold and silver have been · added to the bullion of
the world ! Where is it all? asks the astonished political economist. A very little reflection would tell him
that near that sum was distributed by the five nations
among the Asiatic and African tribes that border on
the Euxine and the Levant, during the Crimean war

—precious little of which has ever found its way back.

Place a piece of gold in the hand of an Asiatic, and it acts like an electric shock. He never forgets the sensation. Like Isaac the Jew, in Ivanhoe, (which, like the conquest of Mexico, was Scott's best work,) 'tis easy to receive the sovereigns, but hard for misers to pay them away— Asiatics and Africans are but misers, since the time that Judas tried to add thirty pieces to his pile, and Esau sold his birth-right for a "hasty plate of soup."

What is a thousand millions of gold when you come to divide it among our little family party ? 'Tis only about one dollar to each individual, after all—and who is there that cannot raise one hundred cents ? In every financial operation, in the Old World, the West has been outwitted by the East. (In the New World 'tis just the reverse. China and India have sold Europe their products at high prices, demanding silver in exchange ; while the Western States are under obligations to the East, for money to build up their fancy cities and complete their fancy improvements. The East has sent out some three millions of people, and furnished them with capital to start them in business in the West; but the speculation, like shipments to the Californian and Australian markets, or like joint stock companies nearer home, does not open up a gold mine.)

England has furnished funds for everybody to open a store, and she must be tired of acting as a special partner. The "Arabia's" news will fall upon the English people like an earthquake. (Dr. Cumming will think that the comet has come.) For a long time they have been deaf to reason, blind to argument, insisting that trade was sound, because the exports were continually increasing.

First a run—then a panic—then a crisis—and the Bank of England, a crippled ship in a rough sea, will run to Government, and Lord Palmerston will do what Lord John Russell did in 1847: write a letter authorizing suspension of specie payments (if necessary), and possibly an issue of small notes again, as they have always done when they were hard up.

The "reserve of notes" on the 2d October, 1847, amounted to - - - $ 17,000,000
The other securities amounted to - 106,000,000
    The discount five and a half per cent.

The "reserve of notes," 3d October, 1857, amounted to - - - - - 23,000,000
The other securities amounted to - 109,000,000
    Rate of discount the same.

On the 30th October, 1847, the reserve of notes fell off to - - - - 5,800,000
And discount went up to 8 per cent.

At this point, out came the Premier's circular, saying that the Government would assist the Bank. This restored confidence; so that, at the end of the year, the reserve had risen to $38,000,000, and the rate of discount dropped to five per cent.

This may be considered the "Railway mania panic." I never pass that magnificent palace on Hyde Park, now occupied by the French Ambassador, without being reminded of its once princely owner,—Hudson, the "Railway King"—who at one time carried all England in his breeches pocket.

Leaving England to make her way into a safe port, if possible, let us follow the tempest to France. Every man who has given any attention whatever to the subject, will agree with me on at least two points: first, that the *Crédit Mobilier* must fail; second, that France has been financially in a bad way for some years.

John Law, the Scotchman, must have laughed in his sleeve in 1719, to see how successfully he duped the French Monarch and the French people with his Mississippi Land Scheme. France was dazzled—poets and statesmen, prince and peasant, duchess and milliner—all bowed before the great financier. Ladies of the highest rank sought to be introduced, and Law became a king among the pigmies. He went up like a rocket and came down like the stick.

Pereire is the Law of this age.

The *Crédit Mobilier* is his Mississippi Land Scheme. The stock has touched two thousand francs, an advance of four hundred per cent. It has fallen to seven hundred within a few months. 'Twas the same with Law's speculation.

The *Crédit Mobilier* is the "Popular Delusion" of the present century; a kiting post for the Cabinet; a stool-pigeon for De Morny, and the choice spirits of the *coup d'état*.

If Pereire has held on to some of the funds of the Austrian and Russian railways, he may have deposits sufficient to outlive the Bank of France. But 'tis difficult to say who is the chief partner, and for whose benefit he is using the money, in the firm of De Morny, Pereire & the French Bank. They are all in the same boat, and Napoleon is the only man on board that understands navigation. Crew and passengers watch with anxious eye every movement of the helmsman. Never before have such stakes rested upon the life of one individual.

No matter where you find him, that same melan-

choly smile sleeps upon his features.   He never changes ;
that face is cold as marble.   Whether standing beside
his mother's grave in Italy, or writing his work on
military tactics; dining at Lady Blessington's table, or
smuggling himself into France with the passport of
a Swedish friend ; taking his frugal meal at a New-
York restaurant, or landing at Boulogne with one
spread eagle ; a special constable in England, or a
prisoner at Ham; throwing himself single-handed on
the bayonets of a French regiment at Strasburg, or
kissing the Queen of England at Dover,—he never
changes.

President of the French Republic, or the Chevalier
of Mrs. Howard—signing the paper to Marshal St. Arnaud, " Burn Paris if necessary," when riding over
the bodies of his countrymen in 1851, or dictating
terms to Lord Palmerston at Osborne regarding the
Principalities—making love to the beautiful Eugenie,
or closeted with Alexander at Stuttgard :—Napoleon,
Emperor of the French, stands at the helm of the
ship of State—with an iron will upon his hardened
face, and that same melancholy smile.   *I can never
forget it!*

The Bourse is the barometer of the Frenchman's
politics, and the Bourse to-day is convulsed—(Read

Mackay's poem, the " Panic on the Bourse.") They are a mercurial people and can make a revolution in an hour. Governments are weakest when they appear most strong. Louis Philippe, the wealthiest, the firmest-seated on the throne, the most powerful monarch of Europe at night, was an outcast and an exile in the morning. Napoleon is made of sterner stuff. He will fight, but never run. Napoleon is brave,—Louis Philippe was a coward. Napoleon is equal to famine, war, pestilence, and inundation ; but take away his money and his power has gone for ever.

Hence to-day Europe rests upon a magazine of powder. The Revolution of 1848 has only slumbered. European diplomatists will tell you it has never died.

Kossuth, Mazzini, Rollin, and thousands of new-born conspirators, still hold their midnight meetings. Dark plans are maturing ; dark deeds will be performed.

All Europe turns to France ! Paris is France. Louis Napoleon is Paris—manifest destiny governs Louis Napoleon :—a chicken bone at dinner—a pistol ball on the *Champs Elysees*—a bayonet at the *Tuilieries*—a run-away horse on the *Bois de Boulogne* (the Duke of Orleans was killed by jumping from his carriage), may deprive France of its best pilot—and the noble ship is wrecked in a sea of blood !

Murat, Robespierre, Danton, and Mirabeau are still walking about the streets of Paris—(Lamartine before staid the fury of the mob. " The *Tri-colored* flag," said he, "has been seen in every land—but your blood-red banner is only known on the Champs de Mars." The Frenchmen listened and rebellion gave way to glory.)

Bonaparte gone—the Count de Morny thinks he can form a regency for Napoleon the Fourth! Count de Paris says, " Stop, 'tis my turn now!" Count de Chambord replies, " Stand back, I've waited for nearly thirty years!" Cavaignac, with his ten thousand Republican majority, rides over them all at the head of the army.

This time no Bonaparte can stand against him as in 1848. Changarnier and Lamoriciere are both ambitious men ; and swarming in the French ranks there are many reckless spirits (who have everything to gain, nothing but life to lose, and life is nothing to a Frenchman) who remember that military scholar at Brienne, who, at twenty-six, was Commander-in-Chief of the grand army of Italy !

France lives in the sunbeam of Napoleon's fortune. Without him she is indeed helpless. No other mind can carry her through the dangerous channel of a crisis.

The first question that the prudent merchant asks when making consignments to a foreign land, is, "Have you a partner?" "No." "Then I cannot trust my property where only one life is at stake."

Louis Napoleon has no partner, and all Europe quakes with fear!

The Emperor has built a palace and filled it with works of art. That palace is a fortress! Look at the gates of the Louvre, examine the roof, and you arrive at the conclusion that Napoleon, with a hundred thousand men, could hold it for three months against all France. New Paris has been built upon a grand military plan. The paving-stones are removed, glass bottle must be taken outside the gates (in 1848 the cavalry refused to charge over a road paved with glass), and carriages are ordered outside the walls the moment of danger. Artillery can be brought in over the *Champs Elysee*—past the *Place de la Concorde*—down the *Rue de Rivoli*—up the *Place de Sebastopol*—through the *Boulevards*—down the *Rue de la Paix*, and the *Rue Castiglione*, to the *Tuileries*. Cavalry have a clear road now. The plan is worthy of a mind like Napoleon's. He made his own throne, and will fight hard to hold it. BUT THE TIMES ARE CHANGING. Ten years is about two-thirds the length of a modern French Dynasty.*

When I remember the fate of that beautiful Austrian, Maria Antoinette, I tremble for the fair Spaniard, the Empress Eugenie.

The French people of 1857 are the same bloodthirsty race as the French people of 1789.

Europe hangs on France.

Italy, like her southern mountains, is volcanic. Poor old land! it is almost dead. Tottering on, a "lean and slippered pantaloon," "sans teeth, sans eyes, sans everything," she stand on the very brink of the grave.

Napoleon wishes to build a palace for the Pope at Jerusalem, but the Pope won't go. He prefers to live at Rome. I should like to see the King of Sardinia President of Italy!

Germany is republican. Her sole ambition is to

---

*Have you ever noticed the singular addition of numbers in connection with the fall of the Dynasties of France?

The French Republic ended.

Dynasty I.:	1794	Dynasty III.:	1830	
	1	(Fall of Charles X.; 2d Revo-	1	
	7	lution.)	8	
	9		3	
	4		0	
Dynasty II.:	1815	Dynasty IV.:	1842	
(The fall of Bonaparte.)	1	(Death of Duc d'Orleans, heir	1	
	8	of Louis Philippe, real cause	8	
	1	of last Revolution.)	4	
	5		2	
	1830		1857	

have the honor of being the fatherland to all the husbands and wives required for the reigning families of England and of Russia.

Austria feels strong since the fall of Hungary, but is not. She was never weaker. Oscar, King of Sweden, is dying, and with the death of the shiftless monarch of Denmark (whose left-hand marriages have disgraced his reign), the son of Oscar, grandchild of Napoleon's old Marshal, Bernadotte, a boy in years, becomes the young monarch of the old Scandinavian kingdoms! The King of Prussia is rapidly approaching the tomb of his ancestors. Perhaps the heir to the throne may retire, and a daughter of Victoria become the Queen of Prussia!

Turkey has been diseased for several generations. Let the "sick man" die. The Emperor Nicholas was right. England will never own it—yet she believes it.

What a miserable farce has been enacted at Constantinople. Lord Stratford de Redcliffe and the Austrian Ambassador dictated to the Sultan in relation to the Principalities. The elections were made to the satisfaction of England and of Austria. Immediately, the French, Russian, Prussian, and Sardinian ministers struck their flags. The telegraph brought the despatch. Napoleon jumped on board a steamer, with Walewski, and three hours later he was at Osborne, arguing with the Queen and Palmerston in relation to Constantinople.

"Change your policy," said Bonaparte to Palmerston, "and quickly, too; I have no time for superfluous conversation."

Off went the despatch—"Give way to France." And the ministers at once resumed their diplomatic functions.

Lord Stratford growls back the defiance: "Recall me if you dare. I have the papers; I have obeyed orders; and if I fall, we must go down together." Lord Palmerston knows that he is dealing with a mind like his own, and save a *Times* editorial—"What shall we do with a refractory Ambassador?" there the matter rests.

The union of the Principalities requires a head—who will it be? Prince Napoleon, or a Prince of Russia? In either case, they become a part of the Russian Empire.*

Russia, to-day, is the strongest government in Europe. "Russia and America," said the Grand Duke Constantine to me, a few weeks since, at Strelna, "must always be friends. You have your destiny—

---

* The grandson of the Emperor Nicholas, the Prince Leuchtenberg, who is also a grandson of the Empress Josephine, is an applicant; so is Prince Murat, another offshoot of Napoleon's family.

we have ours. Your empire is Westward—ours is towards the East." (He spoke of the courtesy of the American Government in permitting his officers to embark in the United States frigate "Niagara; of Captain Hudson's kindness to them; of the salute from the United States ship "Susquehanna;" of the honors paid him by the United States frigate "Congress;" of the American clippers at Cronstadt; of his wish to visit America; of the hope that commercial relations might be extended with the United States; of his war frigate and corvette on the stocks in New-York; and of the Emperor's desire that the good will that has existed between America and Russia since the date of our national history, should continue uninterruptedly through all time.) With all the mental energy, without the physical frame of his imperial father, the Grand Duke Constantine bears the stamp of a ruling mind—an accomplished linguist; a practical soldier as well as sailor; thoroughly educated, under the direction of the Emperor Nicholas, of whom he was the favorite son, the Grand Admiral of Russia will, some day, have his name prominently recorded in the history of Europe. He was too practical to be popular in his late visit to France; and I doubt if anything but an *autograph* letter from the Queen of England would have induced him to visit Osborne.

Constantine's active temperament pines for war.—
Alexander seeks for peace.   But the Crimean war has
created an intense hatred in Russia against England.

The Grand Duke (and a more gentlemanly man I
never met with) appointed his senior aid-de-camp, Col.
Greig, to show me Cronstadt, and gave me an autograph
letter to the Governor General of Moscow.   I was entertained at the Palace of the Empress Catharine, near
St. Petersburg, and at the Kremlin, at Moscow, where
I was surprised to find a full length portrait of Napoleon Bonaparte !

But the most interesting place to me (a graduate
of the counting-house instead of the college) was the
great annual commercial fair at *Nijni-Novgorod*, down
on the banks of the Volga, (a thousand miles east of
Moscow, and two thousand north of Astrakan,) where
sixty million dollars worth of merchandise changes
hands in a barter trade, between the European and
Asiatic merchant, on Russian soil, in six weeks time.
Three hundred thousand Asiatics had assembled, in
their garments of many colors, speaking nearly every
language but those of Europe, (the Russian, to my
ear, so much resembled the Italian that I soon learned
sufficient to be my own courier,) to dispose of their
teas, hemp, iron, feathers, grain, horses, cottons, metals,
cordage, and almost every conceivable kind of manu-

factured goods. Even in this primitive market the expanded credits, and the golden mines of California and Australia, have raised the prices of all kinds of commodities. The Chinese demand silver now on the frontier, and the Armenians had some of the English gold that the allies left in Asia Minor during the war.

Russia to-day is the strongest Government in Europe. Sixty-two millions of people move as one man. Revolution may sweep through Europe, but Russia—all powerful—looks on, and cares not. Religion is the fulcrum. Religion is the lever. The Religion of the Russian is, "Obey the Emperor!"

Russia is desirous of extending her commerce and increasing her navy. New-York is building the pioneer frigate. That finished, she builds the balance at home —all she requires is a model. Russia will shortly have more merchantmen upon the ocean—more men-of-war abroad—more trade in foreign lands.

Russia stands alone. Western Europe waits to see Napoleon's next move on the political chess-board. Some croakers conscientiously believe that England will be checkmated. So long as America is looking over her shoulder, she is all right.

Napoleon scents the financial crisis in the distance.

He knows well that a financial revulsion generally precedes the political storm. Disordered finances in 1825 hastened the Revolution of 1830. The railway panic of 1847 preceded the rather unexpected arrival of Louis Philippe in England; and the " Arabia's" news may distract the diseased minds of European cabinets.

Pereire, in his second financial report to the Emperor, after trying to explain why the public fortunes of France had fallen away some *two hundred million dollars* in *five* months' time, remarks, " *that the budget of fear almost equals the budget of France !*"

The classic author of " Popular Delusions," compares *Law's* plunge from prosperity to adversity to the sensations of the first Indian boatman, whose canoe, gliding over the waters of Lake Erie, suddenly made the fearful leap into the waters of Lake Ontario. Before the bank suspension the world were singing the song of the Canadian Boatman upon a clear blue sea. The crisis (never expected) found them in the rapids. The jump into the waters below—the death-struggle of thousands, and the escape of a few under the " *Suspension*" Bridge to the lake beyond—is still an unopened book in financial history. The *Crédit Mobilier* is the canoe. Napoleon is the boatman.

Pereire, after all, is only a passenger from Rothschild's steamship, who, like the Irishman's ancestor, (at the time that Noah was the owner of the entire domestic and foreign tonnage in the world,) thought "he had a boat of his own!"

> ———Napoleon the modern, mightiest by far,
> Who, born no king, made monarchs draw his car :
> Whose game was empire—whose dominion, thrones !
> Whose table, earth—whose dice were human bones !

Byron describes the Uncle in the "Age of Bronze." Who will describe the Nephew in the "Age of Plaster" ?

The first two lines "are cast in pleasant places." Only one act has been played.

Mark the meeting of Crowned Heads in central Europe.

England was not invited, and she was too proud to buy a ticket. Suspicious of what may be passing, she has her ear at the key-hole. Yet the meeting is all a mystery to her. *She don't understand French !*

What a strange coincidence ? Napoleon the Third met, on the 27th of last September, 1857, Alexander the

Second, at Stuttgard — just forty-nine years, to a day and hour, since Napoleon the First met Alexander the First, at Erfurt.

The old Emperors were surrounded by thirty German Kings and other Potentates.

The new Emperors were alone!

On the 12th October, 1808, a secret treaty was signed between the old Emperors, guaranteeing Finland to Russia, and making the Principalities integral parts of the Russian Empire.

Who will explain to us what has transpired between the new Emperors? Cabinets are mute; statesmen are dumb; the journals of the world are silent—no reporters being admitted, of course I had the door shut in my face. But any one can imagine what passed.

There can be no harm in reporting an *imaginary conversation*. James has done it many a time with only a "single horseman" for an audience.

Brevity is popular. *Telegrams* were invented by William Shakespere.

Giles describes his Shakesperian friend, who printed some of the Commandments in large letters, over the several editions of the great bard, in this wise—

To Actors.

"*Thou shalt do no murder.*"

To Authors.

"*Thou shalt not steal.*"

To Critics.

"*Thou shalt not bear false witness.*"

If I break any of these Commandments, I hope to be forgiven.

The Bonaparte meets the Romanoff; the Hapsburg begs admission; the Prussian King expects the same distinguished regard. (But the door is closed to both in this act. Russia likes not Austria; Russia picked Austria out of the gutter, when she bought Georgey to sell the Hungarian army. Austria, ungrateful, forgot the circumstance during the late war.)

"*Allons! mon cousin!*—now to business," said Alexander.

"Oh! bother business! Let me tell you what a jolly time we had at Osborne," said Bonaparte.

I disagree with *Punch.* The Russian Emperor gave way to the French.

Napoleon was in this case the first spokesman, although generally a listener. "Russia, take Constantinople! It belongs to you as naturally as Cuba does to the Americans! Let Austria have Wallachia and Moldavia. Let Prussia settle that Schleswig-Holstein succession to suit herself. And as France has some one hundred and fifty thousand soldiers in Algeria, she may as well employ the army in 'annexing' Egypt!"

"But what of England?" said Alexander, speaking for the first time.

"England," replied Napoleon, "experienced an attack of apoplexy in the Crimea! The second came with the Indian revolution! The third is paralysis by destroying the power of the 'money king!'"

"That is all very beautiful in theory," said Alexander, "but may prove bad in practice. You should remember that England has always been the strongest when she appeared the weakest.

"The American war did not break her. The Spanish campaign only prevented her army from rusting!

"Your uncle's terrible struggle only placed a laurel round her brow, when she sent the Emperor, Parrhasius like, to die upon a rock in the Southern Ocean."

(Louis Napoleon turned as white as a sheet with rage; but remembering his destiny, that he is to die the sack of London, recovers his color, and resumes the conversation.)

" The war of 1812 was comparatively nothing. Her wealth increased with her debt. John Bull understands kiting better than you and I, Louis."

" Yes ? " (interrogatively) replied Napoleon. " But forty years of peace found England unprepared for the Crimean war. France, as you are aware, occupied the entire *coupe*. England took a back seat in the diligence; and just as she arrived, peace was declared. Speaking of her great wealth, have you ever read Sydney Smith's Apostrophe to Taxes ? "

" True," said the Emperor of Russia ; " but you cannot have forgotten the splendid army that England raised when yours and ours were pretty well used up. I merely mention these things," continued Alexander, "to show you that England is all-powerful, when the world thinks her ruined."

" You make a strong argument for your old friend ; but you should bear in mind," said the Emperor of the French, " THAT THE TIMES ARE CHANGING ! England, before she has recovered the *prestige* lost in the Black Sea, finds her Eastern possessions dissolving away. She has sent her active army of forty thousand men to India. Her colony at the Cape any time may be involved in another Kaffir War. Australia is loyal so long as British regiments keep the miners in check. Remember that forty soldiers were shot from the rebel stockade on the ' Eureka' at Ballarat in 1854.

"The Europeans at Singapore, with a population of eighty thousand Chinese and Malays, have only a Sepoy regiment to protect it. China laughs at the 'pop-gun' attempt of Palmerston to break the Tartar's rule. Mauritius does not feel secure since Canning has taken away the British regiment. The Canadian troops (in several instances) showed disaffection at the very rumor of being sent to India.

"You know as well as I," continued Napoleon, "that this Indian question is the most serious embarrassment England has ever experienced. Notwithstanding the horrible atrocities at Cawnpore and Meerut, constantly kept before the people by the English press, the lower and middling classes consider it no affair of theirs. They say, with some degree of reason, that the Honorable East India Company has always been in the hands of a favored few. The English people have had no share in the spoils, but the glory of the robbery. I doubt if ten thousand volunteers can be raised in England; while a hundred thousand Americans more than were required came forward for the Mexican war, and in that case there were no women to be rescued, no babes to be taken from off the Sepoy's sabre. You, too, must have noticed this apathy. When I contemplate the unheard-of outrages committed upon helpless mothers and children—I would volunteer myself, were I not an Emperor.

"The fact is, THE TIMES ARE CHANGING. For several years England has been so kind as to be governed by my advice. I think I can rule her still. The very rumor of my Uncle's invasion in 1797 caused her National Bank to suspend for twenty-two years. His fleet met in. the West Indies — a storm disorganized his plans. Then it was the 'age of canvas'—now 'tis the 'age of steam.'

"He had only sailing ships—I have steamers; I can land a hnndred thousand men on England's shores in ten hours time, and carry out the Emperor's plan of appealing to the people against the aristocracy. Have you not noticed the rumbling sound of discontent in Ireland? You feel proud of Cronstadt. *You should see Cherbourg.* Your brother Constantine made a few notes when there."

"Certainly," said Alexander, laughing; "you this time have the best of the argument, but still I cannot forget the history of England. My father, the Emperor Nicholas, always respected her greatness, and my uncle Alexander considered it one of the proudest moments of his life when he accompanied Wellington to Paris after the Battle of Waterloo."

"If you mention Waterloo again," interrupted Napoleon, impatiently, "I shall have, in all good nature, to remind you of Moscow. There is much force in what you say, but the fact is, England's strength has gone with her money. I got some of it—America a good deal of it; but you, Alexander, were too late with your railways."

"They will be built, nevertheless," responded the Emperor of Russia; "Russia never attempts anything she does not accomplish; (your uncle once made the same reply to the President of the French Assembly, when asked if he could defend Paris against the mob)."

(Napoleon shudders at the word mob, and begs the Emperor to confine his remarks to England.)

"England," continued Alexander, "may lose to-day, but she will gain to-morrow. About the age which gave birth to three great minds in different lands (your uncle, Wellington, and Mehemet-Ali), England discovered a power that is still in its infancy.

"When the Chathamtonian letters of Junius were being penned—a short time after Lord Clive had gained a colony in the East to compensate for one that Lord Cornwallis was about to lose in the West— Watts with his steam and Arkwright with his cotton-gin were working out a herculean fortune for the British nation. You may be right, but I can't help

thinking that England has something yet in the National Treasury.

"But as you say, my cousin, THE TIMES ARE CHANG-
ING. Who could have imagined such an interview as
this? What would my father or your uncle have
said? Who could have supposed for a moment that
Protestant England would have united with Catholic France, to protect Mahommedan Turkey against
the Greek Church of Russia? Nothing since the Cru-
sades under Plantagenet against Jerusalem has appeared
so absurd. 'Twas a quarrel about the 'holy places'
in each case, and so far as England was concerned,
the result in each case was about the same—nothing!"

"I have listened most attentively," replied Napoleon,
"to what you say—all of which would meet my views,
did I not believe that the TIMES ARE CHANGING.

"The first conquest of Mexico under Cortez was
far different from the second conquest of Mexico under
Scott. The Spaniard encountered an effeminate race, living a life of luxury about the halls of the Monte-
zumas. The Americans met drilled soldiers.

"The first conquest of India under Clive is far
different from the second conquest of India under Canning
—as different as that age compared to this.

"Here the analogy between Mexico and Hindostan
ends—for in the one case Scott had an enthusiastic

nation—every man of which was a soldier—to cheer him on—while Canning thus far has received but forty thousand men. Mexico was near the United States : India is far from England. Mexico is a very little place : India is a very large one. And if England loses India, all the money which she has spent there goes with it.

"England never looks ahead—'sufficient for the day,' &c. Bacon said that knowledge was the result of experience. But Walpole told Chatham there was such a thing as being ignorant in spite of experience."

"I must admit there's method in your reasoning," responded the Emperor of Russia. "My father never for a moment expected that England would so foolishly break their long friendship. It was an oft-repeated remark of his, that when a man had been running at the top of his speed, he must slacken his pace or fall. When prices are inflated beyond a prudent margin, they naturally must depreciate. So when a nation has reached the highest pinnacle of fame, it commences to decay. Venice, Portugal, Spain, and Holland are instances of nations dying out the moment they commence to lose that which made them great—their commerce.

"When a man is at the point of death he must get better or die. Macaulay's singular prophecy of the

New Zealand traveler sketching the ruins of St. Paul's from London Bridge, is in my mind."

"I agree with you, these are natural laws; and while I endorse many of your opinions, I require more reflection on the rest. But at any rate, on the chief points our sentiments are mutual."

"One word," said the Emperor of the French, for the first time looking Alexander steadily in the face—"one word before we part."

"What do you think of America?"

"Simply," replied Alexander, in a quiet and decided way, "that you and I, to say the least, had better leave America to attend to her own affairs."

The Emperors closed the conference. The interview was satisfactory. The two monarchs only argued against each other to agree the better at the conclusion. Both leave the palace with a secret resolve to cripple the power of England forever.

Now comes the issue. America must stand forth and proclaim her sentiments. She must act, not talk.

THE TIMES ARE CHANGING.

Americans must spring to the rescue of the Saxon power.

England has done more for religious freedom and civil liberty than all the world beside.

I speak with the book, and know well what I say. America has followed England abroad and copied her at home. Englishmen should praise rather than censure our nationality; for where is there a people so wrapt up in their national glory as the English.

A little more reflection would convince an Englishman that America must ever be the friend of England. Natural ties are stronger than artificial alliances. Americans are worthy of better treatment, of more respect, of broader sentiments, than Englishmen are disposed to give them. They insist upon judging us by the standard of the "almighty dollar." We have been treated badly by England.

The whole story can be written on a single page.

We commenced our career a shivering band of pilgrims, at Plymouth

Our house was built upon a rock.

We worked—we toiled—we spun. God and the right went up with our morning and evening prayer. By honesty and industry we built up a progressive colony.

A free church, a clear conscience, and just laws, were the daily watch-words of the banished pioneers. Amidst storm and tempest—the bear and the Indian —we increased in numbers and in wealth, and worked hard for that old mother land whose arbitrary laws had driven us from her shores.

We paid the taxes generation after generation. We paid the taxes—for over a century and a-half we paid them—and fought the battles of England. Years passed on. George the Third wanted more money—we paid it. More still—we paid that also. Year after year we paid away our hard-earned gains without complaint. Then tyrannical governors came among us. The Pilgrim Band had become the germ of a great nation. More taxes were wanted for a continental war. Out came the Stamp Act—the Boston Port Bill :—and overboard went the tea—up went the flag—and then came Declaration of Independence—battles—victory !

" There is Concord, and Lexington, and Bunker Hill," said Webster to Hayne, " and there they will remain forever, to prove to the civilized world the justness of our cause."

England admits that she was wrong, that America was right.

" Onward and upward, straight on," we continued our destiny. Washington lived and died, bequeathing the purest name in history to a grateful nation. Adams, Madison, Jefferson, followed, when, waging war with Bonaparte, England again insulted us. Our sailors were ourselves; touch them, you arouse us. The American citizen, on land or on the ocean, must and will be respected. Again we were victorious.

England admits that she was wrong, that America was right.

Then came an age of peace. England sneers at our progress one day, and the next pats us on the shoulder, calling us a saucy little boy. English writers visit our land, but only return to exaggerate our faults and forget our virtues.

"Who reads an American book?" said Sydney Smith.*

---

* "Confining ourselves to our own country, and to the period that has elapsed since *they* had an independent existence, we would ask, where are their Foxes, their Burkes, their Sheridans, their Windhams, their Horners, their Wilberforces?—Where their Arkwrights, their Watts, their Davys?—their Robertsons, Blairs, Smiths, Stewarts, Paleys, and Malthuses?—their Porsons, Parrs, Burneys, or Bloomfields?—their Scotts Rogerses, Campbells, Byrons, Moores, or Crabbes?—their Siddonses, Kembles, Keans, or O'Neils?—their Wilkies, Lawrences, Chantrys?—or their parallels to the hundred other names that have spread themselves over the world from our little island in the course of the last thirty years, and blest or delighted mankind by their works, inventions, or examples? In so far as we know, there is no such parallel to be produced from the whole annals of this self-adulating race.

"In the four quarters of the globe, who reads an American book? or goes to an American play? or looks at an American picture or statue? What does the world yet owe to American physicians or sur-

Marryat came to the United States in the midst of the panic of 1837, to sneer at everything he saw.

"Who fattens on the curse of slavery?" said Dickens; and then there was a distinguished lady writer came Trollop-ing through the land.

The Ashburton treaty was not a generation old when it was broken, but not by us. Our laws were infringed. Enlistment of soldiers in America for the Crimean war would have offended Russia, with whom we have never had an ill-tempered diplomatic note. We protested, but without effect. Back went the British minister. England sent regiments to Canada, and a war-fleet to the Bermudas. Clarendon stormed; Marcy responded, with dignity and with eloquence. The American minister unpacked his trunks, and still remains in England.

England still admits that we were right—that she was wrong.

England should not forget, when shuddering over the atrocity of the Sepoys, that she herself, in days gone

geons? What new substances have their chemists discovered? or what old ones have they analyzed? What new constellations have been discovered by the telescopes of Americans? What have they done in the mathematics? Who drinks out of American glasses? or eats from American plates? or wears American coats or gowns? or sleeps in American blankets? Finally, under which of the old tyrannical governments of Europe is every sixth man a slave, whom his fellow-creatures may buy and sell and torture?"

by, has offered rewards to the North American savage for the "scalps of Americans wherever they may be found." Remember Chatham's eloquent denunciation.

I have merely run my eye along our national history to show that America has not been well treated by England. What are Americans, after all, but Englishmen left to themselves?

With all this bitter remembrance, we are willing to forget and forgive. We are fond of the old land yet —with all her faults we love her still.

England will shortly need our help. *The times are changing.* Our moral sympathy alone may prevent the encroachment of Europe. India hangs by a thread— America can secure the Saxon flag there for another hundred years. Americans are Americans at home— but they are Saxons abroad.

Let England's noble Queen come over to America, and she shall have a welcome such as no historian has ever recorded. A sovereign people know how to welcome a sovereign Queen.

We never liked the Georges. Landor condenses Thackeray's lectures into a thimble.

> " George the Third was reckoned vile;
>   Viler, George the Second.
> And what mortal ever heard
>   Any good of George the Third?
> When from earth the Fourth ascended,
> God be praised, the Georges ended !"

We never liked the Georges; but there is not an American in the land that does not respect Victoria, —the daughter, the wife, the mother, and the Queen— the noblest woman in our Father-land !

Let the Queen of England visit America ! 'Twill heal an age of irritation ; and then one hundred thousand able-bodied soldiers will land in India and in China, to introduce, with cannon, the locomotive, the steamboat, and all the implements of the Saxon's power, to the Asiatic race.

THE TIMES ARE CHANGING.

AN AMERICAN ARTICLE.

European Politics—The Queen's Visit to America—Indian Brutalities—
No place like Home—Bottom out of the Financial Churn—Panic
of 1857 eclipses every other, in the aggregate, for three centuries—
Substitute "Western Land" for "South Sea" Bubble—Panic of
1814—National Bank under Washington, and National Bank under
Madison—Jackson's Veto—U. S. Bank of Pennsylvania—Panic of
'37 compared with Crisis of '57—Meeting of Banking Delegates—
Biddle's struggles to sustain the Bank—Wall street Dodges—
Bankrupt Act of 1841 and '42—Tariff of 1842 and '46—Failures—
Bankrupt Act for *honest men* recommended—THE TIMES ARE CHANG-
ING—How a Bank is got up—Stock Exchange—Bulls break Bears
then Bears break Bulls—State Debts—Depreciation in Property—
Amasa Walker off the Track—Crops Overestimated—What Inter-
ests pay?—When will the Banks resume?—Economy—Factory Op-
eratives—Importations of Grain into England—Everett at Buffalo—
Standing Army of America one million of men—Filibustering—
Cuba; Let the Government buy it, and keep the people honest—
A National Bank Discussed—Jackson versus Biddle—Schuylerisms—
Washington's National Bank — Madison's—Biddle's—Reason why
Jackson removed the Deposits—National Bank preferable to pres-
ent system—Buy Cuba—Build the Pacific Railroad—These two
sums furnish basis for a National Bank—Government must take
care of the People—Free Trade—California—Brigham Young—
Congress of Merchants, &c.—Practical men wanted— Hon. Nathan

Appleton—Chatham's reply to Walpole—Wholesome Reforms—England's Interference with American Slavery—Campbell's Defiance—George Hunt's Retort—Steam and Credit—Slaves better free than Freemen—England's Debt—Blacks more thought of than Whites—Stop the Cotton, and Revolution in England anticipated—Louis Napoleon as Policeman and as Emperor—Reed, the Poet—N. P. Morris—Vigilance Committee.

"HOME AGAIN!"

BUBBLES, — BANKS, — BLACKS.

Having assisted the Emperors of France and Russia
in settling the "disputed points" in European politics, invited the Queen of England, in the name of
the American people, to visit the United States, and
recommended the President to send one hundred thousand of the "unemployed" (for a consideration) to
India, to "assist" the Sepoys in introducing railways,
telegraphs, Christian inventions and Christian laws,
into Hindostan; and to impress upon the mind of the
Mahommedan and the Hindoo, that Saxon children are
not animals of prey, to be bayoneted and butchered
like goats in a Hindoo temple, and that Saxon women
are not to be dishonored by the most terrible crime
that fiends can perpetrate, and then, before life is ex-
tinct, cut into a hundred pieces, and thrown into a
well, as was the case at Cawnpore (the band of Nena
Sahib striking up the music of that beautiful song,
"Cheer, boys, cheer!")—having, I say, gone so far
abroad, and taken a general glance at passing events

in Europe and in Asia, through the magnetic attraction of home, I find myself once more discussing the state of affairs in my native land.

With all due regard for the monuments of the Old World, there's nothing that makes my heart jump so high with delight, after returning from those time-worn turrets, and being tossed about on a rough Atlantic sea for some twelve days, as to see again the great monuments of America, the light-houses along the shore, which at some future day will be the beacons to guide the commerce of the Old World into the harbors of the New.

Just at this particular time, however, I can imagine the surprise that settles over the sunburnt faces of Eastern travelers, who, returning from foreign lands, learn for the first time, when the pilot makes the intelligence known, that, notwithstanding the bottom has dropped out of the financial churn, the commercial dairymen are churning away as blindly as ever, although, every time the dasher goes down it hits the cat and kittens, who are lapping up the skim-milk upon the floor!

The sooner the people of the United States make up their minds that the financial simoom of 1857 eclipses every other crisis since the time that Columbus was under obligations to a North American savage for a raccoon steak, the better.

You may take all the statistics of all the panics for the last three centuries, add them up, and then multiply by two, and you will not make a sum equal to the general depreciation on property throughout the world in the years 1857 and 1858. This may appear an exaggeration, but a little reflection will prove the truth of the assertion.

The panics that followed Columbus—the panics that persecuted the Pilgrims (the tulip mania of Holland exploded just sixteen years after Miles Standish asked the first Indian to take a drink)—the panics that convulsed the old world a century later, born and nursed in the South Sea House, and the *Rue de Quincampoix*—the panics of 1814, '25, '37, and '47, all these panics thrown into the "Vanderbilt" steamer would not be sufficient to make her crank; while the clipper crisis of 1857 will probably be the means of sinking the "Great Eastern!"

Will some one be so kind as to look up the figures, and show in what respect my argument is weak?

In 1814 all the Banks of the country failed except those of New England (*their* paper was worth twenty per cent. above that of the Federal Government; this time I should judge its value was considerably more than that below it). About the time that the Iron Duke prayed "that night or Blucher would come to his assistance," and the "Little Corporal" was straining his eyes through a telescope for Grouché, on the Field of Waterloo, the United States found it somewhat difficult to get a discount, and thousands were made bankrupt.

The war closed; National Bank number two was established; Madison signed the charter, April 10th, 1816. Its capital was thirty-five million dollars.

The charter was for twenty years.

National Bank number one had a capital of ten millions. The charter was signed by Washington for twenty years. About the time that it expired, another Bank was projected, but Clinton's casting vote defeated the bill. The next Congress succeeded in establishing the Bank which has made Biddle famous.

The banks having failed, this great national institution was a blessing to the country.

The other banks struggled hard to keep their heads above water. In February, 1816, the Union Bank tried to resume specie payment; the Virginia Banks copied her example.

In June, 1817, the New-York Legislature passed a bill compelling the suspended banks to pay *twelve per cent. interest* on their notes if they did not resume. (Why are the bill holders not waking up to this forcing process?) Towards the end of the year gold poured in, but the expansion and sudden contraction of the National Bank broke nearly all the merchants.

Paper expansion occasioned the panic.

The National Bank worked much better than the others. I believe the panic of 1825 would have been worse without it. On the 10th of July, 1832, "Old Hickory" vetoed the U. S. Bank bill, and the following October removed the deposits, amounting in the several banks to forty million dollars. That year the thirty per cent. (sliding scale) tariff went into effect.

To prevent a crisis arising from the removal of the specie, Biddle commenced discounting. The extent of the expansion can be seen by the fact that the bank issues increased from $360,000,000 in 1835, to $525,-000,000 before 1837. Of course this expansion drove the specie out of the country to pay the foreign creditors, and buy the foreign grain, and set everybody to speculating in "under water" lands, and all kinds of stocks. 'Tis always so.

To arrest these insane land speculations, General Jackson issued the Treasury Circular 11th July, 1836, providing that all receipts for the sale of public lands must be made in gold and silver. It was afterwards modified, permitting the receipt of the bills of specie-paying Banks. During the balance of the year, the rumbling of the distant thunder announced the approaching storm.

Josephs commenced the ball in March. Their liabilities were some $7,000,000 ; their assets exceeded this sum about a million. About the same amounts were shown by the Ohio Life and Trust Company, and I think they will pay about the same dividend !

Morgan, receiver for the country Banks, came down next.

'Twas the same this time with Thompson. The failures from October, '36, to April, '37, were some $70,000,000.

The failures from August to November, 1857, will amount to some $200,000,000.

Two hundred houses stopped in Boston in six weeks. Specie ranged from ten to fourteen per cent. premium, when out came another Treasury Circular, authorizing Government to receive in payment, on all occasions, the bills of specie-paying Banks. The absurdity of this measure will be observed by remembering that all the Banks had failed—as is the case to-day.

Then the New-York Banks came down on the 10th of May. The Boston and New England Banks followed. This year I remark the same analogy. The next day the Baltimore and Philadelphia Banks broke· This time they preceded New-York.

The merchants' circular to Government, prepared

by the 3d of May Committee, spoke of the great depreciation of property, some thirty to forty per cent., and the terrible effect of the hard times upon the rich as well as the poor.

Twenty thousand men were out of employment. There are twice that now, and the hard times have hardly commenced.

Twelve hundred thousand dollars in specie were sent abroad in August, 1837, and the Government got out their Treasury notes. About the same amount came this way in the "Persia" in October, 1857.

On the 27th of November, 1837, one hundred and thirty-five banking delegates, representing eighteen States, met to discuss the necessity of resuming specie payment. They were in session four days, and adjourned till April, having accomplished nothing but drinking up a good quantity of bad liquor, and eating everything that came in their way, (for the benefit of their shareholders.) Have there been any similar meetings this year?

On the 16th April, 1838, they met again, and advised all to resume on the first Monday of January, 1839. The only result of this second meeting was, the discussing of a few more good dinners. The advice was a dead letter. The banks tried to resume, and failed.

The United States Bank of Pennsylvania suspended on the 9th of September, 1839. This bank, it will be remembered, was raised upon the worn-out fabric of the old National Bank, vetoed by Jackson in 1832, and ex⁃ pired by limitation in 1836.

The National Bank never failed to pay its obliga⁃ tions. The bank that failed bore the same name—was managed by the same President, but existed under a charter from the State of Pennsylvania. Yet foreign⁃ ers cannot separate the two institutions. At this time, everybody looked to Biddle. Biddle struggled hard. His three and twelve months post notes did not work, and 'twas as absurd for him to try and stem the tide by buying up the cotton crop, as for Mrs. Partington to mop away the sea. He tried to resume, and did, on the 15th of January; but down he came again, in February (1841). He fought hard, but the odds were against him. Six millions of specie were paid away in a few days, and all the Wall Street dodges of hav⁃ ing expressmen ride up, and porters carrying in bags of *cents*, &c., were resorted to, without avail. Of course, this knocked all the other banks off the roost except the New-York and New-England institutions.

The Sub-Treasury Law was repealed on the 9th of August, 1841, and, on the 19th of the same month, Congress passed a uniform Bankruptcy Act, to go into operation on the 1st February, 1842, which released between thirty-five and forty thousand bankrupts, and cleared off about five hundred million dollars indebtedness. You never saw a more disgusted set of men than the one million of creditors when they received their dividends.

Kentucky was the only State that made any show at all. To her everlasting credit, she paid eighty cents on the dollar.

Maryland paid ten ; Illinois six-and-a-quarter ; Tennessee four-and-a-half ; Massachusetts four ; New-Jersey one ;—while Michigan, Iowa, Connecticut, Maine, Pennsylvania, Alabama, Virginia, and Washington City, paid so much less than one per cent. on the dollar, it is not worth mentioning.

The " Compromise Tariff " expired in 1842, and the " Protective Tariff " run on to 1846. All the intermediate panics were only the breaking out of the old disease—as Matthews would say, " it was the same drunk ! "

First of December, 1846, this tariff went into operation, and expired June 30th, 1857, when we put in the first free trade wedge.

The total Imports into the country during the ten years and seven months, amounted to $2,504,168,646

Averaging in round numbers, per annum,	$240,000,000
Exports, same time, amount to .	2,429,157,209
Averaging, say, ...	230,000,000
The tonnage employed in foreign commerce was 1,800,000, earning some	225,000,000

I have gone somewhat into details to show how absurd it is to expect for a moment better times for months and months.

If the liabilities arising out of that panic amounted to $500,000,000, will not the liabilities extending over the same length of time, run up to $2,000,000,000 ?

The total value of real and personal property in the United States, January 1st, 1853, amounted to . .	$10,855,636,800
Even *twenty-five* per cent. depreciation would give the pretty sum of .	2,700,000,000

The country did not get a fair start until 1842. What reason have we to expect it to square up and go on again, as many argue, in a few months' time? I should like to hear their side of the argument. Assertions are nothing, without facts.

Bankrupt Acts have generally been made for thieves and scamps. I would suggest now that Congress pass an act for all the States for honest men, and it should be prepared so that lawyers could not drive a Broadway omnibus through it, as they can through a New-York State Legislative Act. A broad, honest, Congressional Bankrupt Law will have to be framed, before the country can make any head-way toward recovery. It is the only " poor man's plaster " that will be in demand.

There are three things that will shortly be fashionable in this country—failures, economy, and, I trust, honesty.

THE TIMES ARE CHANGING.

Heretofore those who were the most extravagant, and had the largest liabilities, were enabled to obtain the greatest facilities from the moneyed interest. A few choice spirits generally club together, get up a bank, and adopt as a motto, when discounts are discussed,. " after number one, the million." And at the present time many say we must save ourselves, if everybody else go to pieces. How natural ?

Now is the time to do unto others (as nearly as possible) as you would have others do unto you. My advice is, if a creditor smite the debtor on the right cheek, give him a chance at the other. But should the miscreant strike him there also—as Scripture don't provide for that alternative—I should decidedly pound him, and give no quarter.

In other words, we require a Bankrupt Act to protect honest debtors and *bona fide* creditors.   The Acts
of 1800 and 1841 can be improved upon, and by taking a leaf or two from the French and English sys-
tems, a sound bill can be framed ; and the debtor and
the creditor (there is little difference this time between the position of the one or the other) can make
a new start in life.

I hope, for a while at least, we shall see no more
of that high pressure system at the broker's board.
For several years the stock exchange has been a disgrace to this country.   The bulls get together and
break the bears, and then the bears club around and
break the bulls.   Wesley gets Little's " nob in
chancery," and of course Little can't sleep till he has
returned the compliment.

The Bankrupt Law will wipe out an immense amount
of corporation rottenness and individual liability.

The total debt of the thirty-one States in

1851, was,   .   .   . $201,541,624
While the assessed value of property was $5,983,149,407

Every dollar of this debt will be paid.

Everything else may depreciate, and insolvency be
general, but I am sure the American people would
bear any amount of just taxation before they will ever
permit another State to repudiate.

In 1837, the liabilities equaled about the amount of the paper money afloat.

Now, the liabilities, most likely, will treble the expansion. While I endorse many of the able comments of Mr. Amasa Walker, on the currency, I cannot agree with him "that the effects of this crisis will be far less lasting than that of 1837, or that a healthy condition of trade will be brought about in a few months."

Almost every financial writer plays upon the same "harp of a thousand strings." They believe the country sound. They talk of recuperative power. They point to the improvements in the country. In what does the soundness consist ? In prices of everything being inflated to a hundred per cent. above their real value ? I am told that the rent-roll in New-York equals the bank capital. Have the landlords made up their minds to a reduction of one half? Have the stockholders in the railways come to the conclusion that one half the roads will better manage the entire business of the country than all do now ? That the falling off in importations and immigration will keep the shipping property poor for many a month ? That land that does not grow grain sufficient to feed a horse, can have but little real value ?

What are our great agricultural resources ? How

much is added to the wealth of the land by growing grain that we eat, and where is the value after
it goes into our mouths?

What we export to Europe I have previously shown
is a bagatelle.   So, after we have obtained what we
shall eat and what we shall drink, and wherewithal
we shall be clothed, the raising of which has given
employment to labor, we want a foreign market for
the surplus.   When labor ceases to be productive, the
produce consumed is wasted.   The stomach is full, but
the pocket is empty.   Therefore, when hundreds of
thousands of laborers are thrown out of employment,
the country loses millions of dollars.   What interest
pays to-day?   Railways?   By no means.   Railways are
mortgaged labor, badly managed by agents general, for
their own benefit.   And even bondholders are governed
by majorities.   Railways have never paid as well as
bank stock, and bank stock is gradually sinking out
of sight.

How many corporations and individuals are hanging
on by their eye-lids in the vain hope that there is "a
good time coming"?

Are factories paying?   I should think not.   When,
as Dr. Cheever says, *ten mills don't make one cent*,
there is something radically wrong!

A reduction of prices cripples merchants, the merchants cripple the banks, the New World cripples the Old : hence, you will see nothing but "crutches" and "cripples" for a long time yet.

Bank notes secured by State stocks may be saved, but depositors may go a begging. Look at the disgraceful statement of the Bowery Bank. Were the directors "Bowery boys" or "Bowery men"? Such disclosures will tend to make Bank and State as unpopular as Church and State.

When will our banks resume ? Echo answers, when? Specie may roll up to $20,000,000 (by keeping back what we owe Europe); what then? Can they get under way again ? I hope so, but certainly it did not work well in 1837.

The moment the billholders and depositors can get the hard eagles, they are bound to have them, and most certainly they have a right to their own vine and fig-tree. Look at the banks of Rhode Island. Loans $18,000,000 against but $3,000,000 in specie !

In all New England there was only $7,000,000 specie to $48,000,000 circulation.

In Boston, a hundred merchants sign a paper, to say they believe the bank notes are perfectly good. The bank notes may be as good as the merchants' notes, but just now it is difficult to say which is

Blucher and which is Wellington. In New-York, the banks prop up the merchants, and the merchants prop up the banks, and both "shake props" together. Make your game, gentlemen. Do you pass? Whist.

This panic may be over, but if it is, there's another close at hand.

All kinds of tricks will be resorted to to stave off the blow. Thus far, we have only seen bank operate on bank, individual on individual, State on State. Wait till the shuttlecock of false credit rebounds from nation to nation.

We must countermand all foreign orders; retain gold (if we can, and pay our debts); cut off all luxuries; reduce necessities; be economical, honestly if we can, but at any rate, be economical. There is one thing worth recording; we have bread and meat enough in the country to feed every soul in the land. A factory girl can board for a dollar and a quarter a week. Six months will cost but thirty-two dollars, and there are few girls that have not got that much stored away, so they are all right for the coming winter. Yet, nevertheless, there must be much misery.

The census of 1850 gives:

	Operatives.
In the New England States, - - -	300,000
New Jersey, - - - - - -	200,000
Pennsylvania, - - - - - -	150,000
Other States, - - - - - -	300,000

In round numbers, a million of people employed in American manufactories.   How many may be discharged?

I hesitate to make the figures.   Truth may prove stranger than fiction.

Already some fifty thousand workmen are out of employment.   A few months later at least one-half of the operatives will be cast adrift.   Think of a half million of men clamoring for something to do—something to eat.   Refuse them bread, and they will give you a stone.   In times of expansion the laboring man fares better than in the hard money days, more especially if his employer pays his board and lodging.

In 1837 the crops were over-estimated.   'Tis the same in my judgment now.

Farmers have given more attention to land speculations than they have to their grain crops.   If our agricultural interests have been neglected, our corn and grain will be wanted at home.   We had no surplus over last year ; and England any way must raise her prices to command any of the present crop.

During the last seven years England has imported from all countries about 40,000,000 bushels of breadstuffs per annum.   This year they will require about the same.   The *Mark Lane Express* makes an estimate of where it is coming from :

	Bushels.
The United States and Canadas,....................	12,000,000
Denmark and the Dutchies, the Hanse Towns, and other parts of Germany,.......................	8,000,000
Southern Russia,................................	5,600,000
Egyptian States,................................	4,000,000
Wallachia and Moldavia,..........................	1,500,000
Turkey in Europe,.......	1,500,000
Northern Russia,................................	1,500,000
Spain and all other countries,.....................	2,900,000
	37,000,000

France, Holland, and Belgium will require all they can raise.

'Tis a fearful thing when a nation is unable to produce grain sufficient for its own population; and it will be a very severe trial for England to have to pay away forty millions this year for bread.

I trust that our crops are not exaggerated, yet I fear they have been; comparatively speaking, nothing has come forward thus far, and as it is, we must wait another season. A bad crop next year would produce in this country a famine. Everett, in his beautiful speech at Buffalo, says: "Stop the production of a dozen articles of breadstuffs for *ten days time*, and eight hundred millions of people will die!"

What shall we do with the unemployed? Five hundred thousand able-bodied men will be soon knocking at the door — "begging for leave to earn their bread."

What is to be done?

First, when England asks us in the proper way, send one hundred thousand of them to India. The preparation of the equipments of the soldiers, their arms and munitions of war, provisions and general disbursements for a long voyage, will give employment to a wide circle of mechanics and traders. Shipping rotting at the wharves will show signs of life at the prospect of a fair freight to the East; and labor is stimulated by getting away the ships, and giving stevedores and sailors something to do. All this to be paid for by England.

Americans are better soldiers than Hessians, Germans, or Swiss. An American is born a soldier. He commences in the cradle with a pop-gun. He shoots a woodcock on the wing at fourteen, and at twenty he is instructed to hit the squirrel in the eye. That story about Scott and the coon is no exaggeration.

America has a standing army of a million of soldiers.

West Point schools the officers; and every State, every city, every county, every township, boasts its volunteer regiments. England can make a sure contract in this country to have India conquered in four weeks after landing in Bengal, for a fair compensation.

America is a military nation; but being a modest, unassuming people, we seldom talk about our standing army.

England is not—never has been—and never will be.
Corporation laws forbid the firing of guns, and the
only sharp-shooters in the kingdom, out of the army,
are the poachers.   Where can the poor man learn to
shoot ?   Out of the British army, they never see a
fire-arm.   Alison says, England is not a military nation.   The people have no woodcocks or squirrels to
shoot.   The game laws were made for the aristocracy.
America has no game laws.   And throughout our
broad domain—from youth to manhood—you cannot
find a young American who does not own a Bible, a
grammar, and a gun.

Well, having dispatched a hundred thousand to
India, how are we to dispose of the rest ?

Americans are prone to exploring expeditions.   When
men have "nothing to do," and "nothing to wear,"
and a prospect of "nothing to eat," they are apt to
turn filibusters.   It will be the case next year.   Central America will be the grave of more Americans.
Walker having *run off* of it, will now *walk* over the
course.   He has not given up the Central American
race.   That land first, and then Cuba.   "There's the
rub."   Cuba we must and will have.   Cuba is only
alluvium washed from the Mississippi ; in fact all
those islands were once a part of our continent.
"What God has joined together let no man put

asunder." The Cubans wish to be Americans. The Americans desire more intimate relations with the Cubans. The pear is ripe and ready to fall. Buy it, or it will be plucked. Let the Government purchase it, and save the national honor. Hesitate, and the " Gem of the Antilles" will be stolen.

The Ostend Manifesto speaks the mind of the President, as well as of the people. The South wish it—the North will not object. Buy Cuba, and Kentucky, Maryland, Delaware, and most likely Virginia, become free States, and free labor will make the wilderness blossom as the rose. Southward the eclipse of slavery takes its way.

Let the Government buy it, and keep us honest. 'Tis wrong to so sorely tempt a filibustering people.

After hard currency has proved the galvanic battery to bring the nation back to its senses, we may require something more portable than specie. Draw for five hundred dollars in an Italian city, and the banker passes over to you a bag of silver that compels you to hire a cart to get it home. This is one of the evils of hard currency. Go into Austria, they give you paper that almost falls to pieces in your hand, and is good for nothing over the frontier. This is one of the evils of paper money.

America, having recovered from insolvency through the medium of hard currency, will require something more workable for the commerce of the country. Without committing myself to the project, I believe the nation will call for a *National Bank;* for the people will be so disgusted with some of the disclosures that will be made by the old banks (the *bona fide Schuylerisms*), that will be brought to light, that they will cry for *change* (small change).

Washington's National Bank, established 1791, expired 1811, succeeded. Then, there were eighty-eight State Banks.

Madison's National Bank, established 1816, expired 1836, also succeeded. Then, there were two hundred and forty-six State Banks. (Now, there are over fourteen hundred.)

But *Biddle's " United States Bank of Pennsylvania"* became a disgrace to the country ; and, because its connection with the National Bank was not well understood, the Government unjustly received a taint upon its credit that will militate against any new project of the kind.

There has been a good deal of talk about General Jackson's patriotism in removing the Deposits. I am a convert to the belief in human frailty, and for some time I have concluded that there is about as much humbug regarding great public acts, public sympathy, and Christian philanthropy, as in everything else.

With all proper respect to their respective memories, I think that "Old Hickory's" spite against old Biddle had more to do with the financial *coup d'état* than any other motive—at any rate, the Bank died a natural death when its charter matured, but not till then. And I see nothing in its funeral sermon forbidding another institution, carefully framed to suit the wants and improvements of the age.

I know it has been fashionable to abuse the National Bank. I think it will, also, shortly be fashionable to abuse the Banking institutions of the present time.

A National Bank would equalize exchanges. We should have then a currency that would take us from Saco to Sacramento, and every holder would feel that the bills were as good as gold. Passing our own domain, foreign nations, oftentimes, would be glad to accept such security. With such a credit the merchant could negotiate at Hakadadi, as well as at Patagonia. It has always been a Buncombe dodge to run down a Bank for the nation. "Too much power," "political agent," "prudence forbids the placing edge tools in the hands of party," and so on.

With proper respect for such arguments, I should say that therein lies the people's best security. If the party in power abused their trust, kick them out at the next election. The people certainly can watch one Bank better than fourteen hundred! We have now thirty-one kinds of paper. A sound national currency would be acceptable to all. The Suffolk Bank, of Boston, is a self-created institution, so far as Country Banks are concerned; and one or two of the New-York Banks take the same position here.

Let a Bank start in New-York with fifty or a hundred millions of capital, the directors would rule the country, all the solvent Banks would have an account there; those in bad odor would be thrown out, and they would fail.

A Bank of this kind could be managed far better by the Government than by such a corporation—we can trust the Government. If they do the country any great wrong, the administration must fall when their term is out. In a National Bank, in case of war, accident—anything to embarrass it, creditors would have no fear. The American Government will always pay. Temporary pressure may create delay, but principal and interest would eventually be paid.

The public lands, the national revenues, the public honor, would be under a guarantee to meet every obligation. The security would be national. The people of this country are Americans, national honor is their proudest right—"America first! America last! America all the time!" should be the heartfelt feeling of every true American. That sentiment must always secure the nation's credit.

What is the basis of such a Bank?

Return to the Cuban question. The President tried to buy it for $150,000,000. Try $200,000,000. Spain owes England and France, England and France are in a tight place just now in money matters. They would wink at a sale now, that at any other time might provoke discussion.

Give, if necessary, $200,000,000, payable fifty years hence, in installments every twenty-five years, making a six per cent. interest.

$200,000,000 at 6 per cent., = $12,000,000.

Under American management, the island could be made to produce $25,000,000 per annum, which would leave the Government a handsome sum in the Treasury, and, long before the debt came due, we should have earned more than enough to pay for half a dozen such islands.

The very soil is saccharine—Cuba can supply the world with sugar, and almost everything you wish to grow. Cuba is a garden land, and soon would pay for itself.

But what will Spain say to the long credit? Does

she want to cash it? There are few foreign capitalists but what would be glad to get such an investment in times like these, when European thrones are crackling under the smouldering fires of Revolution. But in this case, the trouble would be they couldn't get it—the American people wish it for themselves.

Two hundred millions of Government stock is just what we require for currency, (after hard money has restored the country to judgment.) Let that be the basis for a Banking system.

If a modified hard currency system requires any Government help, how easy it would be for the Sub-Treasury to issue certificates of deposit, ranging from ten dollars to a thousand. Deposit your gold with the Government, and take a receipt; that receipt is as good a currency as you require, until the new system is fairly under way. Congress will meet next month and the bill could be passed in an hour.

I simply throw out these hints. Let the statesmen think them over, and make the raw iron into workable *steel*, (that is a bad word.) Discussion must be provoked.

Another point: in connection with giving employment to the workmen, that will soon be making night hideous and day unsupportable.

They must be employed.

The American Government must adopt no picayune policy. Retrenchment in every quarter, but that which throws more labor upon the market. They must support, not depress it.

They must employ, not discharge workmen. The people must be taken care of. France gives them soup. Government improvements must go on. Stop building custom-houses, but nothing else. The last change in the tariff was like knocking out the first block in launching a ship—a touch or two more, another stroke of the hammer, and the splendid clipper ship, "Free Trade," Brother Jonathan, master, is in the market for a profitable charter. Stop building custom-houses, but let everything else go on. Government should avail itself of the material at the reduced prices, to employ at reduced rates the thousands who, next winter, will be in need of bread. This system of work should commence with the Government, extend to the State, the county, the city, and the town. Let each get out of the din of Buncombe politics, and strike into some practical plan to take care of the people, who will be begging for something to do, so that they can get something to eat.

Public buildings, avenues, streets, and roads need attention. Take New-York—some of the streets dis-

grace a civilized land. Outside of the Russian cities,
(where the sharp winter climate prevents improvement,)
I have never seen such filthy, irregular thoroughfares,
as those in this city. In some places, near the wharves,
I doubt whether you would get a colony of well-bred
hogs to settle there, the stench is so unhealthy.
A large number of men can be kept busy, and the
nation enriched by making wholesome reforms. Let
some broad- and practical measures be adopted to provide for the coming winter.

There is still another field for labor, larger than all—
a field that soon must be cultivated. California, as I have
before said, produces, in gold and silver, as much value
as one-third the entire cotton crop. The resources of
that State are astonishing, when you consider that ten
years ago the land was, comparatively, a wilderness.
Already, the Californians have sent some of the surplus crops to the Atlantic markets, and are producing
luxuries as well as necessities at their own doors.

The country prospers. Gold is pouring in upon us
by every mail. We have obtained from her during the
nine months of the present year, $35,262,243, against
$37,285,863 in 1856. The falling off of $2,023,620
may be regained the last quarter.

Thirty thousand majority have just voted to pay
their State obligations. I knew it would be so. Next

election, the vote will be unanimous. Americans would rather put their hands in their pockets, than see their State shirking its debt on some lawyer's quibble.

Our railways extend beyond the Mississippi. Another four thousand miles, and we are on the Pacific. Again, let the Government step out with a bold national plan to bind California to her sister States with a band of iron. It must be done, sooner or later. "Westward the star,", &c. California has now a position in the world. She is located in just the right place to assist in carrying out the destiny of these United States. 'Tis the high road to China and the East, and by the time the railway is completed, the lines of mail steamers are running to China, Formosa and Japan, some of the "Old Colonists," a part of the 100,000 volunteers who settled in the country, after the conquest of India, will desire to return to their Atlantic homes, by the way of the Pacific and the Rocky Mountains.

This road would furnish work for much of the surplus labor of 1858. New countries would be opened up; new life instilled into the country; new resources would be discovered, and we should have a due watch over the Benedict Arnold movements of Brigham Young. "The mountains shall be brought low, and the valleys raised up, and we shall make you a highway of nations."

Private enterprise built the Panama road, every pile of which rests on the corpse of an Irishman. If private enterprise has done all this, what may not Government accomplish in carrying out this grand project of joining the Atlantic and Pacific Oceans?—to employ the labor of the land, and to introduce new channels of commerce—new fields for American enterprize.

The project is worthy of our country. The Government can manage it by supporting individual enterprise. But some *quid nunc* is asking about the money. None is required until the road is built and earning something.

The laborers on the Western Railway by taking State scrip saved Massachusetts from repudiating. What applies to a State, applies to a nation.

No security is better than the United States Government. Buy the iron with scrip. Pay the contractors, the workmen, all hands, with scrip. Buy the sleepers, build the road, with the national signature. No matter if the Government does get swindled out of twenty millions by the contractors. That is nothing compared to the national gain. $150,000,000 builds the road. Make the scrip redeemable as may be arranged. This, added to the Cuban paper, gives $350,000,000—a sufficient bank capital for the wants of the times.

Let some sound financier enlarge upon these points. Discussion these times will bring out some wholesome ideas.

Why not have a congress of merchants, bankers, manufacturers, and farmers?

Pick out your men, your practical men; men who think in the morning and think at night; men who are always thinking, and instinctively too; and who, after reflection, act.

Let worth have the preference over wealth. Choose brains instead of dollars.

In ten days you can bring delegates from every State; and out of a picked assembly there must be some sound opinions.

Don't let it be like that disgraceful exhibition in Wall Street   Don't let it be like that puny affair in Boston; but let it be an assembly of clear-headed, large-brained, intelligent, practical men (who will repudiate nothing except " cut and dried " resolutions). Don't allow any man to enter the debate whose whole life has been devoted to isms. Argue about cause and effect, supply and demand, industry and honesty. Discuss the currency, and don't talk buncombe. Be practical. Admit lawyers, upon the ground that " common law " is only " common sense." Shut the door against politicians. They have no time to be useful; they all expect to be Presidents, and their time is occupied at the wires.

Let Boston and New-York men fight it out by argument in debate, not in letters that irritate without alleviating the disorder.

Mr. Appleton is out in another letter.

He asserts that the banks of New-York have caused the crisis. That history cannot produce another instance of such gross "ignorance" on the part of bank managers. That "circulation and deposits" are one and the same thing. That the suspension was "not the result of natural causes." That "no doubt there are cases in which individuals and banks have extended their credits to their own injury, but the present evil arises wholly from the sudden check or stoppage of the credits which the New-York banks had so freely given."

"The present evil," he says, "*is, not too much, but too little, credit !*"

These points have already been touched upon and replied to in this volume. I need not take them up again only to prove one thing; that, if Mr. Appleton's theory is the true one, our banking system is established on entirely a false basis. If he is right, the currency laws are all wrong. Fifty-five presidents of fifty-five banks never should have possessed the

power to make a nation bankrupt. That the banks
are too greedy, I do not deny. That they have
dealt in stock, all admit. That they have gone far
beyond their means, in inflating everything to unheard
of prices—discounting kites (in some cases so ingeni-
ously made that they thought them legitimate business
paper) on the ground that one half the proceeds should
remain on deposit, to furnish capital on which to base
another transaction of the same nature, in order to
meet dividends—on all which points I agree with Mr.
Appleton. But when he asserts and reasserts again,
that everything is sound at heart, he must pardon me
for not enjoying the same opinions.

The high-toned character which Nathan Appleton has
borne for over half a century, gives weight to his
judgment, and I trust he will not consider it disre-
spectful in me because I have made bold to differ
with him.

I am sure he will not blame me for presuming to
discuss the question with him.

Age before youth, always. Experience is a good
monitor.

Young men, profiting by the experience of the old,
will not be blamed for not being forty years of age.
Chatham once humbled Walpole on that very point.

It has long been a theory of mine that a man's parents solely are responsible for his *age*, his color and his nationality (therefore, why snub a man, when he has no control over those accidents of his life?)

New-York is a central point. Let no jealousy cause delay. The time has come for action. Why not take the "bull" by the horns and teach him how to destroy the "bear"?

There are many that believe that the issues of the State banks are unconstitutional. Certainly they are *since the suspension.* "Gold and silver" are the words in the national law.

Randolph, forty years ago, said a man might as well attack Gibraltar with a pocket pistol, as prosecute a bank, whether legal or illegal. A congress of practical men will suggest reforms. 'Tis time to introduce them.

The practical opinions of the practical men of the country would be of great service to a theoretical administration. Washington is lighted by "Buncombe" gas. Would not daylight be cheaper?"

Party despotism should give way to Republican right. The giant arm of partizan spoil should be broken. Nicholas's conversation with Buchanan was most instructive. Why would it not be well to introduce, if possible, a little more dignity into the management of public affairs? The press of this country think (?) they rule it with a rod of iron. Let them raise the cry of "Government reform, state reform, city reform, and township reform!" 'Tis a crying shame to see armed men parading the streets of Baltimore. 'Tis a pitiful sight to see a great nation at sea without a compass: the compass of right, of virtue, and of truth. 'Tis disgraceful to keep open that Kansas sore. Let us have some practical legislation. Bury buncombe and dig up our Federal nationality. The North and the South must ever be friends; the East and West are brothers. Disunionists may sneer, but nevertheless 'tis true; we all belong to the same family—the family of Washington.

Let us forget the little animosities of partizan feuds. During my lifetime the country has been kept agitated by an *ISM*—a quarter of a century of pro-and-anti talk; twenty-five years of loathsome sectional vituperation.

For twenty-five years the North and the South have been dueling. The principals are all living; the seconds ought to be shot.

Nothing disgusts me so much as the Exeter Hall cant in Sunderland House. England had better let this country manage its own business. 'Tis sometime since we were twenty-one years of age.—

Let her look at home, and tell me which is the
worst, the slavery of the mind or the slavery of the
body.

Many an American has had these lines of Campbell
hissed in his ear:

> United States! your banner bears
> Two emblems—one of fame!
>   Alas—the other that it wears,
> Reminds us of your shame!
>
>   The white man's liberty in types
> Stands blazoned by your stars;
>   But what's the meaning of your stripes?
> Unless your negro's scars!

—and of late years there is many an Englishman
who will remember Mr. Lunt's retort:

> England! whence came that meteor hue
> That tints your flow of meteor light?
>   The streaming red, the deeper blue,
> Crossed by the moonbeams pearly white?
>
>   The *blood* and *bruise*—the blue and red—
> Let India's groaning millions speak;
>   The white, it tells the color fled,
> From starving Erin's pallid cheek.

Go into the manufacturing districts, and then come
over among the Southern planters. Speak plainly;
take facts—observe both classes—and decide which is

the happier of the two. The Honorable Miss Murray says, the slave.

Remember that, (like the fabled blood of Rizzio in Holyrood Palace,) slavery was not our own creation The stain was made by other hands. Under the primogeniture laws of England, slavery was one of the vices which we inherited from the mother land, when we gave a "Shriek for Freedom" in 1776. Our virtues were our own. 'Twas a long time before England abolished the traffic; not until her merchants made themselves wealthy in the slave trade,— and then, with a Wilberforcian horror, she discovers the national sin.

The times are changing. May not anti-slavery England again open up the slave trade? France commenced it last year. The French Government, through the Minister of Foreign Affairs, signed a contract, March 13th, with MM. Régis, to transport 5,000 coolies to Guadaloupe, and 5,000 to Martinique, in 800-ton steamers, for $100 each. Terms, 10 years labor at $2 50 per month, deducting forty cents for passage.

England, I fancy, would like to have, about this time, that one hundred millions of dollars which she paid away to make the garden of her West Indian possessions a barren desert.

Not contented with planting the evil in our soil, she resorts to every possible measure to extend it. Cotton has been paid for on the American plantation with British money—shipped (in former days) in British ships—sent to a British port—carried over a British rail—manufactured in a British factory—sent back again to America—where, after paying a high duty, fabrics formed of our own staple are sold to us at prices lower than we can manufacture ourselves. Anti-slavery England, then, is the real slave upholder. Why was this? Steam and credit. The introduction of the steam-engine reduced labor to a few pence per diem, and credit lowered money to two per cent. per annum. Hence, America has never been able to compete with England. *But now the times are changing.*

Stand from under. The "inverted pyramid" of artificial credit is about tumbling over, on the national and individual debts of Europe. No! England shows as little judgment as genuine philanthropy, in continually meddling with our "Peculiar Institution." Next winter the slaves of the South will be much better fed than the free operatives of Manchester.

England had but 300,000 bales of cotton on hand on the arrival of the last mail; not thirty thousand bales are on the ocean. The planters will not sell (till the price gets down to six cents). Let them keep it back two months longer, and they will cause the most terrible Revolution that England has ever seen. Running at full speed, she has only about six weeks consumption. Retain the cotton, and England trembles as with the palsy. Ten years have hardly gone since two hundred thousand special constables in London were sworn in to keep the peace. Louis Napoleon was one of them. And yet, a few years later, the Queen of England gazed upon the tomb of the banished Bonaparte at Paris, while his Imperial nephew was standing by her side; her special police-man was Emperor of France! To-day that Emperor lives in a glass house.

The domestic peace of England hangs upon our cotton; our cotton remains in the Southern presses, and ships are ready to receive it, but where are the shippers?

Panics are contagious; England has not been vaccin-ated; what is varioloid with us will be the real disease with her. Each European mail will bring startling intelligence from the Old World. THE TIMES ARE CHANGING.

The financial crisis gives birth to the political Rev-olution; Frost is already advocating his Chartist meet-ings; Jones is writing his Reform speeches; Gerald

Massey is preparing his bonfire poems; Ireland is training for the prize fight; yet England sleeps on her National Debt of four thousand millions of dollars as unconscious of the approaching danger as an unborn babe. The people wish to square off the debt and stop the taxes.*

---

* "We can inform Jonathan what are the inevitable consequences of being too fond of glory:—TAXES upon every article which enters into the mouth, or covers the back, or is placed under the foot—taxes upon everything which it is pleasant to see, hear, feel, smell, or taste—taxes upon warmth, light, and locomotion—taxes on everything on earth, and the waters under the earth—on everything that comes from abroad, or is grown at home—taxes on the raw material—taxes on every fresh value that is added to it by the industry of man—taxes on the sauce which pampers man's appetite, and the drug that restores him to health—on the ermine which decorates the judge, and the rope which hangs the criminal—on the poor man's salt and the rich man's spice—on the brass nails of the coffin and the ribbons of the bride—at bed or board, couchant or levant, we must pay. The school-boy whips his taxed top—the beardless youth manages his taxed horse, with a taxed bridle, on a taxed road:—and the dying Englishman, pouring his medicine, which has paid 7 per cent., into a spoon that has paid 15 per cent., flings himself back upon his chintz bed, which has paid 22 per cent., and expires in the arms of an apothecary who has paid a license of a hundred pounds for the privilege of putting him to death. His whole property is then immediately taxed from 2 to 10 per cent. Besides the probate, large fees are demanded for burying him in the chancel; his virtues are handed down to posterity on taxed marble; and he is then gathered to his fathers, to be taxed no more. In addition to all this, the habit of dealing

Pardon me for having run away from the text. The
pen will sometimes play the truant.   When floating
for a long time on an unknown sea, the prudent navigator takes his observation.   That sea is America;
Congress the navigator.

A month hence, and the capitol is full. Now, as
the everlasting discussion of negro slavery has occupied our statesmen, our press, our politicians, for so
many years, without accomplishing anything but to
extend it, I would suggest, as an experiment, a little
practical legislation on our national laws, our foreign
relations, our internal improvements, our currency, and
all subjects of vital import to the American people.
We begin to miss those great minds of the last generation.

> "Lo! Carolina mourns her steadfast pine,
>   Which, like a mainmast, towered above the realm;
> And Ashland hears no more that voice divine,
>   From out the branches of her forest elm!

with large sums will make the government avaricious and profuse
and the system itself will infallibly generate the base vermin of spies
and informers, and a still more pestilent race of political tools and retainers of the meanest and most odious description; while the prodigi-
ous patronage which the collecting of this splendid revenue will throw
into the hands of government, will invest it with so vast an influence
and hold out such means and temptations to corruption, as all the
virtue and public spirit, even of republicans, will be unable to resist."
                    [SYDNEY SMITH.—*Edinburgh Review*, 1820.

And Marshfield's giant oak, whose stormy brow
  Has ofttimes turned the ocean tempest from the West,
Lies on the shore he guarded long,
  And now our startled eagle knows not where to rest."

Since my remembrance, this country has been agitated by legislating for the "blacks." The whites have been neglected. There are about three millions of the one and twenty-five millions of the other. Now, while I have the best possible feeling toward the "blacks," I have also the highest respect for the whites; and as twenty-five millions of the latter have been requested to stand aside, so that the three millions of the former might be attended to, I am an advocate now for a change in our Congressional policy.

Leave the "blacks" alone for the next ten years, and take care of the "whites." The whites deserve more attention than Congress has devoted to them, and having legislated for the blacks for so long a time, they have at least the democratic right of the majority to protest against anything more being done for so inconsiderable a minority in numbers, to say nothing for the question of equality,—at least for some few years.

There has been enough talk on the question to fill the British Museum with reading matter; yet, after all, no one has discovered any invention to bleach a black man white. Next winter, the slaves of the South will be sheltered, clothed, and fed, while multitudes of free-born men are pale with want, demanding labor to purchase bread.

In such times as these, the futile discussion of the slave question had better be thrown under the table, not to be taken up again 'till Congress has legislated on some of the practical questions of the day. The whites demand a hearing.

As the times are changing everywhere, why not give up for a while the continual bickerings on a subject that cannot be touched without provoking unpleasant reflections. Let us be Americans—not Northerners or Southerners—but simply Americans. Union should be the last thought as we sleep—the first when we wake. Let us ever pray for—

> "A *union* of lakes, a *union* of lands,
> A *union* of States, none can sever;
> A *union* of hearts, a *union* of hands,
> And the flag of our *Union* forever
> And ever!
> The flag of our *Union* forever!"

A few months more, and the strong arm of military power may be required to preserve order.

Let us maintain our national rank. We have laws, they must be obeyed. We have laws, but not always justice.

Out of evil good may come—order spring forth from

chaos. California, at one time, was full of evil spirits. The law was ineffectual; then the people rose up in their might, and said, "Let there be justice," and there was justice; and now where can you find a place more orderly and quiet than San Francisco?

There will be no necessity for such measures here. England feeds the poor; France gives them soup. The people are not allowed to starve in Europe, in Asia, or in Africa; nor will they be in America.

Government will do what it can. But when men meet in masses in public squares, and talk sedition, rapine, violence, demand money, (not work and bread,) they must take care that they do nothing more than talk.

In 1837, "Bread, meat, rent and fuel," were on the banners, and "Down with the prices."

In 1857, "Work!"—"*Arbeit!*" are the words on the flag.

Let them break the law—let them step beyond the line of civil avthority—and military power will clear the streets with grape. George the Fourth gave tone to the law—Napoleon knows well its meaning—and the American volunteer militiaman will shoot down his own brother, if that brother dares to place himself beyond the law of right, of equality, or of justice.

Herein lies the strength of the American Republic.

OUTLINE

OF A

GRAND FINANCIAL DRAMA.

CANTO I.

"I had a dream which was not all a dream."

PLACE : A PROSPEROUS COUNTRY.

Time : Indian Summer.   *Hour :* Midnight.

Coming storm.   Whirlwind.

Houses unroofed.   "Doors unlocked."

Devil on two sticks

Discovers some people in other people's beds.   Imp Number One
"chased"—Number Two, *not.*

Offered bribe to keep dark—Accepts, and blabs.

Magazine—Torch.

Falling houses.

CANTO II.

"A change came o er the spirit of my dream."

A COLONY OF CARRION KITES.

History.

Kite Number One proposes to Kite Number Two.

Marriage.   Children.   Old Kites feed Young Kites.

Shows them how to use their *Bills*, and *lends* them their **first**
Notes.

Old Kite fails. O. L. & T. Co.

Western Kites flock in.

Arrival of Credits. Cash balances absorbed.

Collection paper in other Kites' nests.

Neighboring Kites sitting on bad eggs.

Foreign Kites eyes—not open.

Some Home Kites Blind.

Old Kite loses tail feathers.

Young Kite smells rat.

*   *   *

1837, wind raised Kite—1857, Kite raised wind.

Kites fly abroad.

Crows arrive.

Croaks.

Rats.

No hole

*

———

CANTO III.

" A change came o'er the spirit of my dream."

RAILROAD.

Bonds—England.

President makes *tracks*—Directors make *Notes*.

Dividends. Stocks rise.

Board short.

Bridge falls. Train off the Track.

Receiver appointed.

Gratuitous offers to ride Directors on their own *rail.*

CANTO IV.

"A change came o'er the spirit of my dream."

BROADWAY.

Fast Merchant in fast Warehouse desires fast Clerk to keep fast accounts. Advertises.

Elegant man appears.

Good morning. Apply for —— ?—Yes.

Keep horse ?—Yes.

Fast Horse ?—Yes.

House ?—Yes.

Furnished ?—Yes.

Married ?—No.

Fond of female society ?—Yes.

Billiard table ?—Yes.

Diamond ring ?—Yes.

All paid for ?—Yes.

All right—you'll do.

(*Aside to partner*—Has all these things now—good man—won't get them out of us.)

———

CANTO V.

"A change came o'er the spirit of my dream."

GROCERY STORE.

Pious Deacon.

John, watered rum ?—Yes, sir.

Wet Tobacco ?—Yes, sir

Sanded Sugar ?—Yes, sir.

Mixed Coffee ?—Yes, sir.

Oak leaves in Tea ?—Yes, sir.

Charged Cheese ?—Yes, sir.

Charge again before forget it, and come to prayers.

("Old !")

CANTO VI.

More change.

LAWYER'S OFFICE.

Teller Bank, excited.

One hundred and fifty thousand *out*.

Directors informed ?—No.

Take as much more—Position to compromise.

Advice follows.

Compromises for *seventy-five* thousand,

and

Travels on Continent !

CANTO VII.

"*A change came o'er the spirit of my dream.*"

THREAD-NEEDLE STREET—CHESS-BOARD.

Members Exchequer—Exchange Stock on "Stock Exchange."

Bishop behind Queen.

Bustle in Court—Castles in air—Parrus in demand.

Knight approaching—Fair *Exchange* no robbery.

John Bull checkmated.

CANTO VIII.

Dream still changing.

CRICKET MATCH.

All the World against England.
Bank holds stakes.
Nearly bowled out.
"*Small change.*"

TEN PINS.

Head Pin—Bonaparte.
Crisis—First Ball.
Ten strike.
All down.

    •   *   •

A NEW GAME.

CANTO IX.

"*A change came o'er the spirit of my dream.*"

OLD BUNCOMBE—LITERARY CLUB.

Johnson, Speaker.

Goldsmith, review "Rasselas"—I'll review "Traveller."
Garrick, bring "Irene" on stage—speak of you in "Rambler."
Sir Joshua Reynolds, paint my portrait for Town Hall—word for
you in "Spectator."
Bozzy, follow me through Scotland—write—question—answer—go
down to posterity together.
Et cetera.

NEW BUNCOMBE—HOW TO MAKE A PRESIDENT.

Say I'm clever fellow, I'll say you are.

I'll tell everybody you are rich, you tell everybody I am.

Freemasonry—Mum's the word.

"Little Giant."

Kansas.

Talk—Write.

Know "no North, no South, no East, no West."

Make your game.

Choose players.

Four for *Whist*.

Wires.

———

CARDS.

Clubs trumps—*Diamonds* lead.

Hearts lose—*Spades* win.

No *honors!*

———

CANTO X.

(Can—Canto—Canton.)

"A change came o'er the spirit of my dream."

BOOK STORE.—DERBY AND JACKSON'S.

"*Young America in Wall-Street.*"

Observations—Old America, "read it?" Yes.

"Bosh!" Young America, (quietly,) "Good."

Cries—"Put him out." "Gammon." "Gas." "Humbug."

"High-fa-lu-tin." "Lunatic Asylum."

Young America, smiles and passes on.

CANTO XI.

FINANCIAL SERMON.

" He that giveth to the poor, lendeth unto the Lord."

" There's your security:
Down with your dust."—*Dean Swift.*

———

Dream *burst.*

———

Change all gone.

[Printer's boy gives me another hour—another thought or two—another *salmagundian* page—and then *Buon giorno !*]

In after years Young America will decline a crisis, under the credit system, by the rule of three.

> 1851–2–3 — Positive, *Boil !*
> 1854–5–6 — Comparative, *Boiler !*
> 1857–8–9 — Superlative, *Burst !*

Ancient financiers understood the availability of hard currency.

Absalom paid hard cash for Ephon.

Solomon had to fork over silver to finish the temple.

Lycurgus, not considering gold and silver hard enough, made the Spartans use iron.

Chinese " cash" is made of the same material.

Pericles ostracised Cymon for taking a cash bribe. How many members of Congress resigned last session for a similar " indiscretion ?"

Cincinnatus, after he refused the consulship and went to farming, sold his cabbages for the hardest kind of currency. Who would refuse a consulship now ?

Solon's name saved Cyrus from burning Crœsus at the stake, says history. I think, however, it was a question of hard cash.

Demosthenes' virtue was not equal to refusing a " Tip" in hard cash.

Although Euclid gave more attention to logic than morals, he never closed his hand against a little hard cash.

Alfred divided the twenty-four hours into three parts : first, to God; second, to public affairs; third to rest and refreshment.

Alfred's descendants have ᜴devoted their whole time to making money—but not hard cash.

The Bank of Venice, established in 1171, lived six hundred years on a hard cash principle.

Columbus discovered a world, and was sent home in chains!

Scott conquered a nation, and was court-martialed! In both cases, 'twas a question of hard cash.

Cardinal Woolsey's *plate* was only so much hard cash.

Cardinal Wiseman can become a Pope—if he has a sufficient pile of hard cash.

Cromwell's soldiers refused to break into the "star chamber" till they got the hard cash.

John Milton received for the "Paradise Lost" but *seventy-five dollars*, hard cash!

The Bank of Amsterdam, established in 1609, lived till 1795 on a hard cash system. The Bank of Hamburg never has adopted any other.

Chatterton committed the most startling forgery the world ever saw when but seventeen, and then committed suicide—all for a little hard cash.

Surajah-ul-Dowlah marched into Calcutta and murdered the European community, a hundred years ago, to get a little hard cash.

Nena Sahib may be passing over the same road now for a similar purpose.

When Franklin arrived in Philadelphia, with a penny roll, he had *one dollar* in hard cash in his pocket.

Paganini gained by music and lost by gaming several fortunes in hard cash.

When Tom Paine wrote the "Decline and Fall of the System of Finance in England," he advocated hard cash.

Garrick stepped out of a wine-cellar on to the stage in order to make a little more hard cash.

When the natives of Bombay presented Sir Charles Forbes with that magnificent service of plate, it simply proved that in India there was plenty of hard cash.

England broke down the "continental system" of Napoleon at Waterloo through the agency of hard cash abroad, manufactured out of credit at home.

Menschikoff rose from a peasant to a prince by properly understanding the system of hard cash.

Lafitte, the great French banker, who made Louis

Philippe king, might have kept on his feet by the aid of a little hard cash.

But why continue the examples? Some "paper man" will make as good an argument. Nevertheless, money is money, and paper is paper, and always will be, so long as a bargain is like a baby.

Gold stands fire and smoke. Paper is destroyed by the one, and blackened by the other.

Money goes in a circle—from hand to hand—from State to State—from nation to nation; and like the "boomerang" returns again from whence it started. China and India may break the circle for a while, but eventually the money will return. 'Tis not so with paper, a little while, and it wears itself away.

Drop a globule of quicksilver on the table, and it flies into a thousand pieces. But you may gather it all together again. So it is with genuine money.

Paper, when torn, is scattered wherever the wind listeth.

Hard currency cannot be destroyed. You cannot drink it, you cannot eat it. The natural laws of supply and demand send it away and bring it back.

The crisis has only blown away the cobwebs. All the money that was in the country remains here still.

The fabulous fortunes of last year were never made. 'Twas all imagination—air castles—not real brick and mortar. *The money never existed.* Humbug was the foundation, humbug was the first floor, and humbug finished the roof. The ground—the real money—is still a living thing. Years hence, reflecting men will endorse the same opinions.

Kites are not money. Credit is not money. Dombey failed to explain it to Paul. (Toots, when the commercial man at Brighton asked him what he expected England would do with the large quantities of the "raw material" then being received from various parts of the world, replied that he thought she would "*eat it.*")

Gold arrives from England, and the boxes, unpacked, return in the same steamer. More kites?

Letters of deposit from English banks arrive by the same conveyance. We, in our innocence, receive these fictitious values—these well arranged kites—as coined gold! Hedging is what may be called cheating fair—the favorite against the field. "Win this race and you shall have a thousand pounds," said the noble earl. "I will, although I have been offered two thousand not to win," replied the jockey. The immense fortunes in this country were never made. Take sugar; now it goes up, up, up! and now it goes down, down, down!

Above a certain point, consumption falls away. You may raise prices on the Stock Exchange to any margin by continually buying. Commence to sell, and the turn is equally rapid.

All bad news is generally discounted, so far as the public are concerned. The press gets the first intelligence; "a friend" is informed; he buys or sells— tells his friend—who tells another, and their operations has moved the market up or down; so that, when the public rush in, they are just in time to be plucked. What broker will deny the charge? What outsider ever came away from the gaming-table a winner? The race is generally decided before the horses run. The lottery prize (in some cases?) is arranged in advance. The story of the Bottle Imp illustrates the stock operation. So long as the holder of the bottle could sell, he was safe. It was passed rapidly from hand to hand, but Satan caught the hindmost. Some man must be the loser. There is a "Peter Funk and stool pigeon" in every trade— "a skeleton (crinoline?) in every house."

Hard currency will assist the nation in starting afresh. Credit is what Judge Daly would call a "necessary evil;" and the way to get it, said Colonne, is to live extravagantly. It creates—it destroys. It dies a natural death, and is born again.

But the *Fuller reflections* of the late editor of the *Mirror*, may be more acceptable than mine. Hear him—

"Paper *representatives* of money have been mistaken for *property ;* and the whole world of bankers, merchants, shopkeepers, and manufacturers, under the fatal illusions of the credit system, have been ' like little wanton boys swimming on bladders.' Now the bubbles burst ; there is a universal sinking ; the day of settlement and of 'judgment' has come. The smiling wanton, seducing, bedecked and bedezined siren, Credit, wrings her white hands and tears her golden hair.

> " ' Where will this end ? Ye powers of good ! '
>   She weeping cries forever.
>   A voice replies from out the flood,
>   ' Forever—and forever ! ' "

Exaggeration is the fashion—full steam everywhere. English agents force importers to buy—importers force jobbers—jobbers employ drummers to stick western merchants—western merchants buy land and stick them all.

It has been an India-rubber system. Who has forgotten the ten-inch India rubber pantaloons worn with straps ? One strap gives way. Imagine the appearance and sensations of the owner in a crowded street. Only one strap has broken in the crisis.

Bad times make bad men; or rather, good times make them bad, and bad times expose them.

Then both straps are cut.

The London *Globe* announced the other day, under the head of "Fashionable Departures," the names of Paul, Strahan, Bates, Robson, Agar, Tester, Saward and Redpath, all passengers on board the "Nile" convict-ship. (*Punch*, funny fellow, denied it.)

If 1855 and 1856 were so prolific of scamps, what may we expect of 1857 and 1858?

The beauty of the patent hen-scratching machine is in permitting the astonished fowl to quietly scratch herself out of the garden. The "panic detector" is equally effectual in exposing the dishonest servant. The balance sheet of some of the banks will prove a curiosity, when the books are opened. Look at the "Island City." Where's Alibone? where's Clark?

Even Condorcet never could have explained the "integral calculations" of the "Ohio Life and Trust Company." To use the cashier's words, the acounts are "unreliable for any purpose whatever—either to show its debts or credits!" Is this the only company similarly situated?

England, America, and the World are hard up for hard cash. Everybody is "running" everywhere.

An explosion in America must occasion an explosion in England.

Every ten years the grand crisis comes round. The intermediate panics are ripples before the maelstrom. You may go back two centuries if you like.

Child got up the first bank in 1667.

Extravagance of Courts and Dutch invasion caused a run, the first ten-year crisis stampede.

The arbitrary closing of the Exchequer ruined the bankers, five years later.

The National Bank of 1683 broke down, but got under way again in 1694. The Darien and New River Companies were born about same time.

Macaulay gives a graphic account of the suspension when it was only twelve months old. This was the "clipper" coinage age. The Branch project fell through. Hoare and Child took advantage of the Pretender's threatened invasion to run the bank, but a twenty per cent. call upon shareholders saved them. (The Illinois Central only asked for ten.)

The mob of 1709 made a rush for the gold, as the Bowery Boys, in 1837, did for the flour.

The Queen's illness caused another run in 1713, but the moment the Queen got better the bank got well. When the Queen died next year, the bank was taken suddenly ill—only another run.

When George the First rode into power on the waves of rebellion, he only paid six per cent. for interest. Law had just left Scotland for France. His scheme was born, lived and died, in two years time.

This absurd speculation, and the "South Sea Bubble," so well described by Anderson, Smollet, and Mackay, I have touched on in previous pages.

The Pretender was always keeping the Bank Directors in a "coniption." In 1722, the Old Lady was again crowded. Ten years later, that huge pile of uncouth, one-story, square-topped mass of stone was erected, in Threadneedle street, and the founder of the Bank, William the Third, was honored by a statue.

The "sixpenny" dodge of 1745 saved the depositors from breaking the bank. Agents of the bank monopolized all the time of the tellers in receiving sixpences, which they returned by the back door. (What will the directors do this time?)

The panic of 1772 failed a host of bankers, but their entire liabilities would not pay for our annual consumption of European "nothingness."

Lord George Gordon's Protestant riot attempted to relieve the vaults of their bullion, in 1780; this accounts for the soldiers which you see there on guard. Who didn't fail in 1793? 1797 has been discussed before; so has 1814, when the Stock Exchange falsely reported the fall of Bonaparte.

Four years after, five thousand bankruptcies were reported. The run of 1832 rose out of the Reform Bill, and the community were disgusted when they learned how extensively the directors had feathered their nests in 1836. When the forgeries on Continental bankers (using Glynn, Mills & Co.'s name,) were exposed, the London *Times* won laurels; yet they declined to receive a penny, and gave it all to charities. Some*times*, the *Times* is far ahead of the *times*—again, it is *west*-sou'-*west*, half-*west*, Captain *West*.

The Exchequer Bill forgeries of 1841, amounted to some $5,000,000. We shall see something more extensive than that by-and-by.

Commence in 1667 with the first crisis, and end with 1867, when, if history don't lie, we shall have another. Every ten years—this gives twenty panics in all.

Now, I argue that the panic of 1857, in magnitude, will swallow up every other panic—the entire nineteen that have taken place since the establishment of old Childs' Bank—and yet Mr. Appleton thinks there is no serious cause for the crisis but the *sugar speculation!* So do the City Fathers of New-York. Let me introduce a word here in their behalf.

The report of the Financial Committee on the Mayor's message should be framed.

Oh! ye " Bunsbys !" Ye City Fathers ! What reflection ! What wisdom !

I would argue with you, but fear from the tenor of your remarks that you will insist that the " Horse is eighteen feet high." I would argue with you, but cannot reason with your Johnsonian logic, that " He who drives fat oxen must himself be fat."

" In 1837," you say, " the whole country was impoverished."

" That then the South was bankrupt."

" That our foreign debt is less to-day than at that time !"

" That the immense surplus productions from the harvest of the North—*hitherto unknown ?*—will pay all our Northern debts."

Examine closely these points. Each reader of the report has already answered them, proving how slight the fabric upon which their argument is based.

They say that " the gold and silver production has averaged $150,000,000 a year for the last *eleven years !*"

Have the City Fathers forgotten that California only commenced to open her vaults (in quantity) in 1849 ? *Eight* years ago, instead of *eleven !*

Have the members of the Financial Committee also forgotten that Australia commenced her gold export in 1851? *Six* years ago, instead of *eleven!*

Why exaggerate? It weakens—never strengthens—argument.

"The suspension of our banks is a most *fortunate circumstance;* and we hope they will not resume till they are beyond the necessity of another suspension!"

Mirabile dictu! Why, if *one* suspension is *fortunate*, another would be *more furtunate*, according to their reasoning.

> "If a man who oysters *cries*
> *Cries* not when his father dies,
> 'Tis a sign that he had rather
> Have an óyster than his father!"

Again:—" Our indebtedness amounts to little.

"Railroads comprise it. Now confine it to themselves, *in the hands of their creditors*, and nearly all of our debt is '*wiped out!*' "

Are the City Fathers aware that our railways are interwoven with almost every interest in the country? Is it not "so nominated in the bond?"

Listen again to "Bunsby."

" Another erroneous idea is, that luxurious living, extravagant dressing, splendid turn-outs, and fine horses, are the causes of distress to a nation!"

Have the City Fathers forgotten the parable of the prodigal son?

The money expended never existed.   The bursting of the bubble proves it.

They say that "the crisis is simply a panic."   Twelve months later let them make another report.

They say that the distress is "temporary."   So was the Japanese treaty.

They speak of labor in 1837.

Are they aware that all these Park-brawling people (some three millions) were not in this country at that time?

Our City Fathers—like our city merchants and city bankers—are dwelling in the past.   How many more times must I ask them to drop that crisis, and take up this?   They would make in the barn door a large hole for the old hen and small holes for the young chickens, and then make other holes for them to come out again!   They would put the candle to bed and blow themselves out!   They would place the clock in the cradle, and wind the baby up!   They dwell so much in the past, it makes them absent-minded.

The fitful improvements in the money market—like the fire-fly on a summer eve—only makes the night the darker.   A year hence the City Fathers should refer to the opinions which they have published to-day. THE TIMES ARE CHANGING.

Kamehameha IV. was taught sparring by Yankee Sullivan, and a missionary was invited to see fair play.

Seventy-four thousand children were mutilated not long ago because the Sultan of Turkey wished to give *eclat* to the circumcision of his child.

Brady has thrown Daguerre in the shade; steam has shot past canvas.

The stage coach is forgotten in the railway car.

The Bank of England may slide into the Thames in company with the " Great Eastern."

We are living in the age of telegraphs. We walk, we eat, we drink, we sleep by steam. High pressure everywhere—except in the financial reports of the City Fathers.

Thom's colossal statue of Washington in the Park, which for so long a time has been severely staring at the City Hall, with face of stately dignity, (?) has just been knocked down for two hundred dollars, to satisfy a five hundred dollar mortgage. The great Washington —going—going—gone—for only two hundred dollars! What then can be the position of the merchant palaces and the fancy farms? Are they, too, mortgaged? Are we not entering an "interval of indefinite duration," rather than "a mere temporary pressure?"

In 1825, one-pound notes saved the Bank of England from suspending.

In 1847, Russell's letter, (which amounted to about the same thing,) prevented a stoppage.

What will be done the next time? A Palmerston letter? One pound notes again?

Perhaps not. THE TIMES ARE CHANGING.

England is a bundle of hay, and all the asses in the world are tugging at it—(wrote Byron).

The Bank of England assisted the Bank of France in 1847; but when everything is expanded as it is now, if they go to kiting again, they will kite themselves ashore. The Bank of England dare not let the leading houses fall; they are too deeply involved. Gurney gave the directors one hour to decide, in 1847. "Assist me," said he, " or I put up my shutters."

Littledale, of Liverpool, was equally decided.

Lombard, Broad, and Threadneedle Streets, must hang upon the Old Lady. A strong swimmer can carry his wife, and perhaps save his children; but when cousins, uncles and aunts, friends and acquaintances catch hold upon him, down he sinks. The Bank can stand much, but not everything.

" Plenty of ships, and plenty of houses; the best security. Why not draw?" said Mr. W. to Mr. B., in 1837. " True," replied Mr. B. to Mr. W., " but as ships and houses won't meet our acceptances, we, therefore, endure our previous instructions."

India is a bad customer. The whole system is rotten. Piracy, mutiny, and crime. Cimmerian darkness couldn't have been worse. Famine in wheat and rice stares the natives in the face, and rotting potatoes are already making the Irishman speak with a modified brogue.

"*Be assured that this is not a sudden temporary danger, to be repelled by sudden temporary exertion. What at first was a mutiny, has become a Revolution.* Be assured that the military institutions of this country, managed as they now are, are insufficient permanently to supply the number of men required to reconquer what we have lost, and to hold our empire hereafter in security." These words were written by Lord Ellenborough, October 16, just three weeks ago, and the noble Earl is one of the cleverest men in England, and understands Indian affairs better than any man in it, not excepting Lord Dalhousie.

Observe another point in his able letter to the Winchcomb Agricultural Association :—

"*Do you imagine that the great military powers of Europe, always prepared for war, offended by our pride, resentful of our former victories, and coveting our present wealth, would long permit us to enjoy in peace the luxuries we cling to, and the dreams of irresistible strength in which we fatuitously indulge ?*"

The Indian Company have three armies and three Presidencies to manage, besides two outside enemies—the climate and the roads.

" I have two officers that can be depended upon," said Nicholas, during the Crimean war—" General *Janvier* and General *Février.*"

But the former proved a traitor. In the month of January, the Emperor of Russia was placed in the tomb of Peter and of Catherine.

I saw his room at the palace, just as he had left it—bed, clothes, military desk, untouched. No ostentation, no extravagance, *no Fifth Avenue luxury ;* everything as plain as a peasant's habitation.

India is a bad customer. Many expect more favorable news by the coming mail. I hope it may be so.

Delhi may fall, but the effect will disappoint the well-wishers of India. Let the army rescue the Europeans in small stations, who tremble for their fold ; and, when the force is strong enough, attack Delhi, and march in a body through the Sepoy camps—but not before. Take it now, and the mutineers rush out by the Jumna and scatter throughout the land, rushing on such places as Lucknow, Agra, &c. The Sepoys are fighting for life. A highwayman, in desperation, may sometimes kill a dozen policemen. One regiment is nothing—a dozen will make another impression. Remember the Indian's silent example of concentration of forces. The single stick he snapped in twain—the bunch could not be broken. The fall of Delhi would only be the first chapter in the war; the last—the fall of India, without American assistance.

> "Look to the East, where Ganges' swarthy race
> Shall shake your tyrant empire to its base;
> Lo! there Rebellion rears her ghastly head,
> And glares the Nemesis of native dead;
> 'Till Indus rolls a purpureal flood,
> And claims his long arrear of Northern blood."

What would Byron have said when listening to the tragedy of Cawnpore?

England never discounts danger, although the Stock Exchange generally (not this time) anticipates bad news. A lion well represents the national character of the English people. They are a nation of braves. Hence, they are not aroused by minor events. Having lived and moved under a flag of peace for forty years, they couldn't imagine such a thing as war with Russia. When Baron Brunow left London, up went the funds.

Like the Ashburton Treaty, the miserable affair at Naples, they thought as then that the Pen would prove more powerful than the Sword.

Arbitration failed. Then came *battles*, and their usual companions, *loans ;* but not till the Income Tax was doubled, and the English people realize that England was really at war with Russia.

What did they care about the Holy Places?

The Crimean war taking place just after the Californian and Australian gold discoveries, upset the calculations of Commerce, confused all kinds of Trade—false entries, false shipments, false business had to be made, to keep up fictitious values.

The merchant bought the purse with his last shilling. The bottom dropped out of the tub. The credit system was worked down to the last penny. The house was too heavy for the foundation. The ship was crank. Like the nude man trying to hold up the big clock under Tiffany's, the weight was beyond his strength. Who wonders that his legs were bent?

The candle was not only lighted at both ends, but was blazing in the middle. The warehouses were too grand—like their owners, there was an upper story to let.

England must square up and commence again :

Europe must balance the books :

Asia must open a Bank and a counting-house, or Saxon bankers and Saxon merchants will do it for her :

America must go to work once more :—

These are some of the points for contemplation.

Buy Cuba, or it will be stolen. " America should do with Cuba what Russia will do with Constantinople— take it, and ask permission afterwards," was a remark I heard at St. Petersburg. Purchase Cuba and keep the people honest. Central America must be taken care of, any way, whether Government winks at it or not. (Walker is off again—no mistake this time.)

The Pacific Railroad must be built, as a national necessity. Brigham Young must be watched ; and the workmen furnished with the means of sustaining life. England must not be allowed to lose India. America must stand by the grand old land of Alfred, of Shakspeare, and the Queen of Queens—Victoria

Napier well represents his nation. He will shortly ask us for some troops. " Ask, and ye shall receive."

Americans are better soldiers than Hessians, or Swiss and Italian legions.

The pro-and-anti-slavery men, having been charging wind-mills some thirty years, like Don Quixotte, ought to be tossed up in a blanket, as he was tossed, and then let the question be ·quietly put to rest for a few years, just to see how it would seem. The country is tired of hearing anything more about your " Bloody Kansas."

Suppose little Switzerland gets hard pushed by-and-by; without breaking Washington's advice on non-intervention, how would a little brotherly sympathy injure the cause of freedom?

Lafayette represented the principle during the Revolution.

Congress has something else to occupy its attention next session besides the Blacks. The North and South will have something better to do than rap each other over the head in the Senate. The Whites demand a hearing. Toombs mus'nt talk disunion—we will have no more of that—and Seward, one of the ablest men in the Senate, I trust will let his "bleeding Kansas" bleed awhile. 'Twill do her good. In March, 1855, he talked sense; his voice was prophetic. His speech warned the people of approaching danger. I endorse it all—but his Protective hobby.

1856, 1859 and 1860 will be passed in clearing away the rubbish of previous years.   A bankrupt law for *honest* men will do it.   Then the country will shoot ahead again, while the Old World looks on and wonders, remarking, " What a strange people ! "   Touching our obligations to Europe, I would suggest " that we assume a virtue if we have it not."   Issue no more " promises to pay "—but *pay*.

Demosthenes said, *action—action—action*.   Danton, when ringing the same changes, said it was *audace—audace—audace*.   Bulwer, the other day, at the Scottish University, said it was *enthusiasm—enthusiasm—enthusiasm*.   But with the American the cry should be *honesty—honesty—honesty*—and the country will soon have recovered from her confinement.   With *honesty* for the physician, economy the nurse, industry the housekeeper, and good nature throughout the hall, the country must surely recover from having given birth to this, its sixth financial abortion.   Practice honesty, and Diogenes would have no use for his lantern.   As it is, his search would be almost fruitless, although the streets are lighted with gas.

Cain killed his brother Abel, but whom did he marry ?

Solomon had ten times as many concubines as Brigham Young, lived a riotous life, and then gave us the Proverbs—the fruits of his experience—to guide the young American along the steep and slippery path of life. Moses, after taking away the jewels, slew an Egyptian and hid him in the sand. (Professor Webster was hanged for a crime no worse.) David kindly placed Uriah at the head of the army. Napoleon made Marshal St. Arnaud Général-au-Chef in the Crimea for another purpose.

The elders were behind the wall. What for? "Susanna, don't you cry!"

Samson lost his strength with his beard. Young America, take the hint; don't get shaved.

Mrs. Potiphar should also have been placed in the "lock up," while *Lot's* family should have been *cast* into the sea.

(If the "*Woodman*" had "spared that tree," when the "*Caroline*" went over the Falls, would it not have been better for public morals, than to have thrown it in the fiery *Furniss* of public indignation?)

Bad as is our age, theirs was far worse. Young America can improve upon the morals of those old men.

It would seem to me that painters could have selected some more ennobling subjects from out of the inspired pages to ornament the walls of European palaces.

The Old Masters have prostituted their great talents

in representing immorality and vice, instead of honesty and virtue.

The Christian religion was not intended to be portrayed in this manner. Nothing is more sublime— more grand—than to trace its history. Judaism was the caterpillar—slimy, filthy and unclean—out of which sprang the beautiful butterfly of our faith.

Asiatics and Africans adopt our vices, but our virtues are the Drummond lights of the Christian religion, which seldom penetrate the Black Hole of the heathen mind.

Each age improves upon that which went before. The "Young American" of our time may well astonish his grandfather. The parents should feel proud of the progress of their child. Each generation should embody all the good points of those that have preceded them, and try and throw away the bad. The Young Americans of to-day must govern the country in the next generation. Therefore, they should study, work, improve themselves by untiring application.

Cobbett said, "he never remembered the time in which he did not earn his own living." "Early rising, habitual temperance, unrelaxing industry," was the old man's advice to all young men. When Constable & Co. failed, during the panic of 1825, Walter Scott's liabilities amounted to $600,000. "Give me time, and

I'll pay every farthing," said the "old man eloquent."
He was as good as his word. At fifty-five years of
age he went to work again and paid every penny of
his obligations. (Two years afterwards he announced
himself as the author of "Waverly.") Samuel Johnson learned a language after he was sixty. Byron
wrote *Don Juan* at twenty-four. Robert Clive won
the battle of Plassey at twenty-six. William Pitt was
Premier of England at twenty-three. Torquato Tasso
wrote the *Jerusalem Delivered* at twenty-one; and
Napoleon was Commander-in-Chief of the Grand Army
of Italy at twenty-seven.

I have only mentioned these names as a plea for
young men. Let the old remember that they once
were young. Let the merchant reward his faithful
clerk, and encourage him with something more substantial than good advice and promises. The good advice is most acceptable, but back it up with some
good, generous act.

I hope I have said nothing in these pages to injure
the feelings of any man, and trust that I have properly explained to " *Old America* " the reason why I
have so suddenly become a " *Young Fogy.*"

Born beneath the shade of Faneuil Hall, New England's rock-bound shores are very dear to me. Nurtured
on the banks of the Mississippi, I can never forget the

Sunny South; and a traveler throughout our broad domain, I hope that I have at least one friend in every State. Should any of you happen to meet him, give him a dollar, remembering at the same time the language which Marmion addressed to Chester.

When sky-rockety views, written in a sky-rockety manner, are published at a sky-rockety time, the author runs some risk of catching a sky-rockety lecture.

Commendation I cannot expect; censure is more likely to reward a man for being honest in the expression of his opinions. All can sneer; few have the generosity to praise. Let a man speak above a whisper, and down goes the hammer of conventionality. Dare to suggest, and hornets build a local habitation in your breeches. Open the debate with truth, and "buncombe" will close it with falsehood. My object has been, in penning these pages, to awaken, if possible, a little reflection to our present condition and future prospects. I may have expressed myself warmly, but I have done it conscientiously, and with the best intention.

And whereas, sundry individuals may insinuate that some egotism is thrown in the work, this deponent hereby admits the soft impeachment. I have a perfect admiration of my opinions; as the old lady said of her children, "Very commonplace, to be sure, but nevertheless—they are mine!" Should I succeed in opening up a discussion on some of the questions which are of vital import to the nation, I shall feel amply repaid for any abuse that may be showered upon me. To say the least, as a matter of debate, there are two sides to every question. Prove me wrong, and I'll confess the error.

I maintain that the more this question is discussed, the better it will be for the country. Making it an academic argument, there must be pros as well as cons. With Wood " I bet on the bob-tail " against the favorite ; and although, perhaps, standing alone, on all principles of the ring I have a right to demand fair play,—argument, facts, figures—instead of assertion, abuse, ridicule.

Like John Phœnix, I can only say that, should I have offended any one by my style of writing, as I am not at heart a proud man, I am perfectly willing to accept his apology.

Address :—

YOUNG AMERICA,

THREADNEEDLE STREET.

The AUTHOR'S *Compliments*

To the Members of the PRESS :

Hopes to have the Pleasure, &c.

WHEN the *Herald*, with *Trumpet* toned voice, does me the honor to announce from the *Tribune* a book for the *Times*, the *Sentinel*, I trust, will raise the *Banner* of the *Young American*, while the *News* will *Despatch* the *Intelligence* to the *Town*, the *Country*, the *City*, the *State*, the *Union*, and the *World*. The *Clipper Traveler* will *Record* in his *Journal* how a *Youth* was criticised in the *Gazette* for being too *Independent* in discussing the questions connected with the *Plough, the Loom, and the Anvil*—and how a generous *Harper*, a *Christian Advocate*, a *Protestant Churchman*, and *Catholic Emancipator*, came to his assistance as the *Merchants and Bankers Magazine* was about to blow him up in the *Balloon*, charge him in the *Day-Book* and *Ledger*, and cast unkind reflections on him in the *Mirror*.

A *Rambler*, a *Spectator*, and a *Monitor* in Wall street, he could not be an *Idler;* so rushed to the *Press* with a *Leader* for the *Overland Mail* to spread about the *Globe*.

A *Commercial* retrospect, a *Financial* summary, a *Current* glance at *Prices*, and a fair *Market Report*, he thought would help the *Inquirer* and the reflecting *Observer* to *Chronicle* the changes that the *Crisis* has occasioned in the *Shipping*, the *Commerce*, and the *Trade* of the *Country*. If the *Critic* will *Register* a fair *Transcript* of the *Opinions of the Press*, the Author will not regret that he has made bold to play the *Diogenes* in holding the *Lantern*, with the honest hope that free discussion may throw some little *Light* upon this speculative *Age*. He does not profess to be a *Political Economist*, although he has endeavored to be a fair *Examiner* of our financial *Atlas*, in giving a brief *Review*, first, of the rise in the *Thermometer*, and the sudden change in the *Mercury*, with the hope of turning an honest *Picayune* by an *Illustrated* view of a *Pictorial* subject for the *Atheneum*.

An admirer of *Punch* (without taking it), he has tried to keep up with the *Spirit of the Times*, never signing the *Temperance Pledge*, or taking any *Bell* (es) *Life*.

In conclusion, he hopes that some bright particular *Star*, when noting the observations of the *Sun*, will say a kind word for the revolving *Planet*, without *cutting off the entire tail of the Comet;* and would respectfully request that a *Letter* might be sent by the next *Mail*, to every *Whig*, *Democrat*, *Know-Nothing*, and *Native American* in the *Union*, adding that the *Train* has arrived in the *States* from the *Old World*, a good *Patriot* and a *True Republican;* and being a native-born *Citizen*, he maintains that he has a perfect right to discuss any question touching the interests of the *Nation*, or write on any subject that may be unfurled under the

FLAG OF OUR UNION.

From the Edinburgh Review.

(Only Notice Received.)

"There are many things in this book which are GOOD and many things which are NEW; but the things which are GOOD are not NEW, and the things which are NEW are not GOOD." (*Et tu, Sydney ?*)

*** NOTE.—The Author's apology for any inaccuracies that may appear in this edition is, that the volume has been prepared, printed, and published in ten days time.

I intended to have added my Russian correspondence to the *London Times*, but as this volume has already extended beyond my first intention, I must pass it by, although I should have liked to have introduced the statistics of Russian commerce contained therein.

NEW-YORK, November 10, 1857.

APPENDIX.

[*From the American Railroad Journal, N. Y.*]

TABULAR STATEMENT

SHOWING THE NUMBER OF MILES OF RAILROAD IN OPERATION IN THE
UNITED STATES, JANUARY 1ST, 1857.

ROADS.

CALIFORNIA.	Miles.
Sacramento Valley	21

FLORIDA.	
Florida.	35
St. Mark's and Tallahassee	26
Total	61

TEXAS.	
Buffalo Bay, Brazos, and Colorado	40
Galveston, Houston, and Henderson	31
Total	71

DELAWARE.	
Newcastle and Frenchtown	16
Wilmington Branch	6
Delaware	71
Total	93

RHODE-ISLAND.	Miles.
Stonington	50
Providence, Hartford, & Fishkill	32
Providence and Bristol	14
Total	96

MISSOURI.	
Pacific	125
North Missouri	20
Hannibal and St. Joseph	75
St. Louis and Iron Mountain	25
Total	245

IOWA.	
Dubuque and Pacific	25
Rock Island and Muscatine	20
Mississippi and Missouri	88
Burlington and Missouri	50
Des Moines Valley	38
Keokuk and Dubuque	25
Chicago, Iowa, and Nebraska	20
Total	266

MAINE.	Miles.
Androscoggin and Kennebec...	55
Atlantic and St. Lawrence.....	150
Buckfield Branch.............	18
Bangor and Piscataquis.......	12
Kennebec and Portland.... ..	65
Bath Branch.................	9
Portland, Saco, and Portsmouth	51½
Calais and Baring............	11½
Machiasport.................	8
York and Cumberland........	18
Androscoggin...............	20
Penobscot and Kennebec......	55
Kennebec and Somerset.......	37
Total....................	510

NORTH CAROLINA.	
Raleigh and Gaston..........	87
Wilmington and Weldon....	.162
North Carolina Central.... ...	228
Weldon and Ridgway........	25
North Carolina and Atlantic...	30
Total....................	533

TENNESSEE.	
East Tennessee and Georgia...	110
Memphis and Charleston.....	106
Nashville and Chattanooga.....	159
East Tennessee and Virginia ..	50
Tennessee and Alabama.......	28
Memphis and Ohio...........	56
McMinnville Branch..........	35
Total....................	544

MARYLAND.	Miles.
Annapolis and Elkridge.......	21
Baltimore and Ohio......	379
Washington Branch..........	38
Frederick Branch............	3
Baltimore and Susquehanna...	57
Westminster Branch.........	9
Various Coal roads...........	53
Total....................	557

WISCONSIN.	
Milwaukee and Mississippi....	190
Watertown Branch...........	30
Milwaukee and Chicago.......	40
Beloit and Madison...........	20
Milwaukee and La Crosse.....	95
Rock River Valley............	30
Milwaukee and Horicon.......	30
Racine and Mississippi........	72
Mineral Point...............	32
Kenosha and Beloit...........	20
Total....................	559

NEW-HAMPSHIRE.	
Boston, Concord, and Montreal.	93
Cocheco.....................	28½
Concord....................	35
Contocook Valley............	25
Great Falls and Conway......	20
Manchester and Lawrence.....	26½
Northern...................	82
Portsmouth and Concord.... .	47
Sullivan........	26
Wilton.....................	15
Cheshire...................	54
Ashuelot.	23

NEW-HAMPSHIRE—*Cont.* *Miles.*

Eastern.........................	16¾
White Mountain..............	20
Boston and Maine...........	39¾
Merrimac & Connecticut Rivers	58

Total. 609½

MICHIGAN.

Central.	234
Southern...................	212
Detroit and Milwaukee	80
Erie and Kalamazoo..........	33
Detroit and Toledo....	45

Total. 604

CONNECTICUT.

Hartford and New-Haven......	62
Hartford, Providence, & Fishkill	76
Housatonic	98
Middletown Branch..........	11
Naugatuck.	62
New Haven Canal............	62
New-London, Willimantic and Palmer	66
New-Haven and New-London..	50
Norwich and Worcester.......	66
New-York and New-Haven....	76
Danbury and Norwalk..... ..	24

Total....................653

SOUTH CAROLINA.

South Carolina..............	242
Greenville and Columbia.. ...	165
Charlotte and South Carolina..	109
Kings Mountain..............	22

SOUTH CAROLINA—*Cont.* *Miles.*

Laurens.....................	32
Wilmington and Manchester...	171
North-eastern..	50
Spartanburgh and Union......	20

Total..................811

GEORGIA.

Central.....................	191
Georgia.	171
Macon and Western..........	101
Western and Atlantic.........	138
South western..	72
Rome Branch.	20
Muscogee............... ...	70
Atlanta and West Point.......	81
Milledgeville	17
Eaton and Milledgeville.	21
Wilkes County..............	18
Athens Branch..	40
Waynesboro'.	51
Warrentown Branch...	4
Brunswick and Florida........	35

Total...................1,030

VIRGINIA.

Richmond and Danville	142
Richmond and Petersburg.....	22
Cover Hill..................	11½
South Side	133
Manasses Gap...............	74
Petersburg and Roanoke......	60
Seaboard and Roanoke........	80
Winchester and Potomac......	32
Virginia Central, including Blue Ridge	171

VIRGINIA—*Cont.* *Miles.*

Virginia and Tennessee.......205'
Orange and Alexandria........ 97
Richmond, Fredericksburg, and
    Potomac................... 76
Greenville and Roanoke....... 21
Roanoke Valley.............. 22
Salt Works Branch..... 9
North-Western...............104
                  ————
    Total. 1,259½

MASSACHUSETTS.

Berkshire................... 21
Boston and Lowell.......... 28
Boston and Maine........... 44½
Boston and Providence....... 55½
Stoughton Branch 4
Boston and Worcester........ 68
Cape Cod.................. 68
Dorchester and Milton........ 4
Eastern........ 60
Essex (Salem to Lawrence).... 21
Fitchburg..... 69
Fitchburg and Worcester...... 14
Lowell and Lawrence......... 12½
Nashua and Lowell.......... 15
New Bedford and Taunton..... 21
Newburyport. 27½
Old Colony and Fall River..... 88
Peterboro and Shirley........ 14
Pittsfield and N. Adams.... ., 19
Providence and Worcester..... 43½
South Shore................ 11½
Stoney Brook............... 13
Western (Boston to Albany)....117
Worcester and Nashau........467
Vermont and Massachusetts.... 77
Housatonic Branch.......... 11

MASSACHUSETTS—*Cont.* *Miles.*

South Reading Branch........ 9
Salem and Lowell........:.... 17
Georgetown.................. 14
Grand Junction.............. 9½
Harvard Branch........... .. 1
Lexington and West Cambridge 7
Boston and New-York Central. 74½
Medway Branch.............. 3½
Saugus Branch.............. 8½
South Reading Branch........ 8
West Stockbridge............ 3
Connecticut River............ 52
Charles River Branch......... 9
Stockbridge and Pittsfield...... 22
Danvers.................... 9
Danvers and Georgetown...... 12½
Agricultural.................. 15
Amherst and Belcherton....... 20
Easton Branch.............. 4
Fairhaven Branch............ 15
Hampshire and Hamden....... 25
Merboro' Branch............. 4
Middleboro' and Taunton...... 8
                  ————
    Total..................1318

INDIANA.

Columbus and Shelbyville..... 24
Evansville and Crawfordsville..109
Indiana Central....... 72
Indianapolis, Pittsburgh, and
    Cleveland................ 84
Jeffersonville................. 77
Lafayette and Indianapolis..... 64
Madison and Indianapolis...... 86
Martinsville.................. 27
New Albany and Salem. 288

OHIO—*Cont.*	*Miles.*
Cleveland and Toledo, S. Division.	72
Cleveland and Toledo, N. Division	107
Columbus and Xenia	55
Columbus, Piqua, and Indiana.	72
Dayton and Michigan	28
Dayton and Western	42
Findlay Branch	16
Greenville and Miami	47
Hamilton, Eaton, and Richmond	45
Carrolton Branch	20
Iron	13
Little Miami	84
Mad River and Lake Erie	193
Mansfield and Sandusky	56
Newark and Mansfield	61
Ohio and Pennsylvania	187
Ohio and Mississippi	20
Ohio and Indiana	131
Scioto and Hocking Valley	56
Dayton and Xenia	19
Marietta, Hillsboro' and Cincinnati	193
Steubenville and Indiana	124
Springfield, Mt. Vernon, and Pittsburgh	50
Springfield and London	20
Toledo and Illinois	76
Northern Indiana	72
Total	**2,850**

AGGREGATE IN THE UNITED STATES.

States.	*Miles.*
California	21
Florida	61
Texas	71
Delaware	93
Rhode Island	96
Missouri	245
Iowa	266
Louisiana	251
Kentucky	286
Mississippi	413
Alabama	454
Vermont	471
New-Jersey	478
Maine	510
North Carolina	533
Tennessee	541
Maryland	557
Wisconsin	559
New-Hampshire	$609\frac{1}{4}$
Michigan	636
Connecticut	653
South Carolina	811
Georgia	1,030
Virginia	$1,259\frac{1}{2}$
Massachusetts	$1,318\frac{1}{2}$
Indiana	1,901
Pennsylvania	2,041
Illinois	$2,571\frac{1}{2}$
New-York	2,757
Ohio	2,850
Total	**24,310**

WEEKLY STATEMENTS

OF THE

CONDITION OF THE NEW-YORK CITY BANKS.

FROM SEPT. 20, 1856, TO NOV. 7, 1857.

	Loans.	Specie.	Circulation.	Actual Deposits.
Sept. 20, '56	$109,715,435	12,270,685	8,760,385	65,866,422
Sept. 27, '56	108,992,205	10,873,220	8,665,193	63,661,172
Oct. 4, '56	107,961,707	11,015,184	8,330,628	62,052,546
Oct. 11, '56	107,147,392	10,382,751	8,748,930	60,078,367
Oct. 18, '56	105,918,836	10,847,010	8,697,417	60,304,883
Oct. 25, '56	104,156,483	10,580,795	8,649,802	58,696,457
Nov. 1, '56	103,142,093	11,057,675	8,636,935	58,024,115
Nov. 8, '56	102,503,639	11,513,420	8,946,721	56,938,387
Nov. 15, '56	103,554,450	12,258,722	8,850,971	58,942,050
Nov. 22, '56	104,504,919	12,971,868	8.848,378	60,154,121
Nov. 29, '56	105,536,476	12,110,884	8,610,256	61,614,348
Dec. 6, '56	106,998,534	12,278,847	8.071,753	62,823,968
Dec. 13, '56	108,335,580	10,832,548	8,516,854	62,854,772
Dec. 20, '56	108,334,593	11,151,310	8,397,448	66,265,756
Dec. 27, '56	108,527,429	10,392,428	8,387,167	62,239,391
Jan'y 3, '57	109,149,153	11,172,244	8,602,113	63,677,829
Jan'y 10, '57	116,150,234	11,090,108	8,328,395	64,316,551
Jan'y 17, '57	110,860,401	11,955,054	8,047,065	66,076,937
Jan'y 24, '57	111,094,415	11,633,924	7,879,027	66,877,231
Jan'y 31, '57	111,785,838	12,191,325	8,024,948	67,241,670
Feb. 7, '57	112,876,713	11,148,894	8,426,817	65,997,160
Feb. 14, '57	112,722,799	10,497,832	8,151,799	55,943,490
Feb. 21, '57	111,773,572	10,432,158	8,106,074	65,098,895
Feb. 28, '57	111,137,717	10,065,254	8,159,275	64,627,069
March 7, '57	111,399,649	11,707,846	8,465,457	64,894,958

NEW-YORK CITY BANKS—Continued.

	Loans.	Specie.	Circulation.	Actual Deposits.
March 14, '57	$113,250.989	11,077,732	8,452,541	66,694.525
March 21, '57	113.443,692	11,291,373	8.494,238	65,975.946
March 28, '57	112,884.025	11,325,738	8.473,829	66,223,415
April 4, '57	114,833,902	11,538,732	8,812.325	66,834.089
April 11, '57	115,374,717	10,834,400	8,787,344	67,042,863
April 18, '57	114,398,174	12.061,372	8,770,823	67,547,241
April 25, '57	113,391,910	11,827.861	8,736,763	67,068,424
May 2, '57	114,409.275	12,009.911	9.006,566	68,078,676
May 9, '57	115,068,822	12.011.401	9,182,733	67,954,466
May 16, '57	114.620,042	12,543,694	8.935,297	68.595,165
May 23, '57	114.049,103	13.126,734	8.738,025	68,517.283
May 31, '57	114,049,633	12,815.515	8,696.692	68.565,903
June 6, '57	115,338,502	13,134,715	8.838,573	69,233,090
June 13, '57	115,412.541	11.974,378	8,696,893	68,111,334
June 20, '57	115.119,690	12.790,456	8.593.801	68.781.446
June 27, '57	115.015,504	10,901,081	8,505.065	67,213,111
July 4, '57	115,044,303	12.837.346	8,901.590	65.387.584
July 11, '57	116,028,618	12,666.146	8.693.578	65,702.597
July 18, '57	117,365,321	13.594.606	8,443,838	67,005,589
July 25, '57	118.848.131	12.956,855	8.528,814	67,377,055
Aug. 1, '57	120,597,050	12.918.013	8.665,422	68.682,039
Aug. 8, '57	122,077,252	11.737,367	8.981,740	67,372.940
Aug. 15, '57	121,241,472	11.360,645	8,780.012	66.814.931
Aug. 22, '57	120.139.582	10.097,178	8.694,011	64.241.471
Aug. 29, '57	116.588,919	9,241,376	8,671,060	59,690.311
Sept. 5, '57	112,221,365	10,227,965	8,673,192	57,260,609
Sept. 12, '57	109,985,572	12,181.857	8,322,316	57,334,121
Sept. 19, '57	108,777,421	13,556,186	8.073.801	57.851,931
Sept. 26, '57	107.791.433	13,327,095	7.838.303	56.918.863
Oct. 3, '57	105.935,499	11,400.413	7.916.102	52.798.365
Oct. 10, '57	101.917.569	11.476.294	7.524.599	48.745,176
Oct. 17, '57	97.245.826	7.843.230	8.087.441	42.696.012
Oct. 24, '57	95.593,518	10.411.643	6,884,739	47,873,900
Oct. 31, '57	95.317,754	12,883.441	6,334,748	51,853,158
Nov. 7, '57	95,866,241	16,492,152	6,434,312	56,424,973

STATEMENT

OF THE

CONDITION OF THE NEW-YORK CITY BANKS.

7TH NOVEMBER, 1857

	Loans.	Specie.	Circulation.	Nominal Deposits.
America	$4,559,400	1,085,119	52,171	4,421,435
American Exchange	6,076,493	1,052,923	120,885	4,477,890
Artizans'	575,039	62,626	49,453	183,749
Atlantic	495,335	61,375	95,323	237,018
Broadway	1,686,936	241,332	212,523	1,100,786
Bull's Head	203,616	30,394	124,030	132,992
Butchers'	1,314,807	81,213	138,050	713,733
Chatham	404,789	32.932	90,747	162,502
Chemical	1,206,848	575,461	186,856	1,525,191
City	1,829,618	597,958	17,154	1,953,800
Citizens	521,889	73,916	131,256	340,286
Commerce	10,970,275	2,009,656	2,095	5,777,137
Commonwealth	889,897	118,151	45,773	768,342
Continental	2,407,510	493,490	98,413	1,553,235
Corn Exchange	1,353,112	146,719	91,515	1,133,674
Dry Dock	361,017	57,080	39,354	125,917
Fulton	1,346,872	253,575	90,968	1,255,410
Greenwich	548,166	118,211	110,769	455,751
Hanover	1,062,070	98,473	55,953	585,460
Irving	613,426	121,379	93,659	425,561
Importers' & Traders'	1,696,283	229,542	102,907	794,401
Leather	1,698,288	289,922	250,107	1,383,413
Manhattan	4,390,177	638,291	329,037	3,485,622
Merchants'	4,127,576	1,204,013	284,624	3,813,063
Mechanics'	3,595,283	391,206	341,099	2,655,067

NEW-YORK CITY BANKS.—Continued.

	Loans.	Specie.	Circulation.	Nominal Deposits.
Merchants' Exchange.	1,612,740	153,900	87,169	1,015,779
Mechanics' & Traders.	639,723	86,406	109,684	342,765
Metropolitan.	5,431,484	731,413	238,926	4,271,398
Market.	1,398,693	131,372	160,650	863,857
Marine	745,636	63,687	59,507	382,974
Mercantile..	1,573,383	272,395	43,984	1,304,795
New-York.	3,270,270	547,627	353,023	2,132,132
National.	1,783,223	543,053	117,907	1,138,211
North America	1,395,886	202,200	38,955	1,162,160
Nassau.	1,079,236	157,967	75,919	670,312
New-York Exchange.	223,141	35,129	96,361	162,762
New-York County	266,519	34,808	99,200	132,811
Oriental	424,818	62,237	103,149	244,207
Park	2,687,754	350,592	110,965	1,520,128
Phenix	2,739,546	577,719	79,597	2,158,816
Ocean	1,148,915	165,221	71,724	683,353
Pacific.	803,794	113,079	114,219	551,046
People's	488,295	46,097	97,678	237,265
Republic.	3,308,925	393,910	87,666	2,514,173
Seventh Ward	891,099	249,175	113,936	562,070
State.	3,440,350	503,632	431,308	2,595,795
St. Nicholas	791,677	55,704	91,299	345,446
Shoe and Leather.	2,371,633	419,143	106,271	2,117,530
Tradesmen's	1,166,251	102,627	297,193	575,902
Union	2,248,508	430,102	93,301	1,737,652
Total.	$95,866,241	16,492,152	6,434,312	68,884,773